Advance Praise

"Dr. Tokuhama-Espinosa has bridged the gap between cognitive science and pedagogy with clarity and grace. I highly appreciate the difficulty of translating the complexity of this topic in a language which can be understood by a broader audience. Her work has proven very useful for our own foresight study on the nexus of human cognition and machine learning. Her five pillar structure provides a critical transdisciplinary lens to both diagnose and communicate such interdependent relationships."

—Mark Azzam, Dr.-Ing., Executive Board Representative Digitalization and Head of Think Tank at the German Aerospace Center (DLR)

"Tokuhama-Espinosa presents a game-changing theory about how humans think and learn, appealing to researchers and lay readers alike with her succinct yet comprehensive writing. Characterized by transdisciplinary thought and real-world examples, the author's ideas apply not only to a myriad of disciplines, but also to our everyday life. Connecting topics such as the mind, brain, and learning to everything from sand dunes, to stingrays, music, emojis, and math, this book is undoubtedly worth the read."

—Cynthia Borja, Ph.D., professor and Dean of the School of Psychology, *Universidad de Las Américas – Quito*, co-founder of and researcher at *Connections: The Learning Sciences Platform*

"With depth and brilliance, Tokuhama-Espinosa has created a masterwork with *Five Pillars of the Mind*. She proposes a fresh taxonomy for our time replacing antiquated curriculum models with neurologically anchored "pillars." Look for Symbols, Patterns, Order, Categories, and Relationships to be the new fundamental launching points for the design of contemporary learning experiences. In exquisite detail, she explores what replacing with an upgrade to the pillars would literally look like in our education settings. Moreover, Tokuhama-Espinosa dives into the connections between brain research and how it must be reflected directly into our education models of practice. I recommend this engaging and mind-opening book to educators at all levels seeking fresh curricular possibilities."

—Heidi Hayes Jacobs, Ed.D., President, Curriculum Designers, Inc.

"One paragraph and I was hooked. One chapter and I was jumping up in excitement. For a teacher like me, with a passion for brain sciences and whose life mission is to 'relieve the suffering of the classroom,' this book is a godsend. Tracey, a true teacher's teacher, has shown us the path to making education effective; and more, to making it humane."

—Curtis Kelly, Ed.D, founder of the JALT Mind, Brain, and Education Special Interest Group

"Among a cacophony of voices telling us that education is in desperate need of change, *Five Pillars of the Mind* emerges as a logical and systematic framing of that important change. Tokuhama-Espinosa's brilliant concept of the five 'pillars' is founded in deep reading of neuroscience, education, and psychology literature, the combination of which is known as the field of Mind Brain Education. Tokuhama-Espinosa has a unique and remarkable talent to balance the theoretical and the applied, a great service to her readers. Whatever our position in education—school leader, teacher, parent, school reform activist, or just curious onlooker—this book provides us with a fascinating and inspiring thought exercise, supported by page after page of practical examples, about how school can better serve students."

—Emily McCarren, Ph.D., Principal, Punahou School

"*Five Pillars of the Mind* presents a sophisticated and provocative conception of learning with profound implications for educational curricula, assessments, instruction, and the very structures of schooling. Citing multi-disciplinary sources from cognitive psychology, educational neuroscience, and studies of student achievement, Dr. Tokuhama-Espinosa offers a framework that will likely challenge your mental constructs and question many established practices. Get ready for a deep dive!"

—Jay McTighe, M.Ed., educational author and consultant; co-author of the *Understanding by Design®* series

"This book places learning and teaching in a whole new, brain-friendly light! Tracey's compelling thesis—that all learning is the learning of symbols, patterns, order, categories, and relationships, and that learning outcomes will improve by aligning curricula and teaching to these five pillars of the mind—is a must read for researchers in psychology, neuroscience, and education, as well as for pioneering practitioners keen to develop curricula and methodologies better suited to the learning brain."

—Dieuwerke Rutgers, Ph.D., Postdoctoral Research Associate, Faculty of Education, University of Cambridge

"The author has done a breath-taking examination of the literature and engaged with a score of experts in neuroscience and education around what she identifies as the Five Pillars concept. Not only does she join the dots convincingly between neuronal networks and decades-long educational theory, she engages in appropriate inquiry around teacher development and curriculum: usually a no-go zone for researchers, most of whom do not wish to disturb the status quo. Refreshingly, Tokuhama-Espinosa tackles the idea of how the Five Pillars concept might look, if we were to apply it to curriculum design. The author acknowledges next steps to test the model thoroughly, and outlines a number of challenges, none of which are insurmountable. In sum, this book merits consideration by leaders and practitioners, as we ask ourselves how best to prepare our young people in this age of exponential learning. Perhaps the answer lies in (the structure of) our brains."

—Kevin J. Ruth, Ph.D., Executive Director, ECIS, the Educational Collaborative for International Schools

"In this brief but mighty volume, Tokuhama-Espinosa proposes a new way of processing, probing, and understanding the world around us—and of structuring teaching and learning. Drawing on insights from psychology and neuroscience, she presents five organizing pillars to deepen learning, develop reason, and facilitate meaning-making for teachers and students alike. This is the most thought-provoking and innovative book about education I have read in a very long time."

—Carol Ann Tomlinson, Ed.D., William Clay Parrish, Jr. Professor, Curry School of Education, University of Virginia

"Tokuhama-Espinosa has written a cutting-edge book that has the potential to change the way educators think about designing and teaching the curriculum. Teaching relationships using the five broad pillars makes infinitely more sense in this day when most content can be found by 'Googling.'"

—Pat Wolfe, Ed.D, author of *Brain Matters: Translating Research to Classroom Practice*

Five Pillars of the Mind

Norton Books in Education

Five Pillars of the Mind

Redesigning Education to Suit the Brain

TRACEY TOKUHAMA-ESPINOSA

W. W. Norton & Company
Independent Publishers Since 1923
New York / London

Note to Readers: Models and/or techniques described in this volume are illustrative or are included for general informational purposes only; neither the publisher nor the author can guarantee the efficacy or appropriateness of any particular recommendation in every circumstance.

Printed in the United States of America
First Edition

For information about special discounts for bulk purchases, please contact W. W. Norton Special Sales at specialsales@wwnorton.com or 800-233-4830

Manufacturing by LSC Willard
Production manager: Katelyn MacKenzie

ISBN: 978-0-393-71321-3 (pbk.)

W. W. Norton & Company, Inc., 500 Fifth Avenue, New York, N.Y. 10110
www.wwnorton.com

W. W. Norton & Company Ltd., 15 Carlisle Street, London W1D 3BS

1 2 3 4 5 6 7 8 9 0

Contents

Figures

Tables

Dedication and Acknowledgments

Upon a visit to the Caixa Museum in Barcelona, a wonderland labyrinth of science, I was guided to an original, interactive exhibit on fractals—the repeated patterns that design nature in the form of ferns, nautilus shells, snowflakes, broccoli, crystals, leaves, and peacock feathers, and which inspire art, design, and architecture. My guide was a family friend, **Hernán Jaime Crespo**, who helped design the exhibit with world-famous architect Jorge Wagensberg, which reminded me of other exhibits that **Xavier Bellprat**, another amazing architect and designer, had shown me as we developed Planète Exploration in Switzerland (later fused with KinderCity), an interactive children's science museum on the environment and sustainable development. The multiple ways fractals help shape the world led me to observe my own surroundings in more detail. Transported, childlike, into seeing the world differently opened my eyes to the five pillars as I reviewed **Stanislas Dehaene**'s discoveries of neuronal pathways that were the same for mathematical numerals as for reading symbols, and other studies by **Michael Posner**, as I learned how distinctly functioning attention systems could be so much the same, yet so different. **Howard Gardner** and **Art Costa** helped me understand the relationships of multiple parts in complex systems, and **Helen Quinn** showed me the aesthetic order of physics and thinking like a scientist. These mentors and giants in academia are inspirations, and their perspectives added to my understanding of the five pillars concept. Thank you.

In addition to these inspirational people, I also wish to thank other insightful friends and colleagues who offered feedback on the concept paper and who encouraged me to write up these findings, including **Sashank Varma** (educational psychologist, University of Minnesota); **Jay McTighe** (educational consultant and author); **John Hattie** (educational researcher, University of Melbourne); **David Daniel** (professor of psychology, James Madison University); **John Bruer**, (president of the James S. McDonnell Foundation, adjunct professor of philosophy); **Sonia Guerrero** (former project leader, CERI, OECD, currently UNESCO education); **Dee Rutgers** (educational researcher, Cambridge University); **Usha Goswami**, (researcher, professor, and director of the Centre for Neuroscience in Education at St. John's College, Cambridge, formerly of United College of London); **Julia Volkman** (mentor, Montessori teacher, and teaching fellow at the Harvard University Extension School); **Judy Willis** (neuroscientist and teacher); **Jelle Jolles** (director, Centre Brain & Learning, LEARN! Research Institute, University of Amsterdam); and **Mariel Hardiman** (vice dean, Johns Hopkins University School of Education). Each of you added new dimensions to the pillars and helped complete the vision. Thank you for your collegial support and intellectual generosity, which are vital for nurturing ideas.

Special thanks to my dear friends Pablo, Alejandra, Giselle, Ricardo, Christine, Barbara, Lisa, Laraine, Silke, Ruth, Martina, Claudia, Ana, Drew, Cynthia, Monse, Isa, and Mishel for listening to various iterations of these ideas.

Love and gratitude to Cristian, Nati, Gabriel, and Mateo for letting me experiment on you.

Much appreciation to Mom, Dad, Nick, Vera, Amie, and Miko for always being both eternal cheerleaders and critical friends who continue to sculpt my ability to think.

Finally, I would also like to thank the team at W. W. Norton: Deborah Malmud, Kate Prince, Sara McBride, Mariah Eppes, Carol Collins, Kevin Olsen, and Nicholas Fuenzalida for being the most supportive and clever minds in the business.

Five Pillars of the Mind

Preface:

The Origins of the Pillars

A few years back I was asked to do a study for a Central American government that suspected that children's lack of academic success in the early years was due to a failure to strengthen certain brain networks during preschool experiences (0–6 years old). This intriguing hypothesis led to the documentation of 16 neuronal networks needed for pre-numeracy and pre-literacy preparedness, more than half of which were *not* stimulated enough in the preschool settings we observed in regular practice (Rivera, 2013; Tokuhama-Espinosa & Rivera, 2013a). It appeared that the hypothesis was correct: Early development of key neuronal networks needed for reading and math was not rehearsed enough, which probably contributes to school failure in the primary years. This finding was important because it highlighted at least two aspects of the teaching-learning process that have only just begun to be incorporated into modern teacher training based on Mind, Brain, and Education science (MBE).

First, learning does not take place in single isolated spots in the brain, nor due to a singular type of experience, but rather through a series of connections gleaned from a variety of moments that link areas and networks together to create the potential to learn. These neuronal networks, or basic brain circuitry, are inherited through our genes and (hopefully) strengthened through our daily life experience. Learning can be improved depending on the type of stimuli a person receives in his or her environments, including home, school, the wider community, informal contexts, as well as the surrounding culture. The exciting conclusion drawn from this new information is that we teachers can improve student learning outcomes by taking advantage of a better understanding of these neuronal networks, followed by the use of methodologies that correctly stimulate them in an orderly way. The appropriateness of the methodologies depends on determining this "orderly way," however, which unfortunately, has yet to find full consensus in the world of academia. Having said that, we are getting closer, thanks to better documentation of classroom practices and findings in neuroscience, which, together, supply evidence for a new way to devise learning in schools.

This leads to the second finding that reveals what appears to be a new dimension to learning previously undocumented in the literature. After sorting them, I found that the 16 neuronal networks needed for pre-literacy and pre-numeracy skills fell into just five distinct types of studies, shedding light on a different way to structure research and teaching that may be more natural than our current journal classifications or curriculum divisions by subject or domain areas. Upon review of a thousand articles on the reading brain and the early-forming math brain, it became apparent that all these studies could be divided into just five "pillars," which were related to one another in an iterative design and through a constructivist hierarchy.

The five pillars—**symbols, patterns, order, categories and relationships**—were a surprising find. They not only offered an organizing concept for existing theories of learning, but also suggested evidence and answers to ideas and challenges in education that have existed for decades, ranging from difficulties designing mastery instruction to improved diagnosis of learning problems. As it seemed either too good to be true or too good to be original, I emailed 31 experts in neuroscience and education and asked them for feedback. Shortly, I heard back from 20 of them, each confirming the potential of the five pillars concept.

This book will first describe the five pillars, explain their complementary nature to current models of teaching and learning, and offer evidence for their existence in distinct domains. We will then hypothesize about what they would look like if applied in our schools today. We close with a reflection on the potential implications of the pillars in educational practice and an invitation to radically rethink education. For readers interested in the neuroscientific angle and curious about the 16 neural networks mentioned above, I invite a close reading of the Appendices as well.

Introduction:

Elegant Complexity

Often, the simplest solutions are the best.

The mystery of how humans learn has generated hundreds of theories over the centuries, ranging from the philosophical to the neuroscientific. Ideas from as far back at the Greeks (*all learning comes from the senses,* as Aristotle believed) to more current views from neuroconstructivism ("the experience-dependent development of neural structures supporting mental representations" [Westerman et al., 2007, p. 75]) are testaments to a human desire to know ourselves better. The Theory of the Five Pillars of the Mind, based on studies from Mind (psychology), Brain (neuroscience), and Education science, indicates that everything humans learn is either a symbol, and/or a pattern, and/or an expression of order, and/or a category, and/or a relationship. This book is about the Theory of the Five Pillars, how it complements previous schemes of learning, what scientific evidence exists to support it, and the potential implications this has for education, schools, teaching, and specifically, curricular design.

Lots of Improvements in Education, but Few in Curriculum Design

Schools and formal education have been around for a very long time, and there have been significant advancements in teaching methodologies, knowledge about the brain and learning, technological contributions to education, and instructional design. There have been many keen insights over the years by educators whose work has helped us get to the heart of good teaching. Most of these efforts relate to **teaching methods** (e.g., Nuthall, 2004), **strategies** (e.g., Schroeder et al., 2007), **tools** (e.g., Davis, 2009), **technologies** (e.g., Bishop & Verleger, 2013), interventions and **activities** (e.g., Tokuhama-Espinosa, 2014), **habits of mind** (e.g., Costa & Kallick, 2009), **best practices** (e.g., Zemelman et al., 2005), **routines** (e.g., Ritchhart et al., 2011), **mindsets** (e.g., Dweck, 2006), **design** (e.g., Wiggins & McTighe, 2005), **attitudes** (e.g., Esquith, 2007), **techniques** (e.g., Lemov, 2010), **instruments** (e.g., Feuerstein & Jensen, 1980), **motivational tools** (e.g., Cushman, 2012), **teacher-student relationships** (e.g., Fink, 2013); **differentiation** and **inclusion** (e.g., Tomlinson, 2014), **management and engagement** (e.g., Fisher, et al., 2017), **teacher education** (e.g., Darling-Hammond, 2016), and/or **teaching to the whole child** (e.g., Perkins, 2010). Most of these insights are applied through a **constructivist educational philosophy** (e.g., Ultanir, 2012) and have achieved good results. They should all be applauded.

There have also been excellent frontline interventions by classrooms teachers themselves who approach their daily work from imaginative perspectives. Quinn's pyramid model based on Reggio Emilio formats (i.e., Quinn, personal conversation, October 23 2013) in San Francisco, the Wisconsin Innovative Schools Network (Stout, personal conversation, April 18, 2015), Hawaii's Punahou School efforts to teach community members about Mind, Brain, and Education (McCaren, personal conversation, February 8, 2017), the International School of Bangkok's work to engage and motivate (Scott, personal conversation, November 30, 2016) and the International School of Geneva's interest in modernizing educational design (Hawley, personal conversation, January 17, 2018) using information from neuroeducation and technology offer testament to the change underway in education. The Deans for Impact initiative in the United States (2015) and the OECD (Organisation for Economic and Cultural Development) recommendation to its 34 member countries, including the U.S., for teachers' new pedagogical knowledge (Guerriero, 2017) are forging a path in educational policies and redesigning education's best practices. All of these contributions add to our general understanding of the teaching and learning processes and celebrate innovation in schooling.

To the best of my knowledge, however, while there have been a number of attempts at modifying the **curriculum** over the past 100 years (Common Core; International Baccalaureate; various state standards), there have been only small dents in its **subject-oriented design**. In international comparisons of school curriculum, there is a surprising amount of similarity in content. All school systems around the world teach some form of language, math, social studies (history or civics), art, science, and physical education (health), and nearly all require a second language. Some schools offer technology/computers, and moral or ethical studies. About half of the school systems surveyed teach work-related or vocational skills, as well as the aforementioned courses. This means that all around the world, school curriculum has been and remains focused on the instruction of specific academic subjects with content delivery in domain areas of knowledge such as math, language, science, and art for centuries.

Subject-focused curricula are the norm around the world. This book explores an alternative to traditional curriculum structure.

The Five Pillars: A New Way of Looking at Human Learning

The nearly one thousand neuroscientific studies I have reviewed over the past decade about the brain as it learns math and language can be sorted into (1) **symbols**, (2) **patterns**, (3) **order**, (4) **categories**, and/or (5) **relationships**. Some concepts only fit in one pillar, while others fit into all five pillars. For example, the letter "s" is a symbol, but it is not a pattern, order, category, or relationship, whereas the concept of "addition" involves symbols, patterns, order, categories, *and* relationships. I refer to these groupings as "pillars" because each can be considered on its own and stand firmly without external support; however, when combined, they can sustain even larger structures, in this case, human learning.

In the literature, there are hundreds of studies about how the brain encodes, recalls, recognizes, shapes, and creates ***symbols*** such as letters and numbers (e.g., Smolensky et al., 2014; see Table 7 for more examples).

Similarly, there are a myriad of reviews of the brain's ***pattern***-seeking mechanisms from those in nature, to sentence structuring, analogies and behaviors (e.g., Long et al., 2015; see Table 8 for more examples).

Likewise, studies showing the struggles of the brain to structure its world as it learns that "Tom likes Sally" is very different from "Sally likes Tom" show that true learning relies, at least in part, on ***order*** (e.g., Dunn et al., 2011; see Table 11 for more examples).

Table 1. Subject Areas Covered in Curriculum Around the World

	Language A	Math	Social Studies/ History	Art	Science	Personal, social, and physical education	Language B	Technology skills	Ethics	Work-related learning
International Baccalaureate	X G1: Studies in language and literature	X G5: Math	X G3: Individuals and societies	X G6: The arts	X G4: Experimental sciences	X G4: Health science	X G2: Language acquisition	X G5: Computer science		X Community, Action, Service
Common Core (U.S.)	X	X	X	X	X	X	(X)	X		
National Curriculum for England	X English Key Stage 1, 2, 3, 4	X Key Stage 1, 2, 3, 4	X Geography; History Key Stage 1, 2, 3 Citizenship 3, 4	X Music; Art and Design Key Stage 1, 2, 3	X Key Stage 1, 2, 3, 4	X Key Stage 1, 2, 3, 4	X Key Stage 2, 3,	X Key Stage 1, 2, 3, 4 (Computing) design and technology Key Stage 1, 2, 3		X
Australian Curriculum	X English F-10; 11 -12	X Math F-10; 11-12	X Civics and citizenship 3-10; Economics and business 5-10 Geography F-12 History F-10, 11-12	X Arts F-10	X Science F-10, 11-12	X Health and Physical Edu F-10	X Second language F-10	X Technologies F-10		X Work Studies 9-10
Japan National Curriculum	X Japanese	X Math	X Social studies (civics, geography; Japanese history; World History, Sociology; politics/ Economics	X Art, music	X Science	X Physical education	X English		X Moral studies	

Canadian Curriculum	X English language arts	X Math	X Social studies	X Arts, music	X Science	X Physical education, health education	X Second language (French)	X Technology education	X Ethics	X Home economics; carpentry; automatic tech
Philippine Curriculum	X Mother tongue language and literature; communication	X Math	X Social sciences		X Natural sciences		X English and Filipino		X Philosophy	
Finnish Curriculum	X Mother tongue and literature	X Math	X History, social studies	X Music; visual arts; crafts	X Environmental and natural sciences; Biology (and geography); Physics and chemistry	X Health education; physical education	X Second national language; foreign languages	X (Information and computer technology – cross curriculum)	X Religion; ethics	X Home economics; Educational and vocational guidance
French Curriculum	X French	X Math	X Humanities; history; geography; citizenship; civics	X History of the arts; Arts and crafts; music	X Science (biology; geology); physics and chemistry		X First foreign language; Second foreign language (Latin and ancient Greek optional)	X Technology	X Philosophy	

SOURCE: TOKUHAMA-ESPINOSA, 2017

There are also numerous studies that explain what at first seems like the brain's ability—but later is recognized as the brain's *necessity*—to create ***categories*** in the world of physical things as well as ideas and intangible concepts (e.g., Kourtzi & Connor, 2011; see Table 14 for more examples). The seemingly intuitive manner in which semantic memories are grouped physically along similar or neighboring neuronal pathways, for example, suggests that the brain facilitates learning by economizing networks and expediting retrieval by clustering together similar schematic representations.

Finally, it became apparent that ***relationships*** are fundamental to learning concepts, both within and outside of school settings (e.g., Baumann, et al., 2012; see Table 18 for more examples). Understanding magnitude, measures, and proportions enables humans to connect ideas and link their surroundings in ways that explain natural phenomena, as well as the world of ideas.

My initial study focused on pre-literacy and early math skills in preschool children. I then expanded my review of the literature to include math and literacy from the early years through adulthood. When I found that these studies could also be grouped into the pillar structure, I expanded my search to include other academic fields. After researching nearly 2,000 more studies related to human learning, it appears that just about anything that can be studied and learned can fit into the five pillars. These five basic pillars of human learning—symbols, patterns, order, categories and relationships—appear to be the foundations for all subject area study as far as the brain is concerned, not only language and math but every other domain area taught in school.

My review of the cognitive neuroscience literature from 1997 to 2017 on human learning found studies that considered the **arts** (e.g., Mell et al., 2003; Segev et al., 2014; Vessel et al., 2012; Zeki & Nash, 1999); **history** (e.g., Kennerley & Kischka, 2013; Thomson, 2011); **physical activity** (e.g., Castelli & Hillman, 2012; Erickson et al., 2015; Staiano & Calvert, 2011; Zatorre, et al., 2012); and **science** (e.g., Gray, 2013; Lipko-Speed et al., 2014; Wagenmakers et al., 2012) could all be documented showing symbols, patterns, order, categories and relationships. Nothing fell outside of these five pillars. *But why would this occur?*

It appears that different types of learning, as documented by brain connectivity and circuitry, tend to travel similar pathways to take advantage or economize the process of learning itself. I wondered, *Is it possible that this is accidental?* Or is the brain far too efficient for such a coincidence? Independent of domain content information, there is evidence that similar types of learning travel similar pathways in the brain.

After comparing academic fields typically found in K-12 education, I then asked friends in architecture, gender studies, design, museology, peace studies, administration, economics, international trade, communications, technology, artificial intelligence, and neuroscience if their fields could similarly be divided into area knowledge using the five pillars, and found initial puzzlement and then amazement as we found that *anything* they considered field knowledge could, indeed, fall under the same five pillars. I then asked gardeners, grocery store owners, bank tellers, journalists, and babysitters the same question: *Does what you do fall neatly into the five pillars?* It appears that just about everything humans can learn can fit into these five pillars, so long as the definition of these groupings is agreed upon in a broad way. I suggest the following sub-pillar divisions:

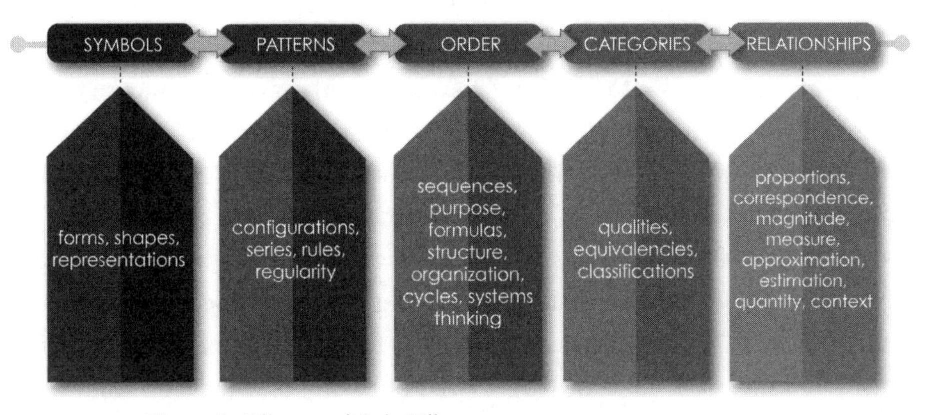

Figure 1. Pillars and Sub-Pillars. SOURCE TOKUHAMA-ESPINOSA, 2015

Core Concepts, Key Notions

The exciting idea here is that the pillars are core concepts—in fact, they may be *the* core concepts often alluded to when teachers lament missing student skill sets. Every area of knowledge hinges on the basic notions embodied in these concepts. For example, human babies have a general number sense about quantity, even before they can speak. The general notion of order in size, for example (small, medium, large; a lot, a little), is in place before kids develop a mental number line and before they get to school and start to use a physical number line. If the number sense is missing, children cannot develop a mental number line. If they have no mental number line, they cannot learn to add. If they cannot learn to add, they cannot learn to subtract, and so on. Missing notions—basic conceptions or beliefs about something—cause academic failure.

In another example, a basic notion in language is a "language sense" that implies a pre-verbal conception of communication (Berwick & Chomsky, 2015; Chomsky, 1967; Davies, 2003; Hauser et al., 2002; Pinker, 2003), without which words have no meaning. Without an understanding of words, there can be no implicit understanding of morphology, and without morphology there is no understanding of syntax. If there is no understanding of syntax, no one can understand semantics, and pragmatics depend on semantics, and so on. This means that the basic notions (core concepts and basic knowledge) precede and establish a kind of hierarchical understanding of everything. Humans develop these core notions thanks to adequate stimulation, rehearsal and contextual placement. But, as many teachers note, sometimes they are missing. Kids can miss out on normal stimulation (with parents who don't talk to them to develop the basic notion of language, or play peek-a-boo with objects so they see how "something" can turn into "nothing") and they can have gaps in core notions. Some kids can be born with problems and imperfect neuronal circuitry that can also lead to missing core notions. It is not unusual to hear teachers in just about every setting and level of education lament that some of their student are missing some basic concepts and therefore cannot grasp higher-order ideas. The pillars can serve to mediate the teaching-learning processes of this basic comprehension of notions, which is needed for deeper thinking by explicitly laying out a hierarchy of knowledge based both on current curriculum design and on neuroscientific studies (*neuroconstructivism*, which will be explained in Chapter 7).

The Five Pillars vs. Traditional Domain Areas and Models of Teaching

Cumulatively speaking, I propose that it is possible to analyze all human learning through symbols (forms, shapes, representations); patterns (configurations, series, rules, regularity); order (sequences, purpose, formulas, structure, organization, cycles, systems thinking); categories (qualities, equivalencies, classifications); and relationships (proportions, correspondence, magnitude, measure, approximations, estimation, quantity, context). I suggest that the pillars serve as a complementary system that can accompany any existing curriculum, teaching, evaluation, or research structure. I hypothesize that using the five pillars can improve learning outcomes because they reinforce what the brain already does intuitively—organizes and aligns certain ways of knowing. Unlike other learning theories, which sometimes contradict one another, the five pillars do not dispute, negate, or challenge other types of learning theories, but rather complement them by adding a new dimension to their usefulness in academia. Neuronal networks develop as a consequence of potentiating genes through experiences, which may occur along physical divisions in the brain based on the pillars. The pillars explain a natural order of knowledge networks, which complements—and does not compete with—other ways of describing how the brain learns.

The brain is complex, and its processes are often hard to imagine because they are invisible to the naked eye. The pillars offer an explanation of the holistic functioning of the brain and learning, which is composed of concepts that make sense, even to the youngest of minds—a kindergartener understands "symbols," "patterns," "order," "categories," and "relationships." Not only are the pillars comprehensible, they are complementary to one another. The pillars are not constrained by distinct methodological approaches, learning environments, techniques, materials, or routines, but rather they add to existing processes. For example, the traditional way of organizing classrooms based on *cognitive stages* of development, as suggested by Piagetians, can be complemented by the pillars. Likewise, the decision to divide children by level groupings and mastery goals can also be complemented with the pillars. The pillars can be used independent of the *curriculum design* or in concert with them. These will all be explained in more detail as we talk about each of the pillars in the coming chapters. For now, it's important to understand that the pillars add to current educational structures—they do not detract from them, but they can, possibly, replace them as we will see in Chapter 8.

Ages vs. Stages

We currently divide kids into age groups in our schools. We do this based on a logistical need created by the implementation of universal education at the end of the 19th century, which forced us to make a decision about how to divide our overcrowded classrooms. While dividing children by their birthdates may seem logical at first *(after all, it's the way we have always done it)*, we often forget that cognitive development is not always in parallel with chronological age (Boula et al., 2017). In fact, there are numerous studies indicating that some key goals for school success, such as reading, are normal if taught in schools anywhere between three and nine years of age (Tokuhama-Espinosa, 2008b). Similarly, most teachers can share at least one, if not multiple, examples of a kid in their class that would likely have found more success if they had just been given a bit more time. Competency-based learning tried to respond to this challenge.

Competency-based Learning and Attending to Different Rates of Learning

The creation of gatekeeping standards may often spell failure for some who develop differently, or those we call "late bloomers." "Both age and education are associated with hierarchical development" (Dawson-Tunik et al., 2005, p. 11), but age and subject area content do not always align for student success in our classrooms. The pillars can be used to refocus efforts of mastery learning, rather than just on meeting standards.

If one reviews failure rates in schools, startling patterns emerge about who usually misses the standardized test score minimums (see Lucio et al., 2012; Oyserman, 2013). It is interesting to note the populations of students who are naturally "slower" on the comparative scale of achievement in the early years: boys, who genetically mature slightly more slowly than girls (see Marceau et al., 2011); bilinguals, whose vocabulary evens out at a slightly slower rate in the earlier years than monolinguals but usually ends up being superior in the later years (see Poulin-Dubois et al., 2013); subsequent children as compared with first children (e.g., Berglund et al., 2005); minorities (e.g., Appel & Kronberger, 2012); and children from low socioeconomic status (SES) groups (e.g., Currie & Thomas, 2012). Some of these differences are merely developmental and go away on their own, leaving no perceivable signs by mid-primary school. In other cases, the transformational impact of great teachers can reduce the gap between these slower starters and other children, sometimes availing such extreme benefits as to reduce perceivable differences between these groups after high-quality intervention over just a few years (Stigler & Hiebert, 2009).

Even if we accept that there is a natural "evening out" of the playing field over time, for some children it is often too late as their initial failures in school spiral into long-term underachievement. Early labeling can end up being a self-fulfilling prophecy (Hattie, 2009) in which the student views the condition or label as his identity. This is especially evident for students with a fixed mindset who consider their potential to be tied to factors outside their control (Dweck, 2006) such as in heredity traits, rather than believing their environments or their free will can influence their learning outcomes. The label turns into an indication of perceived inadequacy, leading to low self-esteem, and subsequently, academic failure. Many children, labeled as "slow" too early in their academic careers, are potentially superior learners, but due to our zeal to "treat early" we mistakenly mark them, which can lead to a downward spiral in self-efficacy and/or academic failure (Hudak, 2014). Once a child has been labeled, he has to struggle his way back up to even. Unfortunately, we sometimes limit the chances of slower starters to show us what they know because we pollute their self-perception as learners with the suggestion that they are "behind" or are somehow less intelligent or less ready than their peers. Since a student's self-perception as a learner is one of the greatest influences on student learning outcomes (Brophy, 2013; Hattie & Anderman, 2013), it is sad to watch how some children mistakenly misjudge their own potential to learn because they are slightly behind the developmental curve. Had we personalized their learning a bit more, would we be met with less failure? I propose that if students were allowed to advance through different levels of *mastery* based on a pillar hierarchy, rather than being grouped by age, there would be less school failure.

Prior Experience

The speed with which a person can recall information can be directly related to the level of repetition received for that information (Voelker et al., 2017; Zatorre et al., 2012). The myelin sheath that insulates the axonal connections between memory hubs in the brain is responsible for how quickly a person can "find" the right information (Hartline, 2008). We all have habituated actions that seem ingrained in our intuitive behavior, but which have actually been cemented into memory due to the high level of repetition (think of driving, for example). A certain amount of repetition is required for true learning to take place (Rock, 1957). We know that different kids will enter our classes with different amounts of prior experience due to their life conditions. This makes some kids seem exceptionally intelligent (or slow), even though their outcomes can be chalked up to experience, not to intelligence. People can appear to be experts or even gifted in a skill set based solely on a large amount of practice. Ericsson and colleagues (2007) suggest that with "10,000 hours" of practice a novice can appear to have expert skills, which clearly demonstrates the key role of prior experience in learning outcomes.

The order in which skills are learned is more important than one's age, meaning that the alignment of cognitive development and past experience is most indicative of a child's potential to learn. For example, a child who has been read to since birth will have more connections in place in key neuronal networks when it comes time to learn to read in school than a child who has ever been read to before at home (Bus et al., 1995). Constructivism, both as a pedagogical concept as well as a neurological reality (more on this in Chapter 7), explains why experiences create the building blocks upon which new learning can occur. Without proper prior knowledge, new learning is slowed. A child who knows how to add will be able to learn how to subtract in a relatively short period of time compared with a child who does have sufficient practice in addition. The prerequisite knowledge that comes from prior experience is a gatekeeper for learning.

There are thousands of kids who fail in school, not because they lack the intelligence to succeed, but rather because they don't have the necessary prerequisite knowledge upon which to build learning (and this is usually not due to any fault of their own). Happily, this can be remediated relatively easily, if students are given more practice with the learning concepts in a constructivist design. The pillar structure provides such scaffolding.

Transdisciplinarity

Transdisciplinarity's goal is to ensure that multiple lenses are used to approach a single problem, that every lesson considers a variety of viewpoints and that, most importantly, learners habitually take into consideration different *ways of knowing* as they undertake challenges (Gibbs, 2015). Transdisciplinarity differs from interdisciplinarity in that it appreciates the use of a single multifaceted lens for thinking rather than adjoining distinct fields as separate views of the problem. Rather than take a problem like urban trash collection, for example, and think about it as a politician, a home owner, an economist, or a public health worker (which would be problem-based learning), transdisciplinarity asks the individual to *think* from all of these visions at once as a habituated practice of thinking. This requires a shift in mentality about how problem solving, learning, and academic prowess emerge that moves away from specializing in one area alone to habitually taking into consideration various ways we humans can know the world. While counterintuitive, transdisciplinary thinking is actually more natural than single-disciplinary thinking, as all problems in the world are better resolved with multiple viewpoints than from a single perspective alone.

Table 2. Transdisciplinary Thinking

Diagram	Type
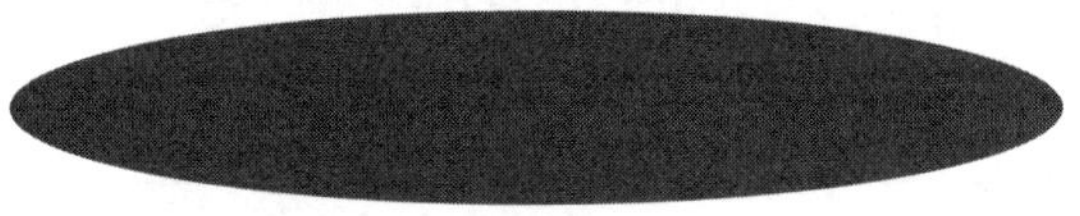 (one large dark ellipse)	Transdisciplinarity
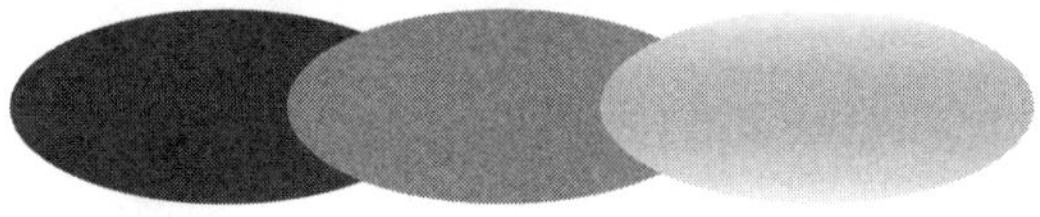 (three overlapping ellipses)	Interdisciplinary
(three circles connected by lines)	Multidisciplinary
(three separate circles)	Disciplinary

SOURCE: TOKUHAMA-ESPINOSA, 2018 BASED ON DRAKE, SAVAGE, REID, BERNARD & BERES, 2015

Imprinting the regular use of cross-disciplinary thinking rather than thinking solely like a chemist (or a botanist, mathematician, or artist), for example, improves the chances of reaching a sustainable solution, a creative answer, and/or a holistic, empathetic vision of the world. For example, if I want to resolve school attendance issues, traffic congestion, food security, child well-being, climate change, or research an unknown, it would be hard to find anyone to defend that a single vision—thinking like a biologist, engineer, environmentalist, educator, parent, politician or professor alone—would be superior to thinking through multiple lenses simultaneously.

In early childhood education, we often seamlessly integrate the physical sciences with art, language with math, and music with history in a transdisciplinary way (for an example, see Brooks-Gunn et al., 2013). Young kids are also often encouraged to compare their neighborhoods, homes, and other institutions with school learning, something that is often absent in upper grades. This natural integration of disciplines in the early years facilitates student recall for concepts and better reflects the child's world in an authentic way, which will hopefully lead to greater interest in school-taught content (Willingham, 2009). The division of six years of primary education, in which topics are seamlessly integrated, with six years of secondary education, in which topics are purposefully divided, is a curricular decision. Presumably, this is done in the higher years to permit students to dig deeper into content areas; however, it can be argued that the best way to foster deep understanding is by learning concepts in authentic contexts, which are naturally transdisciplinary. The five pillars motivate transdisciplinary thinking because, rather than using curriculum divided by subject areas (which habituates single lens thinking), they unite multiple disciplines under them. For example, we can use **symbols** to see just how different and how alike language, math, biology, art, and all other subject areas actually are. Or think of **patterns** that exist in nature, history, philosophy, psychology, literature, or any other academic field, and then move on to cross-fertilize with other fields or concepts. If all levels of education were approached through symbols, patterns, order, categories and relationships, the connections between subject areas would be more transparent. Thinking across and among disciplines enhances problem-solving skills and leads to more innovative thinkers, something that most societies view as being a goal of modern education.

The pillars help bridge disciplines in context. The commonality of symbols, patterns, order, categories, and relationships that are found in the classroom, the lab, and in society helps **reinforce basic notions**. The benefits of viewing problems with multiple lenses (e.g., Ciesielski et al., 2017) motivate broader transdisciplinary thinking, which is desirable, but often hard to operationalize in classrooms. The pillars can help. For example, rather than teach the alphabet in a vacuum, small children could be asked to explore as many symbols as they can in their school, home, and natural environments and consider how they are used globally *before* teaching letter-to-sound/phoneme recognition. Or, rather than talk about the stages of a caterpillar turning into a butterfly as an isolated event, **order** and processes can be explained more broadly *first*, such as what order do they tie the laces of their shoes, what happens before a baby bird hatches from an egg, or how bread is made by first mixing ingredients then baking the dough. Any experience that reinforces the basic notion of any symbol, pattern, order, category or relationship lays a firmer foundation for future learning in that pillar.

The pillars also offer a new way to think about theory-to-practice, planning-to-execution, and research-to-application models. An example of the research application of the transdisciplinary use of the pillars is shared below in the section on *How the pillars can help researchers* at the end of this chapter.

Analogies and the Mind

Learning can be difficult and often feel foreign, forced, and unnatural, as many school kids will attest as they grab their heads in anguish, perceived or real. As I wrote in *Making Classrooms Better* (2014), thankfully the brain is efficient in its dealings with new information. The natural pathway of a perceived stimulus makes its way into the brain with first stops in memory hubs to compare what is already known to the new information: All new learning passes through the filter of prior experience, as studies with two different international Delphi panels on Mind, Brain, and Education determined (Tokuhama-Espinosa, 2008a, 2017). This is why, when the brain is faced with something with which it does not already have some kind of reference point from past experience, one of the best ways to approach it is through analogies (Ragni & Strube, 2014). Learning through the pillars is learning through the analogical references of prior symbols, patterns, order, categories and relationships, which can potentially speed the process of learning while also make learning more authentic.

> Eggen and Kauchak (1998) suggest that the introduction of new content should always be done within a familiar frame of reference. When direct links to past knowledge are not available, the use of analogies is key: 'The closer the fit of the analogy, the more learning is facilitated' (Eggen & Kauchak, 1998, pp. 295–296). Ever since human communication has existed, analogies have been used to help learners connect with unknown concepts by offering 'parallel' ideas (Harrison & Croll, 2007). Before the written word existed, Aesop's fables, Bible lessons, and almost all forms of teaching were passed down through stories, a special type of analogy (see Hulshof & Verloop, 2002, for concrete examples of analogy use in language teaching).

> Being able to piece together knowledge from past experiences is a fundamental aspect of all new learning and vitally important in developing thinking skills. (Tokuhama-Espinosa, 2014, p. 213)

Analogies are the best way to learn anything new when we have no familiarity or prior experiences to scaffold understanding. Pillars thinking is analogous thinking.

Feedback and Metacognition

In addition to acknowledging the role of analogies in new learning, it is also important to remember that feedback and metacognition are intractably linked and can also be facilitated by the pillars. The brain can't help but learn, but it does not reach levels of higher order thinking or metacognition without training and guidance received through feedback (Tokuhama-Espinosa, 2014). External feedback and questioning help develop habituated, intrinsic thinking patterns and improve the internal metacognitive processes of learners. Teachers can use the pillars as an additional way to give feedback that assists children in viewing their world. Some of the best forms of feedback are through Socratic questioning in which the teacher guides the learner to identify missing information for herself: "*What other **relationships** do you see here? How are they similar to something you already know? In what ways are they the same, and do they differ?*" Guided feedback from teachers to students develops the internal dialogue students need to eventually become autonomous learners with a high degree of metacognition. Rehearsal of these feedback exchanges over time eventually leads to a child's own internal self-talk and metacognitive skills. This means the pillars can be used to leverage the natural feedback-metacognition development cycle.

If we were to teach children to identify the symbols, patterns, order, categories, and relationships around them in a routine fashion throughout their early years and education, they would then naturally call upon this way of thinking as they approached anything new throughout their lifetimes (Squire, 1987). Guided feedback from teachers improves metacognitive abilities in students—*how* they think about *what* and *why* they think. I suggest that if teachers regularly include references to the pillars in their classroom teaching ("*What other **categories** do you see here?*"; "*How is this order similar to other expressions of*

***order** you already know?"; "What is different about this **symbol** or similar about this **pattern**?"*) they would deepen students' understandings of new information because their prior knowledge would become more visible, thanks to rehearsal of feedback dialogues that lead to metacognitive skills.

Explicit and Implicit Learning

The five pillars have the additional benefit of taking advantage of both implicit as well as explicit instruction to enhance learning.

The difference between implicit and explicit forms of learning was first discussed in detail in the 1970s (e.g., Brooks & Miller, 1979; Reber & Lewis, 1977). Reber noted that implicit learning displays a lack of consciousness of what and how something is learned (in DeKeyser, 2008), whereas explicit learning moments include mnemonics and strategies as well as representational systems (Reber et al., 1980). An example of implicit learning is the use of authentic, real-life contexts to learn something meaningful to the learner, such as when a child learns to ride a bike for the first time both because he wants to and because it is important to him to do so. An example of explicit learning includes classroom settings with typical methodologies, such as precise discussion strategies to highlight a specific type of vocabulary in a foreign language. An interesting thing about the pillars is they can be used to enhance both implicit as well as explicit learning.

The understanding of symbols and the recognition of patterns are both implicit and explicit, depending on the methodology employed. This is also true of order, categories, and relationships. For example, whereas the understanding of patterns is normally an implicit aspect of learning—perceived by the learner but not explicitly taught by the teacher—the use of the pillars would make it an explicit learning tool as well. The use of both implicit and explicit learning enhances the probability of recall. As memory and attention are vital for all learning, both implicit as well as explicit teaching should be used. The pillars facilitate this.

Implicit and explicit memory systems are distinct neuronal networks in the brain (Dennis & Cabeza, 2011), however, there is speculation by Dew and Cabeza (2011) that "under certain circumstances, there may be an important and influential relationship between conscious and nonconscious expressions of memory" (Dew & Cabeza, 2011, p. 174) that suggest these systems are

Table 3. Explicit and Implicit Knowledge in the Pillars

HOW THE PILLARS MERGE EXPLICIT AND IMPLICIT LEARNING		
Pillar	**Example of Explicit Question**	**Example of Implicit Question**
Symbols	"What symbols do you see?"	"How would you label that?"
Patterns	"What patterns are there?"	"How does this seem similar to . . .?"
Order	"What expressions of order can you detect?"	"How does this formula differ from other formulas you have seen in the past?"
Categories	"What categories are there?"	"How would you group these ideas?"
Relationships	"What relationships do you see?"	"Do you think X and Y the same as A and B?"

SOURCE: TOKUHAMA-ESPINOSA, 2018

naturally linked in the brain. It can be speculated that, as the use of the pillars is habituated over time, the interface between implicit and explicit learning can be enhanced, leading to improved uptake and recall. It is important to note that this has not yet been proved, though promising research is underway (e.g., Chafee & Crowe, 2017). What does seem clear is that **content knowledge** (in the domains of math, language, history, health, science, art, and so on) and **non-domain-specific cognition** (reasoning, imagining, reflecting, memory, attention, executive functioning, and so on) will find greater overlaps when the pillars are used. This suggests the pillars can be used to mediate normal pathways for learning specific content as well as general cognition.

How the Pillars Interact with Each Other

It is important to remember that the pillars are mutually interdependent and are not necessarily regulated by a hierarchy themselves. Categories, for example, are dependent on patterns; patterns in turn rely on symbols; order depends on relationships, and so on. But none of the pillars must be situated in any particular order in relation to the others. All the pillars can precede and succeed one another.

In many cases it might seem logical to first consider symbols as conceptual representations that usually precede patterns, order, categories, and relationships. However, this is not always true. For instance, there are no symbols in some patterns, such as those that occur in time and space—as with weather

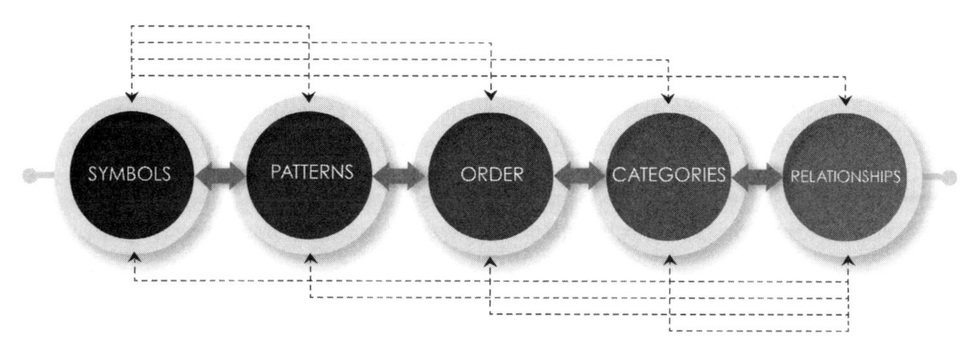

Figure 2. Interrelation of Pillars. SOURCE: TOKUHAMA-ESPINOSA, 2015

patterns, heartbeats, sleep patterns, historical patterns, orbital patterns, and so on—that do not necessarily depend on a symbol for their existence. Similarly, while it might seem predictable that relationships and categories always occur together, this is not necessarily true either. Animals, vegetables, and minerals are categories, but they do not necessarily display a relationship among themselves, for example.

This reminds me of road trips we used to take as kids. "Twenty questions" is a guessing game we used to play as a family on long rides. When it was my turn, I was prompted to think of *anything* in the whole wide world. My mother would always begin by asking if what I was thinking was an "animal, vegetable, or mineral?" This ***categorizing*** tool quickly narrowed down the seemingly infinite number of options. She would then inevitably ask if what I was thinking of was something we could see, or something we had in our house, or something I liked. This determined the ***relationship*** I had with the unknown object. Both the categorization question ("animal, vegetable or mineral") and the relationship questions (something visible, something at home, something I liked) were helpful in narrowing down the choices, but they were not mutually dependent. This is an example of how the five pillars do not always exist together, but when they do, they are always complementary.

How the Pillars Can Help Researchers

Peer-reviewed journals are often held up as the gold standard for evidence-based information. Researchers of teaching and learning processes find that studies in our field are often grouped into journals to respond to specific stages of development (e.g., *Early Childhood Research Quarterly*); cognitive abilities or domain areas of study (e.g., *Journal of Research in Mathematics Education*); problem areas, human variance or ranges in the spectrum of intelligence (e.g., *Gifted Child Quarterly; European Journal of Special Needs Education*); explanations of the physiology of learning (e.g., *Cerebral Cortex*; *Genes, Brain and Behavior; Neuron*); the teaching-learning process, teaching techniques, and best practice (e.g., *American Educational Research Journal; Perspectives in Pedagogy*); field tendencies (*Trends in Cognitive Science; Frontiers in Education*); and even research tools (*Journal of Magnetic Resonance; Brain Topography; Journal of Qualitative Studies in Education*). While logical, this peer-reviewed journal categorization does not lend itself to the intriguing potential of elegantly separating these same studies into the ways that the brain itself might actually subdivide networks or webs of knowledge: symbols, patterns, order, categories and relationships. It's easy to argue that the current research divisions are helpful and necessary for publication processes, editorial division, and grant awards, and can aid researchers in delving deeply into areas of expertise in highly specific aspects of the learning process. I suggest that the five pillars can help us not only to structure learning moments better, but also help structure research better. *How?* In very much the same way: explicitly reminding ourselves to think through the pillars.

The pillars do not reject the existing division of research and teaching-learning practices, but rather *expand their use* by adding the pillars to our thinking constructs. The pillars complement the characteristics of existing research structures by **adding a new dimension** to how they can be used. This means we can read Patricia Kuhl's *Early Language Learning and Literacy: Neuroscience Implications for Education* (2011) not only with her original intent as a comment on the importance of learning in social contexts, *but also* as a study related to **patterns**; part of her work considered infants' computational abilities and the normal language processing (the regular patterns of development) of monolingual and bilingual children. Similarly, we can read Rueda, Checa, and Cómbita's study on improved executive functions (EFs) in children (*Enhanced Efficiency of the Executive Function Attention Network After Training in Preschool Children* [2012]) both as a confirmation that EFs can be enhanced through training *and* as a study of how the brain manages congruences and incongruences through the pillars of **order** and **relations**. This means that the rich body of literature already available that examines specific aspects of the brain's learning mechanisms can be extended in use by applying the pillars as an additional dimension for analysis. Not only can neuroscientific articles be interpreted this way, but articles from all fields benefit from this added dimension.

An example from education is Schleppegrell's *Content-based Language Teaching with Functional Grammar in the Elementary School* (2014), which can be read for its original focus on teaching foreign languages through school subjects, but can *also* be interpreted as a study on **symbols** (written expressions in different languages); **patterns** (similarities between language systems); **categories** (grammatical rules; schematic understanding of content concepts); or **relationships** (how content knowledge in one domain can be used to learn a new language). In another example, Smolleck and Nordgren's study on hands-on, inquiry-based learning in science (*Transforming Standards-Based Teaching: Embracing the Teaching and Learning of Science as Inquiry in Elementary Classrooms* [2014]) can be read as an article on best-practices in science education and *also* be viewed as a study of scientific **symbols** and **patterns** of inquiry, the **order** of scientific methodology, **categories** of hands-on experience that enhance scientific learning in middle school students, and the **relationships** between observation and evidence.

The main idea is that *all* journal articles, independent of the field of study, can be interpreted through the additional lenses that the pillars provide. ***This does not require any specialized knowledge of the field, but rather an openness of mind.*** With a little imagination and a certain level of rehearsal, anybody can learn to think through the lenses of symbols, patterns, order, categories, and relationships, and in doing so, expand the utility of existing research by adding a new dimension of interpretation.

How the Pillars Can Bridge Education and Neuroscience

The pillars can potentially bridge the fields of education and neuroscience, both in research and practice, by offering a common space for analysis. For example, studies on executive functions (EFs) training (e.g., Diamond, 2012) can retain their original purpose of showing the benefits of training but can *also* be viewed through the pillars of order (motivation *leads to* more time on task which *leads to* learning) and relationships (mutual strengthening of working memory, cognitive flexibility, and inhibitory control; as well as the relationship between EFs and decision making). Yuan and Raz's work (2014) on structural neuroimaging of executive functions in adults can be seen as a general meta-analysis of the "bigger is better" hypothesis of prefrontal cortex volume and thickness as it relates to EFs, *and* it can be seen as a study of the relationship between age and EFs, or the categories of tasks used to measure EFs. Viewing them through the pillars, we can analyze these two research areas together to see whether the types of studies that are used in Yuan and Raz's meta-analysis to measure EFs in adults correlate with the types of real-world experiences children have in classes shown in Diamond's work. This means that existing studies will take on added value and can have extended comparative use. These different studies show that—independent of what type or aspect of learning is considered (domain area instruction, methodologies or activities, neuronal correlates of learning, and so on)—the pillars can serve as an additional lens through which to view the data.

Building Logical Pathways in the Brain

A final introductory idea of the five pillars is that different types of learning tend to follow multiple, predisposed, "logical" neuronal networks similar in all humans, though individual variances are also notable in the specific neuronal pathways that branch from the networks. There are different neuronal networks for different aspects of learning. When a student learns to do math, multiple networks are used simultaneously. For example, semantic recall (e.g., Flegal et al., 2014); affective learning (e.g., Berridge & Kringelbach, 2013); implicit memory dependent learning (e.g., Curran & Schacter, 2013); Bayesian learning (e.g., Gopnik & Wellman, 2012); symbolic and nonsymbolic representation learning (e.g., Gullick et al., 2011); and auditory and visually stimulated learning (e.g., Altieri et al., 2013) are all different networks, yet all play a role in learning math formulas. Furthermore, when two students learn that same math formula, the precise pathways branching from these networks are likely to be unique, as they depend on an individual's prior experiences (which are unique to the individual). This, according to Sirois and colleagues (2008), is in part how neuroconstructivism works: "Activity-dependence is one part of a feedback loop with morphology, with each affecting the other" (Sirois et al., 2008, p. 321). Learning is an iterative process where different pathways systematically interact with one another, the environment, and the experiences of the learner. While no two human beings appear to follow identical routes, *similar* neuronal pathways are easily identified in large-scale studies that indicate general human tendencies for network development. Some impressive documentation of these networks can be found on the Human Connectome Project webpage (http://www.humanconnectomeproject.org/) in which hundreds of healthy subjects are scanned while conducting the same activities using different imaging techniques to document neuronal network use. This means that not only are the pillars a neat way of organizing curricula, they also appear to mirror the way the brain aligns like-elements in neuronal networks. These studies permit the identification of the types of networks that tend to cluster together in similar brain areas, but which are actually unique to each individual based on their life experience, which supports the idea of a neuroconstructivist hierarchy for learning. We will come back to this idea in detail in Chapter 7. We now turn to a description of each of the five pillars.

1. Symbols

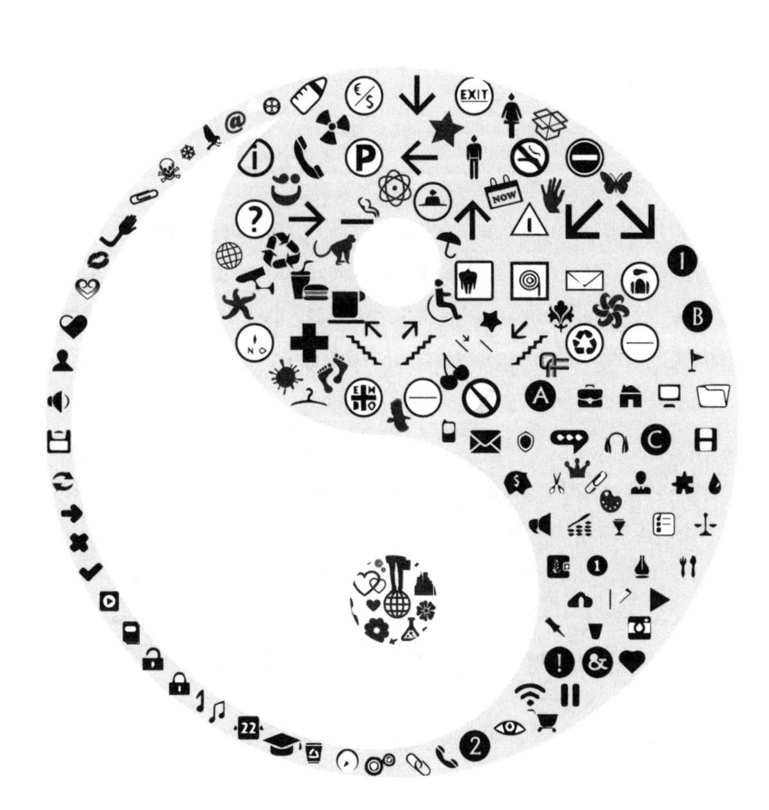

What is a Symbol?

Symbols are characters used in place of conventional representations to signify meanings, functions, processes, feelings, or objects, including words. A symbol can be a simple mark or letter, but it can also be an emoji or ideogram; anything that stands for something else, including emblems, street signals, company logos, and other visible signs. Symbols can also be intangible, as in "literary symbolism," including events or even a simple spoken word, which can be used to give an entirely different meaning to a specific context. As a verb, to *symbolize* can mean to suggest, signify, embody, denote, indicate, mean, epitomize, or imply. Some of the manifestations of common symbols is offered below.

Forms

One kind of symbol is a form. Forms are configurations that represent the external appearance of an object and can be used to make shapes. Forms offer outlines of structures and can be used figuratively or literally. Two of the clearest examples of forms are language and mathematical forms.

Language

There are between 2,500 and 7,000 languages in the world, depending on whether we count pidgins and creoles, which in turn have a total of around 50 different alphabets. Letters are found in many languages that often (but not always) have symbol-to-sound references. Other languages use characters, which represent pictographs (logographs), ideograms, and/or sounds. For example, Japanese has two syllabaries (*katakana* and *hiragana*), which represent sound-to-symbol forms, but it also has *kanji*, which are based on Chinese pictographs, as well as *romaji*, which is the alphabet based on Roman or Phoenician letters (A, B, C). A single Japanese sentence can include all these forms.

English uses the Phoenician alphabet, also referred to as the Latin alphabet. There are many languages with other traditional scripts, such as Arabic, Greek, and Chinese, which have in some cases adopted Latin letters for popular press. Some cultures use their traditional script as well as an international language in their social communication. For example, in Lebanon people speak Arabic and French, and use both these scripts in their everyday writing, such as in newspapers.

Figure 4. Japanese Alphabets. SOURCE: LEOPOLDO PEREIRA, 2018

Figure 5. Lebanese Newspaper. SOURCE: GOOGLE TRANSLATE

Languages are made up of many other forms aside from letters, including punctuation marks. We use symbols such as "?" and "!" to convey questioning or exclamation. We note who is speaking to give agency by using quotation marks (". . ."), and give pause by integrating commas (","). We use parentheses to give clarification "(. . .)" and highlight concepts by using **bold** or *italic* script. There 14 common punctuation marks used in English (apostrophe, bracket, colon, comma, dash, ellipsis, exclamation mark, period, guillemet, hyphen, question mark, semicolon, slash, and backslash), as well as another two dozen used less frequently but which are part of common literacy (including the ampersand, asterisk, at sign, backslash, bullet, number sign, copyright sign, and registered trademark symbol) (Your Dictionary, 2017). A little fewer than half the languages of the world do not have written forms. According to Ethnologue, of the "7,099 living languages, 3,866 have a developed writing system" (Simons & Fenning, 2018, p. 1). Letter forms from the Latin alphabet are among the most important symbols in the West in traditional education, as all subject-area teaching is mediated through language. Other common forms in educational settings are numerical forms.

Mathematics

A number is an arithmetic value and can be expressed by a figure (e.g., 3), a word (e.g., three), or another symbol (e.g., ***). The earliest numerical system was a simple tally notation:

Table 4. Tally Marks

Western	Asian
I II III IIII ~~IIII~~	一 丅 下 𤴓 正

SOURCE: TOKUHAMA-ESPINOSA, 2018

Numbers can be categorized in many ways, including natural, integers, rational, real, and complex, among others. Rational numbers can be expressed as fractions, and real numbers can include numbers requiring a decimal point as well as square roots. Each of these uses a different symbol.

Table 5. Mathematical Symbols

EXAMPLES OF MATHEMATICAL SYMBOLS				
Addition	**Subtraction**	**Multiplication**	**Division**	**Positive and negative numbers**
$+$	$-$	$\times$	$\div$	-1, 0, 1
Fraction	**Equivalencies**	**Fraction to decimal**	**Pi**	**Square root**
$\frac{a}{b}$	$\frac{24}{30} = \frac{12}{15}$	$\frac{1}{4} = .25$	$\pi = 3.1415$	$\sqrt{4} = 2$

SOURCE: TOKUHAMA-ESPINOSA, 2017

Math symbols can represent a specific idea or schema, or they can indicate a process or property. In math, we use symbols to explain whole processes, such as the use of the number line to explain addition or subtraction: 1 2 3.

Math symbols are also used to explain formulas or processes that are used to do things such as calculating volume or area:

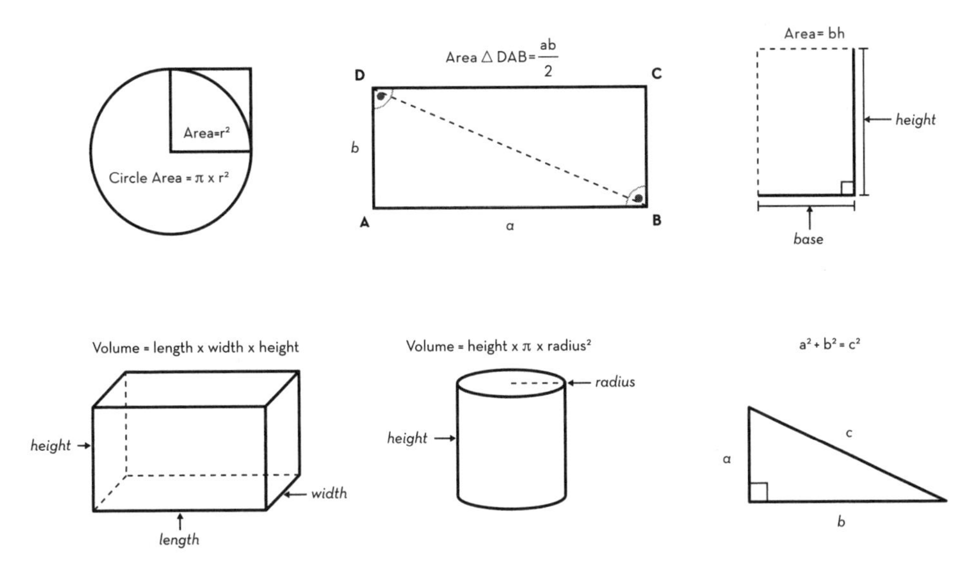

Figure 6. Basic Geometric Formulas. SOURCE: TOKUHAMA-ESPINOSA, 2018

It is interesting that, while there are around 50 written language systems, there are just 20 or so numerical systems. Globally, Western Arabic numerals (1, 2, 3, 4, 5, 6, and so on) are the most commonly used in education. Other systems include Eastern Arabic, Thai, and Greek.

Table 6. Numerical Forms

Eastern Arabic	Thai
٩ ٨ ٧ ٦ ٥ ٤ ٣ ٢ ١ ٠	๐๑๒๓๔๕๖๗๘๙
A	B
Greek	**Chinese, Japanese, Korean**
ōαβγδεϝζηθι	〇/零 一 二 三 四 五 六 七 八 九 十
C	D

SOURCE: (A) ARABIC NUMERALS, WIKIPEDIA, HTTPS://EN.WIKIPEDIA.ORG/WIKI/FILE:ARABIC_NUMERALS.PNG (B) THAI NUMERALS, WIKIPEDIA, HTTPS://EN.WIKIPEDIA.ORG/WIKI/THAI_NUMERALS; (C) GREEK NUMERALS, WIKIPEDIA, HTTPS://EN.WIKIPEDIA.ORG/WIKI/GREEK_NUMERALS; (D), CHINESE, JAPANESE AND KOREAN NUMERALS, WIKIPEDIA, HTTPS://EN.WIKIPEDIA.ORG/WIKI/CHINESE_NUMERALS

Japanese language symbols have evolved from Chinese and are different. However, the numerical symbols are still shared, and are also used in Korea, though some textbooks use Arabic numbers as well. Numerical forms, along with language forms, are the most common symbols used in education today. Other symbol systems are also based on math.

All musical scales are based on math, for example. Music is arguably a universal language, which is supported by the fact that its symbols have strikingly less variation than written languages or mathematical languages. Music, like spoken language and mathematical reasoning, does not need to be written down to exist, but in doing so, creates documentation and therefore a memory, making replication possible. While musical instruments have been found dating back 40,000 years (see information on the Divje Babe flute), symbolic forms for musical notation have only been in existence since approximately 2,000 BC (in the form of a cuneiform tablet created at Nippur in Sumer, or present-day Iraq [The Oriental Institute of the University of Chicago, 2018]). Symbols to write music only became commonly used in a consistent way in the West from about the midpoint in medieval times onwards (around 900AD). Monks like Guido d'Arezzo, who laid out the first musical stave in five lines and wrote the first notes (*do-re-mi-fa-sol-la-si-do*), or the heptatonic scale (seven-note) (Lyons, 2007), were largely responsible for devising the symbols we use to compose music today. Current musical notation uses both ancient symbols, such as the stave that structures the musical piece (𝄚), as well as modern notation, such as the notes themselves (♪). Musical symbols can represent the sound, meter, pitch, mode, tempo, duration, repetition, signatures (flat or sharp keys), articulations, and volume or intensity of a musical line (Gerou & Lusk, 1996). There are symbols used to indicate "breath marks" and pauses, and others that show the relationship between notes (𝄚). There are additional special symbols for different instruments (percussion, string, brass, woodwind, and keyboard).

It is interesting to note that Chinese symbols parallel d'Arezzo's scale but do so in numbers 1-7 (do=1; re=2; mi=3; fa=4; sol=5; la=6; si=7), which is really a translation scheme as much Eastern music is based on a pentatonic scale with just five notes. While different countries such as Korea and Egypt have additional symbol systems for music (with different placement of similar symbols mentioned above, or with the use of colors that replace some of the symbols [Hickman, 1980]), music is almost universally written today using western symbols.

Other symbolic forms include computer languages. For example, there are hundreds to thousands of programming languages, depending on categorization schemes. The sub-set of computer languages are less numerous; there were an estimated 715 languages in use in 2018 listed on Wikipedia, with more being written every day. Computer languages use a combination of symbols from language and mathematics. For example, BASIC (**B**eginner's **A**ll-purpose **S**ymbolic **I**nstruction **C**ode) was one of the first computer languages to be widely used and combines alphanumeric symbols as do most codes used today. Other symbols are found in physical forms.

Physical Forms

Other forms can be found in *molds, blocks,* and *blueprints.* These are used to create consistent versions of a desired form.

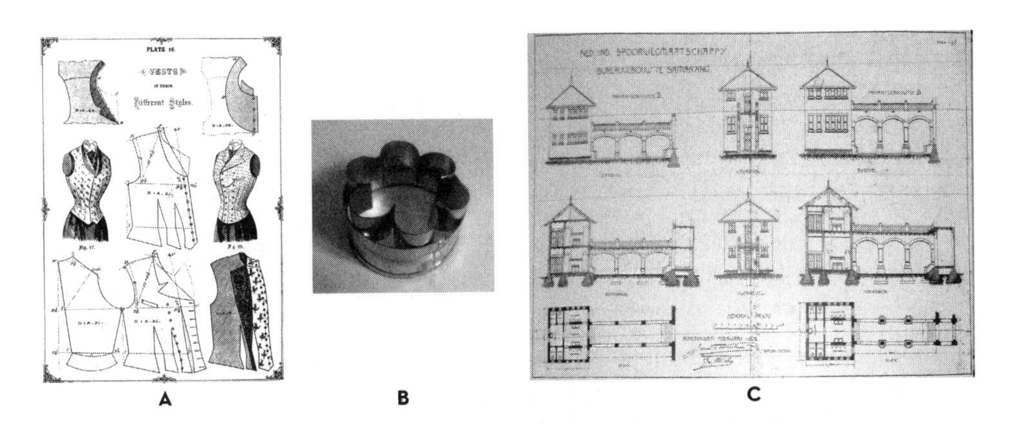

Figure 7. Forms: Stencils, Molds, and Blueprints. SOURCE: (A) ENGLISH: THE CUTTERS' PRACTICAL GUIDE TO THE CUTTING OF LADIES' GARMENTS BY W.D.F. VINCENT, INTERNET ARCHIVE IDENTIFIER : CUTTERSPRACTICAL00VINC [PUBLIC DOMAIN], VIA WIKIMEDIA COMMONS; (B) MINORQUIAN COOKIE MOLD, BY SLASTIC (OWN WORK) [PUBLIC DOMAIN], VIA WIKIMEDIA COMMONS; (C) BLUEPRINTS FOR LAWANG SEWU, PICTURE BY J. F. KLINKHAMER AND B. J. QUENDAG, IN AMSTERDAM [PUBLIC DOMAIN], VIA WIKIMEDIA COMMONS

Forms are the most useful symbols in educational contexts, but *shapes* and *representations* also account for a large number of symbols found in everyday life.

Shapes

Other symbols are found in shapes. It can be argued that there are an infinite number of shapes. Some of the most basic examples include the following:

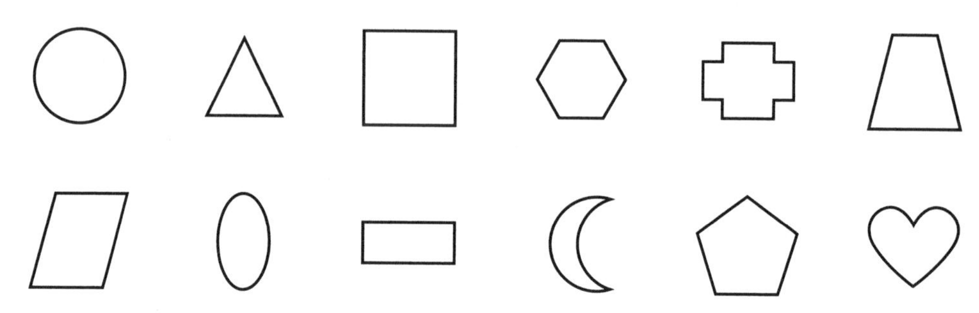

Figure 8. Basic Shapes. SOURCE: TOKUHAMA-ESPINOSA, 2018

Shapes can be combined to create elaborate forms, and all design depends on their conjoint representations. A house can be drawn, for example, by combining the basic shapes of triangles, rectangles, and squares.

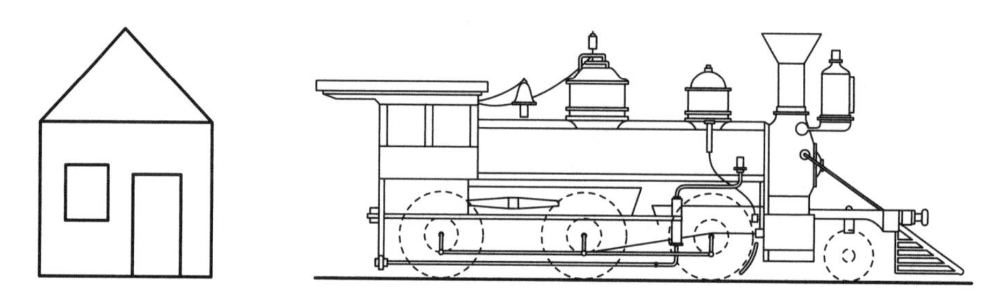

Figure 9. Objects Drawn from Basic Shapes. SOURCES: (A) TOKUHAMA-ESPINOSA, 2018; (B) DANIEL KINNEAR CLARK, 1822—1896 [PUBLIC DOMAIN] FROM WIKICOMMONS

Everything in the visible world is composed of shapes, from the food you eat to the transportation systems you ride, the house you live in, and the clothes you wear. Shapes describe people, nature, animals, cloud formations, and the city around you. Everything found in the physical world can be expressed in shapes. In schooling, shapes are among the first things small children learn, along with numbers and colors. Shapes are used in geometry, physics, math, art, design, architecture, and can express processes, concepts, and ideas. Shapes can also be used figuratively, as in "it hurt like an arrow through my heart," "he was straight as a rod," or "she was such a square." Shapes precede language forms, as they are often more intuitive than letters, which are arguably abstract.

Representations

Symbols can also be representations. A representation can be a picture or a model that depicts a similarity or likeness to another thing. Representations can also be portrayals or figures used to convey a meaning. Representations can be simple, for example a silhouette of men and women can be used to indicate bathroom divisions, or the use of a map or globe to represent Earth.

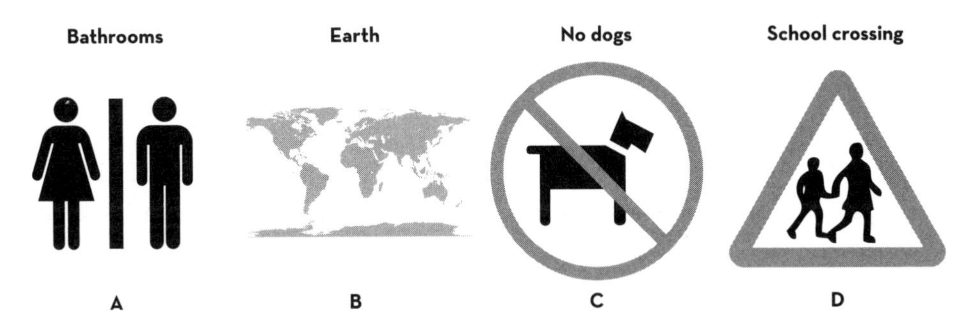

Figure 10. Examples of Representations. SOURCES: (A) BY AIGA [PUBLIC DOMAIN], VIA WIKIMEDIA COMMONS WIKIMEDIACOMMONS; (B) BY CRATES (OWN WORK) [GFDL (HTTP://WWW.GNU.ORG/COPYLEFT/FDL.HTML) OR CC BY-SA 4.0-3.0-2.5-2.0-1.0 (HTTPS://CREATIVECOMMONS.ORG/LICENSES/BY-SA/4.0-3.0-2.5-2.0-1.0)], VIA WIKIMEDIA COMMONS; (C) BY SLOMOX [PUBLIC DOMAIN], VIA WIKIMEDIA COMMONS; (D) BY WOODENNATURE (OWN WORK) [CC BY 3.0 (HTTP://CREATIVECOMMONS.ORG/LICENSES/BY/3.0)], VIA WIKIMEDIA COMMONS

Street signs represent things such as children crossing the road, or rocks falling, but can also be abstract as in a triangle used to mean "yield." A skull-and-crossbones represents "death" and can be used to show poisonous contents, while a line drawn through an object represents "no" or "not allowed." Graphs can be pictorial representations. For example, representations of the world's population can be expressed in pie charts, bar graphs or other elaborate forms.

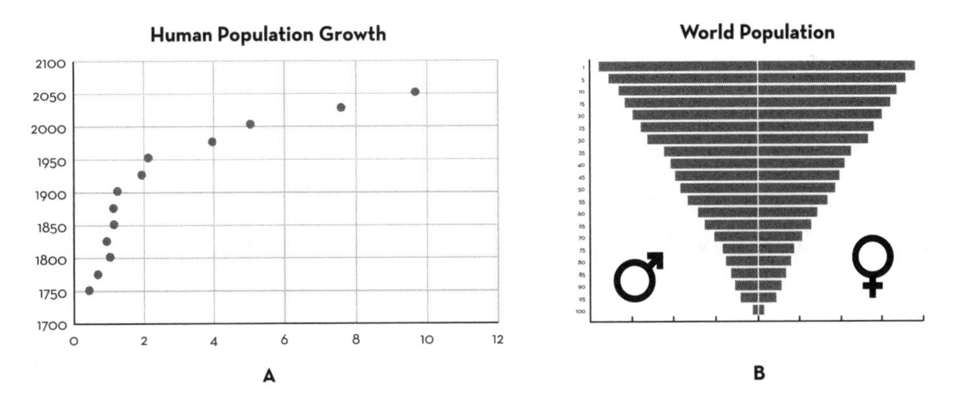

Figure 11. Representations of the World's Population. SOURCE: TOKUHAMA-ESPINOSA, 2018

Symbolic representations can be used to express chemical compounds, physics formulas, math problems, or biological gene labels.

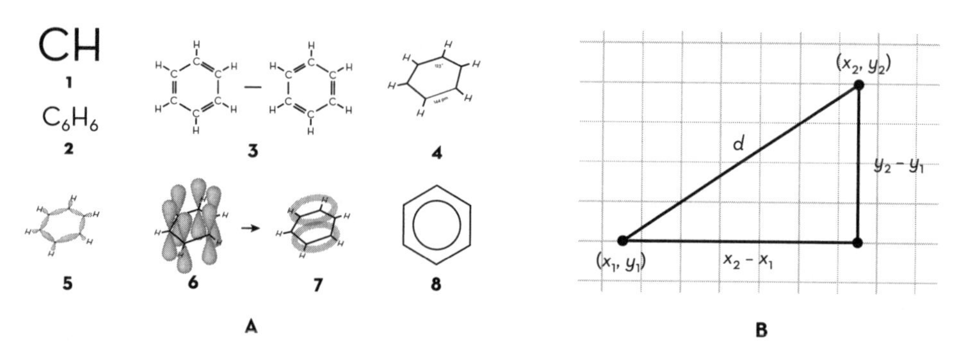

Figure 12. Scientific Representations. SOURCE: (A) BENZENE REPRESENTATIONS VIA WIKIMEDIA COMMONS; (B) DISTANCE FORMULA VIA WIKIMEDIACOMMONS

Representations can use one medium to represent a distinct object or belief in another, as when an origami paper crane or a turtle represents "long life" in some cultures. Similarly, "peace" can be interpreted as a dove, as the Christian church has done since the 15th century, or as a circle with three legs, originally used as an anti-nuclear symbol in the late 1950s.

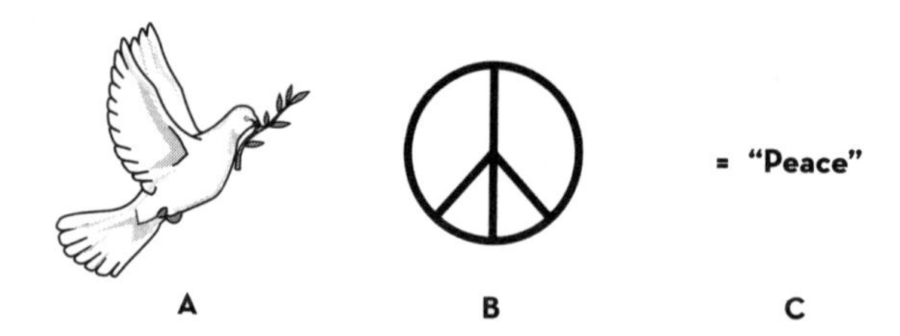

Figure 13. Conceptual Representations of "Peace." SOURCES (A) BY ELEMBIS A DOVE CARRYING AN OLIVE BRANCH. 7 JANUARY 2007 [PUBLIC DOMAIN], VIA WIKIMEDIA COMMONS; (B) TOKUHAMA-ESPINOSA, 2018

Fashion and style also represent elements of time, values, or attitudes. Dressing like a hipster or a businessman represents very different perspectives on the world, for example. Representations are also seen in company logos, which use symbols to convey memorable ideas or names. The designs on flags represents countries, including their values and histories as expressed through basic symbols, such as the red circle in the Japanese flag, which represents the rising sun and is part of the name *Ni-hon* or "Land of the Rising Sun." Our favorite sports teams all have colors, mascots, or other symbols to represent their core values ("Guardian Angels"; "Fearless Bobcats"; "Mighty Warriors"). The six most adhered-to religions have symbols that represent some aspect of their history or values.

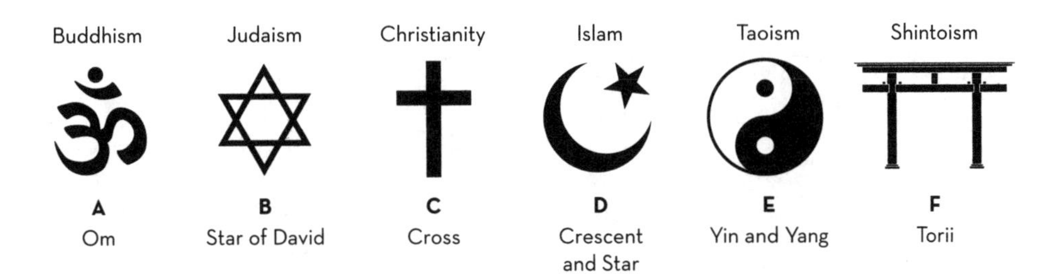

Figure 14. Religious Symbols. SOURCE PUBLIC DOMAIN, VIA WIKIMEDIA COMMONS

Representations can also be found in things like advertisements and infographics, which use symbols to convey messages. Some of the newest representations are found in *emojis*, which range from images of happy faces, "thumbs up" to any number of foods, animals, or emotions.

Figure 15. Examples of Expressive Symbols. SOURCE: TOKUHAMA-ESPINOSA, 2018

Finally, there are abstract representations, which are imprecise renderings of the original that are purposefully created for art's sake, such as when an artist interprets a woman's form.

In academia, students are taught to use and interpret symbolic representations not only in art, but also in literature, history, graphic design, and the social sciences. Different branches of psychology interpret different symbolic representations in objects or actions. Hand gestures can represent sentiments and values, such as that of a salute, handshake, or "OK" sign. Symbols, expressed

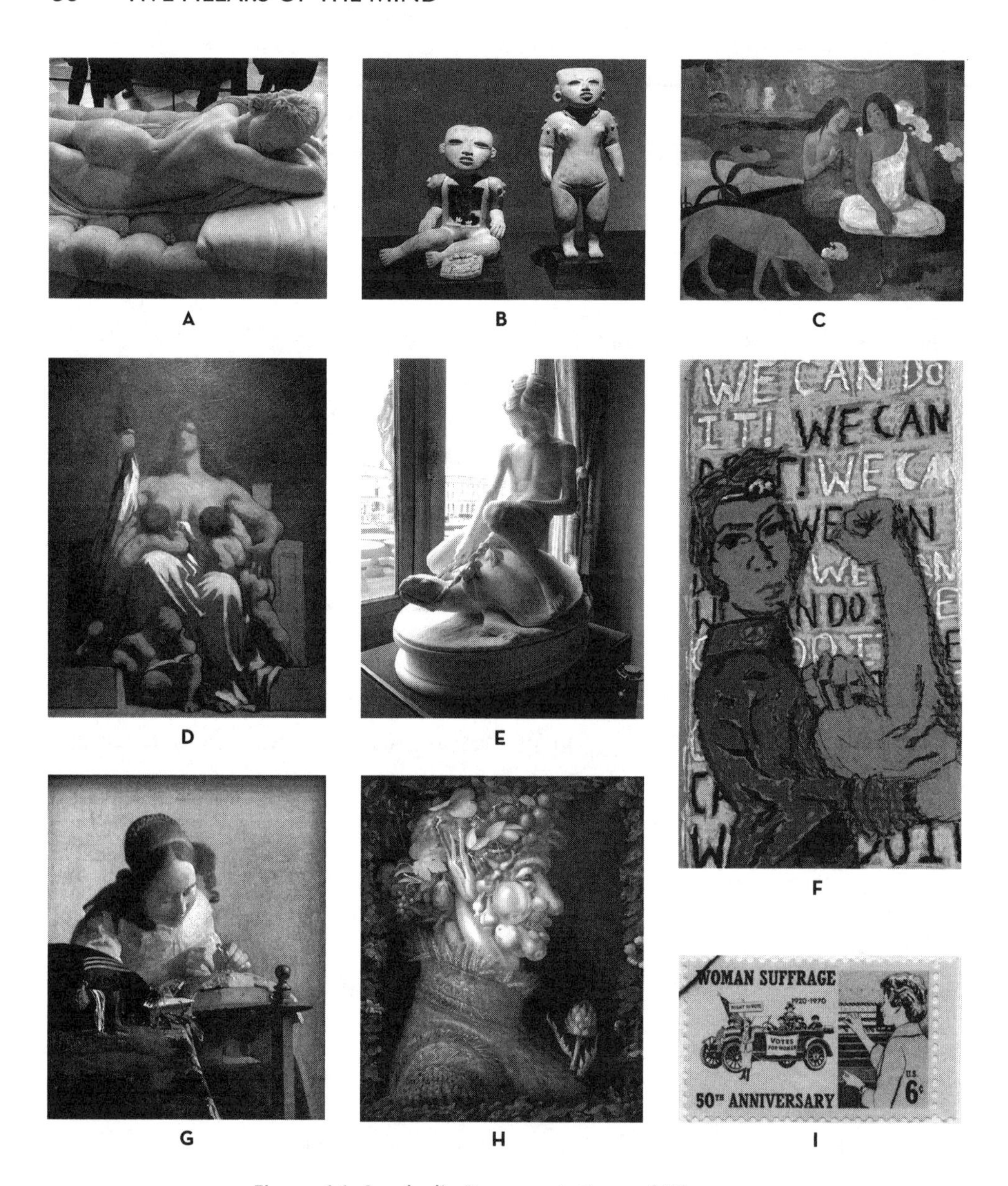

Figure 16. Symbolic Representations of Women.

SOURCE: PHOTOS BY TOKUHAMA-ESPINOSA: (A) HERMAPHRODITUS ASLEEP. ARTIST UNKNOWN. GREEK MARBLE, ROMAN COPY FROM THE IMPERIAL ERA (2ND CENTURY CE) AFTER A GREEK ORIGINAL, NOW AT THE LOUVRE, PARIS. (B) SCULPTURES IN THE TEOITHUACÁN STYLE, CLASSIC PERIOD FROM THE 6TH AND 7TH CENTURY FROM THE STATE OF MICHOACÁN, MEXICO. UNKNOWN ARTIST. MUSÉE LE LOUVRE, PARIS, FRANCE. (C) PAUL GAUGUIN, MUSÉE D'ORSAY, PARIS, FRANCE. PUBLIC DOMAIN VIA WIKIMEDIA COMMONS. (D) HONORÉ DAUMIER, PUBLIC DOMAIN VIA WIKIMEDIA COMMONS. (E) PIERRE HÉBERT, ENFANT JOUANT AVEC UNE TORTUE 1849 LE LOUVRE, PARIS, FRANCE. (F) GABRIEL ESPINOSA, WE CAN DO IT. PERSONAL COLLECTION. REPRINTED WITH PERMISSION OF THE AUTHOR. (G) JOHANNES VERMEER, PUBLIC DOMAIN VIA WIKIMEDIA COMMONS. (H) GIUSEPPE ARCIMBOLDO, L'ÉTÉ, SIGNÉ ET DATÉ, 1573, MILAN. LE LOUVRE, PARIS, FRANCE. (I) BY WARD BRACKETT, DESIGNER, PUBLIC DOMAIN VIA WIKIMEDIA COMMONS.

as forms, shapes, and representations, are fundamental in communication and define our world both literally and figuratively.

There are more writings about **symbol** representations in the brain than in any other pillar. Some representative research articles on this topic can be found in Table 7.

How the Pillar of Symbols Economizes Learning

Looking at the world through the pillar of symbols economizes learning, as many symbols share similar or neighboring neuronal pathways. This suggests that once a certain symbol or group of symbols is known to the learner, other symbols that follow the same or similar neuronal tracts can be learned faster, even if they come from different disciplines or fields. There is evidence that letters cross over and share some pathways with numerical symbol understanding (Pinel & Dehaene, 2010), though the precise symbols in questions are key. Arabic numerals and the Phoenician alphabet show greater overlay than Chinese symbols with Arabic numerals, for example. There are studies that indicate that numbers are not processed the same as words (Carreiras et al., 2015), however, numbers and *letters* (not words), appear to share networks. There is also evidence that there is a relatively high correlation of people (40 percent) with problems in language (dyslexia) who also have problems in math (dyscalculia), suggesting that there are identical or overlapping pathways for some aspects of math and language ("comorbidity"). Zebani and Ansari (2012) showed that people who can read have different neuronal pathways than people who cannot read, and they process numerical magnitude estimations differently if they are expressed in symbols. This means that there is no difference between literate and illiterate individuals when it comes to nonsymbolic numerical processing, but people who can read have different neuronal pathways to process quantity that depend more on the symbol used to do that processing.

Overlapping pathways economize learning. Letters (A, B, C . . .), linguistic and mathematical symbols (+, -, . . .), and numerals (1, 2, 3, . . .) have some overlap in processing, meaning the brain quickly categorizes these elements together. The hypothesis is that symbols that overlap with other pillars also economizing learning. For example, a square is a shape (a type of **symbol**) but can also be interpreted as parts of **patterns** (⚃), parts of **categories** (four-sided shapes), or **relationships** (four equally sized lines joined at 90-degree angles yield a square). Use of the pillars enhances recall for these like items. Memory is vital for learning, and speed of recall influences cognition, meaning habituated review of the **symbols** pillars can improve the probability of long-term learning.

Implications for Student Learning

Symbols surround us and are part of our academic world, in our natural world, as well as in the ways our imaginations unify ideas. Symbols distinguish humans from other animals, much in the same way that language does, and extend the way thoughts can be expressed. Symbols can be transparent and direct, as in a single tally mark signifying "one," or they can be interpretative and nebulous, as in Edgar Allan Poe's artistic symbolism of "the raven" in his poetry.

Look up from your book right now. What symbols can you see, aside from the letters and numbers on this page? The logo on an object? A chart or graph? A geometrical symbol? Now, what do they all have in common? How are they different? Habituating your mind to survey your surroundings for **symbols** will improve your ability to see them effortlessly in the future. Once habituated, you will naturally begin to see the symbols without prompts. This will lead to a more transdisciplinary vision for problem solving, and hopefully, if prompted to think of an innovative new software language, business logo, architecture, design, or clothing line, you will be better equipped for the challenge if you have learned to think through the pillars. Table 7 offers some example studies of how symbol systems have been documented in the brain.

Table 7. Example Studies of Symbols in the Brain

FURTHER READING ON THE SCIENCE OF SYMBOLS IN THE BRAIN
Math Symbols
Amalric, M., & Dehaene, S. (2016). Origins of the brain networks for advanced mathematics in expert mathematicians. *Proceedings of the National Academy of Sciences, 113*(18), 4909–4917. Ansari, D. (2015). Number symbols in the brain. *Mathematical Cognition and Learning, 2,* 27–46. Goffin, C. & Ansari, D. (2016). Beyond magnitude: Judging ordinality of symbolic number is unrelated to magnitude comparison and independently relates to individual differences in arithmetic. *Cognition, 150,* 68–76.

Krause, F., Lindemann, O., Toni, I., & Bekkering, H. (2014). Different brains process numbers differently: Structural bases of individual differences in spatial and nonspatial number representations. *Journal of Cognitive Neuroscience, 26*(4), 768--776.

Lyons, I. M., Ansari, D., & Beilock, S. L. (2015). Qualitatively different coding of symbolic and nonsymbolic numbers in the human brain. *Human Brain Mapping, 36*(2), 475-488.

Mathieu, R., Epinat-Duclos, J., Sigovan, M., Breton, A., Cheylus, A., Fayol, M., . . . & Prado, J. (2017). What's behind a "+" sign? Perceiving an arithmetic operator recruits brain circuits for spatial orienting. *Cerebral Cortex, 28*(5), 1673-1684.

Sokolowski, H. M., Fias, W., Mousa, A., & Ansari, D. (2017). Common and distinct brain regions in both parietal and frontal cortex support symbolic and nonsymbolic number processing in humans: A functional neuroimaging meta-analysis. *NeuroImage, 146*, 376-394.

Vogel, S. E., Goffin, C., & Ansari, D. (2015). Developmental specialization of the left parietal cortex for the semantic representation of Arabic numerals: An fMRI-adaptation study. *Developmental Cognitive Neuroscience, 12*, 61-73.

Language Symbols

Asano, M., Imai, M., Kita, S., Kitajo, K., Okada, H., & Thierry, G. (2015). Sound symbolism scaffolds language development in preverbal infants. *Cortex, 63*, 196-205.

Dehaene, S. & Cohen, L. (2011). The unique role of the visual word form area in reading. *Trends in Cognitive Sciences, 15*(6), 254-262.

Dehaene, S., Pegado, F., Braga, L. W., Ventura, P., Nunes Filho, G., Jobert, A., . . . & Cohen, L. (2010). How learning to read changes the cortical networks for vision and language. *Science, 330*(6009), 1359-1364.

Kherif, F., Josse, G., & Price, C. J. (2010). Automatic top-down processing explains common left occipito-temporal responses to visual words and objects. *Cerebral Cortex, 21*(1), 103-114.

Kovic, V., Plunkett, K., & Westermann, G. (2010). The shape of words in the brain. *Cognition, 114*(1), 19-28.

Madec, S., Le Goff, K., Anton, J. L., Longcamp, M., Velay, J. L., Nazarian, B., . . . & Rey, A. (2016). Brain correlates of phonological recoding of visual symbols. *NeuroImage, 132*, 359-372.

Price, C. J. & Devlin, J. T. (2011). The interactive account of ventral occipitotemporal contributions to reading. *Trends in Cognitive Sciences, 15*(6), 246-253.

Pulvermüller, F. (2013). How neurons make meaning: Brain mechanisms for embodied and abstract-symbolic semantics. *Trends in Cognitive Sciences, 17*(9), 458-470.

Revill, K. P., Namy, L. L., DeFife, L. C., & Nygaard, L. C. (2014). Cross-linguistic sound symbolism and crossmodal correspondence: Evidence from fMRI and DTI. *Brain and Language, 128*(1), 18-24.

Numerals, Letters, and Other Symbols

Carreiras, M., Monahan, P. J., Lizarazu, M., Duñabeitia, J. A., & Molinaro, N. (2015). Numbers are not like words: different pathways for literacy and numeracy. *Neuroimage, 118*, 79-89.

Carreiras, M., Quiñones, I., Hernández-Cabrera, J. A., & Duñabeitia, J. A. (2014). Orthographic coding: brain activation for letters, symbols, and digits. *Cerebral Cortex, 25*(12), 4748-4760.

Holloway, I. D., Battista, C., Vogel, S. E., & Ansari, D. (2013). Semantic and perceptual processing of number symbols: Evidence from a cross-linguistic fMRI adaptation study. *Journal of Cognitive Neuroscience, 25*(3), 388-400.

Park, J., Berg, B., Chiang, C., Woldorff, M. G., & Brannon, E. M. (2017). Developmental trajectory of neuronal specialization for letter and number visual processing. *Developmental Science, 21*(3), e12578. DOI: 10.1111/desc.12578

van Atteveldt, N. & Ansari, D. (2014). How symbols transform brain function: A review in memory of Leo Blomert. *Trends in Neuroscience and Education, 3*(2), 44–49.

Zvyagintsev, M., Clemens, B., Chechko, N., Mathiak, K. A., Sack, A. T., & Mathiak, K. (2013). Brain networks underlying mental imagery of auditory and visual information. *European Journal of Neuroscience, 37*(9), 1421–1434.

Forms and Shapes

Amedi, A., Stern, W. M., Camprodon, J. A., Bermpohl, F., Merabet, L., Rotman, S., . . . & Pascual-Leone, A. (2007). Shape conveyed by visual-to-auditory sensory substitution activates the lateral occipital complex. *Nature Neuroscience, 10*(6), 687.

Cavina-Pratesi, C., Kentridge, R. W., Heywood, C. A., & Milner, A. D. (2010). Separate channels for processing form, texture, and color: evidence from fMRI adaptation and visual object agnosia. *Cerebral Cortex, 20*(10), 2319–2332.

DiCarlo, J. J., Zoccolan, D., & Rust, N. C. (2012). How does the brain solve visual object recognition? *Neuron, 73*(3), 415–434.

Georgieva, S., Peeters, R., Kolster, H., Todd, J. T., & Orban, G. A. (2009). The processing of three-dimensional shape from disparity in the human brain. *Journal of Neuroscience, 29*(3), 727–742.

McManus, J. N., Li, W., & Gilbert, C. D. (2011). Adaptive shape processing in primary visual cortex. *Proceedings of the National Academy of Sciences, 108*(24), 9739–9746.

Milner, D. & Goodale, M. (2006). *The visual brain in action*. Oxford, UK: Oxford University Press.

Orban, G. A. (2011). The extraction of 3D shape in the visual system of human and nonhuman primates. *Annual Review of Neuroscience, 34*, 361–388.

Silson, E. H., McKeefry, D. J., Rodgers, J., Gouws, A. D., Hymers, M., & Morland, A. B. (2013). Specialized and independent processing of orientation and shape in visual field maps LO1 and LO2. *Nature Neuroscience, 16*(3), 267–269.

Stilla, R. & Sathian, K. (2008). Selective visuo–haptic processing of shape and texture. *Human Brain Mapping, 29*(10), 1123–1138.

Welchman, A. E., Deubelius, A., Conrad, V., Heinrich, H. B., & Kourtzi, Z. (2005). 3D shape perception from combined depth cues in human visual cortex. *Nature Neuroscience, 8*(6), 820.

Representations and Objects

Amedi, A., von Kriegstein, K., van Atteveldt, N. M., Beauchamp, M. S., & Naumer, M. J. (2005). Functional imaging of human crossmodal identification and object recognition. *Experimental Brain Research, 166*(3–4), 559–571.

DiCarlo, J. J., Zoccolan, D., & Rust, N. C. (2012). How does the brain solve visual object recognition? *Neuron, 73*(3), 415–434.

Huth, A. G., Nishimoto, S., Vu, A. T., & Gallant, J. L. (2012). A continuous semantic space describes the representation of thousands of object and action categories across the human brain. *Neuron, 76*(6), 1210–1224.

Kozhevnikov, M., Blazhenkova, O., & Becker, M. (2010). Trade-off in object versus spatial visu-

alization abilities: Restriction in the development of visual-processing resources. *Psychologic Bulletin & Review, 17*(1), 29–35.
Mahon, B. Z. & Caramazza, A. (2011). What drives the organization of object knowledge in the brain? *Trends in Cognitive Sciences, 15*(3), 97–103.
Mazza, V. & Caramazza, A. (2011). Temporal brain dynamics of multiple object processing: The flexibility of individuation. *PloS One, 6*(2), e17453.
Mudrik, L., Lamy, D., & Deouell, L. Y. (2010). ERP evidence for context congruity effects during simultaneous object–scene processing. *Neuropsychologia, 48*(2), 507–517.
Rousselet, G. A., & Pernet, C. R. (2011). Quantifying the time course of visual object processing using ERPs: It's time to up the game. *Frontiers in Psychology, 2*, 107. DOI: https://doi.org/10.3389/fpsyg.2011.00107
Sehatpour, P., Dias, E. C., Butler, P. D., Revheim, N., Guilfoyle, D. N., Foxe, J. J., & Javitt, D. C. (2010). Impaired visual object processing across an occipital-frontal-hippocampal brain network in schizophrenia: An integrated neuroimaging study. *Archives of General Psychiatry, 67*(8), 772–782.

We now turn to the pillar of patterns.

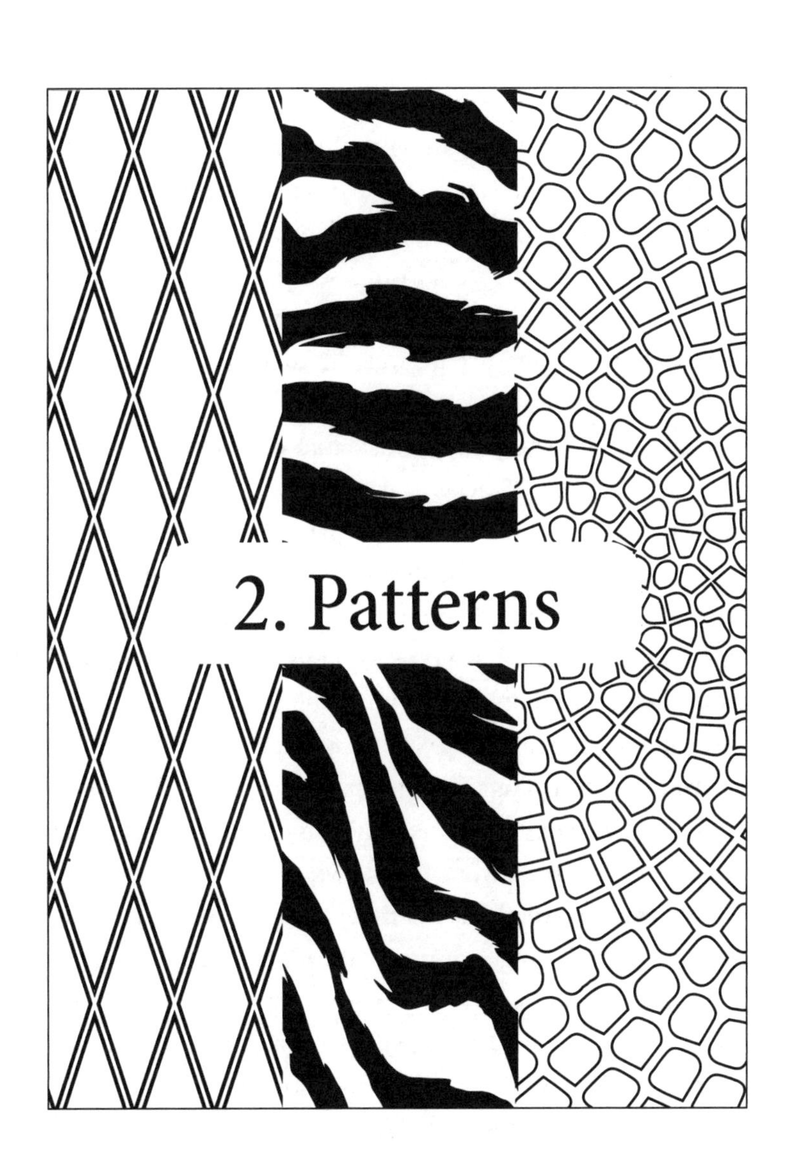

2. Patterns

What is a Pattern?

Patterns are models or recurring designs, or organizational structures used to guide people in the completion of a task, as in work patterns, school schedules, good (bad) behavior, and other routines. Patterns also create expectations (*global warming has changed normal weather patterns*). Patterns are often used to assist people in imitating an action or process and to set up expectations of behavior (as in *typical life patterns*), which can be applied to people as well as to societies (*the pattern of tit-for-tat conflict is common in warring factions*; *there is a pattern that when unemployment goes down, the stock market goes up*). Patterns are also artistically related to endeavors in painting, sculpture, architecture, music, and literary structures, which are genres that display similar design. An inexperienced eye can see the difference between modern art (Banksy, for example) and Cubism (Picasso, for example). An experienced eye can see the difference between paintings, architecture, and music in a Baroque style from other time periods, such as Gothic or Neoclassical movements. Patterns also occur frequently in nature, in plants, animals, and earth formations (sand, mountains, clouds, the ocean). Patterns can be expressed as configurations, series, rules, and regularity, and be based on temporal and/or space divisions.

In neuroscience, patterning is a type of "physical therapy especially for neurological impairment based on a theory holding that repeated manipulation of body parts to simulate normal motor developmental activity (such as crawling or walking) promotes neurological development or repair" (Merriam-Webster, 2017, p. 1). Social *patterning* explains why some people might make illogical choices or decisions (such as what to eat, when to sleep, how much exercise to get, or how to treat women) based on decades of repeated behavior in their communities rather than on good information or research. Patterning can be used synonymously for modeling, copying, or imitation (as in patterning the teacher's dance moves to learn the steps). As a verb, *to pattern* means to model, to imitate, to decorate, or to give a regular or intelligible form. **Patterns** can be expressed as configurations, series, rules, regularity, or expected mental schemas and can exist in time or space, both, or neither. A few examples of each are mentioned below, along with examples in and out of school, starting with configurations.

Configurations

Configurations are patterns that are arrangements of elements in a specific combination. Configurations can be designed by humans or develop in the natural environment. Design configurations are often seen in human creations such as art, architecture, urban planning, clothing, computer programming, and psychology. Natural configurations include the ways clouds group together at specific times of the year based on the temperature and winds, how a snowflake is created, or emerge in how land masses evolve over time. Natural configurations exist in macro structures, such as the general relative position of stars, or the atomic spatial arrangements in chemical bonding.

Figure 18. Cloud Configurations. SOURCE: TOKUHAMA-ESPINOSA, 2015–2018

Configurations are easy to detect, so much so that even very small children can identify them in natural objects such as cloud or leaves, even when they are not identical. A child can intuit that leaves, for example, share similar characteristics, making them easy to identify based on their general configuration and despite their great variety.

Figure 19. Leaf Configurations. SOURCE: TOKUHAMA-ESPINOSA, 2013—2018.

Configurations are also visible in in things as varied as music composition, war tactics, cinematography design, floral arrangements, and cemetery layouts.

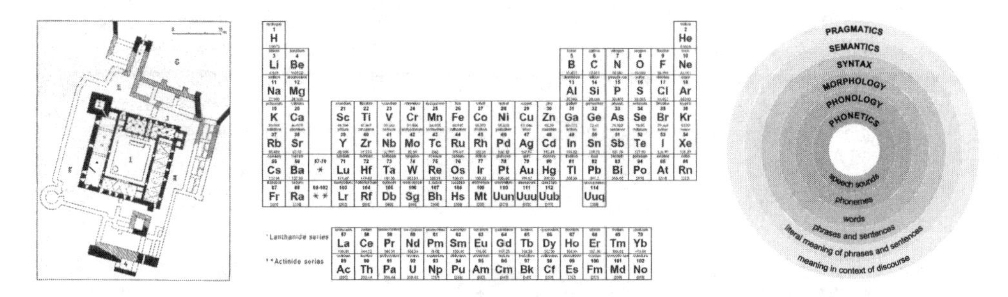

Figure 20. Urban Planning, Chemical, and Language Configurations. SOURCES: (A) BY KARL WOLDEMAR VON LÖWIS OF MENAR (1855–1930). PUBLIC DOMAIN VIA WIKIMEDIA COMMONS; (B) BY LEVANHAN, MODERN PERIODIC TABLE 2008; (C) BY JAMES J. THOMAS AND KRISTIN A. COOK (ED.) DERIVATIVE WORK: MCSUSH, MAJOR LEVELS OF LINGUISTIC STRUCTURE, PUBLIC DOMAIN VIA WIKIMEDIA COMMONS

Chemical elements also have predictable configurations, as do cities, religious factions, and military organizations. In school, we can teach configurations through language patterns (as the way verbs are conjugated, for example), and as parents we can call attention to changing weather patterns based on the seasons. When the coach asks basketball players to line up in *a 2-1-2 configuration*, players understand the pattern associated with it (two guards, a center, two forwards). Political structures (parliamentary democracies, communist governments, monarchies) also have predictable configurations.

Series

Series are another type of pattern that create expectations. When there is a break with a normal series, dissonance occurs. For example, if we hear a particular musical scale in a series, and an unexpected note is struck, the brain's attention system is alerted. This means that patterns are important for learning based on serial expectation—the brain seeks out patterns and is alerted to novelty (Tokuhama-Espinosa, 2008a, 2017).

Series are key to many math procedures, including calculus and statistical analysis. Series normally have a beginning and an end, as in the series of outdoor performances in the park this summer; the series of medical tests the doctor ordered for the patient; or in collections of books, cars, or designer fashions—a limited series. Series can be seen in the patterns found in intricate Persian rug designs, or other textiles.

Figure 21. Rug Patterns. SOURCE: TOKUHAMA-ESPINOSA, 2017

Life can be said to have some predictable series of events, especially due to cultural norms and age (celebrations of birth, coming of age, marriage, death). A series is different than a rule, though they share the expectation of patterns.

Rules

Rule expressions are also examples of patterns. Grammatical rules, for example, create an expected pattern of word order, and math formulas express quantitative rules. Numerical methods are based on rules, as are computer programming formats, parliamentary procedures, and rules that govern scientific methodology. These patterns of procedures are all based on expected behavior or outcomes. Rules also guide mathematical, historical, artistic, and linguistic interactions. There are data input and logical rules (if, then, if, then . . . patterns), not unlike rules for patterns of expected behavior in civil society.

In school, kids learn lots of subject-based rules. For example, there is a rule on how to "round up" decimals, rules about how to conjugate irregular verbs, and the rule of thirds in photography layout. Rules bind patterns. While many rules are created by humans, some rules come from nature. Examples include patterns of birth, death in the animal kingdom, and dominant and subdominant species. Laws of nature are the rules by which events occur in expected order, and the "unseen rules in nature" are generally accepted as those dictated by ecology and ecological systems, which seek a balance or homeostasis among creatures.

Regularity

Regularity suggests a consistent repetition, such as patterns of events in which certain actions typically occur after other actions in a repeated and prescribed way. Regularity is often associated with bodily health as in having good eating, sleeping, and bowel movement patterns. Regularity is also associated with desirable traits and mental states, as in having a regular rather than an erratic temperament. In contrast, irregularity is generally undesirable: Irregular menstrual cycles, mail delivery, and in-law visits are usually disagreeable. Some patterns of regularity are developed unconsciously, such as the pattern of your bathing routine. Most people lather up in the same way every time they bathe, but they rarely recognize this until they break an arm and have to change their regular routine. Almost all expressions of pattern regularity are also expressions of order, which will be discussed in Chapter 4.

Vygotsky (1998) suggested we order our world based on ***mental schemas***, which are types of patterns that describe the way the mind builds up expectations. Very small children devise an understanding of their world based on their experiences, and then generalize on past experiences to anticipate future events or to categorize types. As young children learn to read, prediction exercises push them to anticipate patterns of events, which enhances comprehension. Pattern recognition is only possible if there is regularity. For example, there is an "axiom of regularity" in mathematics, and "statistical regularity" associated with probability theory and regularity associated with linguistic structure, all designed to clarify expectations.

Time and Space

Some expressions of patterns occur in time sequences. Patterns can be objects or verbs and can be expressed *over* time and space. For example, the change of seasons, the cycle of a day, and a person's sleep pattern all occur over time. Time binds growth patterns in humans, as well as social customs, such as the nearly universal celebration of birth, adolescence, marriage, death, and in cultural events, like holidays. There are also disease patterns associated with times of the year (Jeong et al., 2013), and higher crime rates during certain months (Field, 1992). Time also regulates the phases of the moon and the changing of the tides. Many patterns in time also correlate with space patterns.

Space provides for expected patterning, which occurs regularly based on natural as well as manmade structures. In school, aside from content-oriented information, there are patterns of attention system stimulation based on timing (Petersen & Posner, 2012), and studies in chronobiology that show that the time of day can influence academic outcomes (Roenneberg, 2013). Natural

Figure 22. Patterns in Nature. SOURCES: (A) BY NATIONAL PARK SERVICE, 2006 [PUBLIC DOMAIN], VIA WIKIMEDIA COMMONS; (B) TOKUHAMA-ESPINOSA, 2017, LAUSANNE, SWITZERLAND; (C) PUBLIC DOMAIN, VIA WIKIMEDIA COMMONS; (D) TOKUHAMA-ESPINOSA, 2018. CHICAGO, ILLINOIS; (E) TOKUHAMA-ESPINOSA, 2018, QUITO, ECUADOR; (F) PUBLIC DOMAIN VIA WIKIMEDIA COMMONS

space patterning can be found in cells, plants and animals in which regular distribution of content can be seen due to external forces or internal generic determinations.

There are also certain spaces that lend themselves to refugee clusters, human trafficking, civil war, high school dropout rate, and entrepreneurship, creating patterns of human behavior in areas that lend themselves to specific actions. Additionally, there are patterns in the way animals build their habitats, including how, why, and where they do so. Nesting patterns for birds and burrowing habits of rabbits follow seasonal trends, and the structural design of beehives and complex egg laying rituals of turtles all follow patterns, many of which are innate.

Spatial patterning created by people is found in architecture, geography, and population distribution, and can be related to weather and climate, among other things. The designs with which humans decorate their habitats is unparalleled and goes well beyond basic functionality expressed by other animals, sometimes using elaborate decoration, as in the collection of doors seen in Figure 23.

Humans are unique among animals in pattern choices. Trends are a type of pattern, which can defy logical choices. Trends point to patterns of human behavior that are highly volatile and can be shaped by thought leaders or frequency of messaging. For example, consumer spending patterns might be tied to yearly holidays, but what trends as a popular purchase can be shaped by the patterns of advertising or what a celebrity wore to a party. This is a far cry from patterns of human behavior in childhood, which are more predictable.

Toddlers are taught to identify patterns early in their development. Some of the easiest patterns to grasp are those that combine time and space, such as in music. Musical rhythms are patterns. The most primitive music patterns are similar to heartbeats and can be expressed through percussion instruments, like drums and tambourines. Young children are often introduced to patterns first by ear (listening to music) and by touch (clapping out rhythms), then in primary school they learn written patterns, and eventually they learn patterns through subject area, which are often more abstract.

Students are taught the general pattern of a good essay, which does not always have the same structure, but it does have the same order (more about this in the pillar of **order**). Children are also taught patterns of interaction through verbal discourse, as well as patterns of social expectations and behavioral

Figure 23. Doors. SOURCE: TOKUHAMA-ESPINOSA, 2015—2018. (A) GATE NEAR MUSÉE RODIN AND PARC CHAMP DE MARS, PARIS; (B) CHURCH OF ST. AUGUSTIN, MANILA, PHILIPPINES; (C) CUENCA, ECUADOR; (D) GENEVA CATHEDRAL MAIN ENTRANCE; (E) PARIS, FRANCE; (F) PARIS, FRANCE; (G) MUSÉE RODIN, FRANCE; (H) NEAR MUSÉE RODIN AND PARC CHAMP DE MARS, PARIS, FRANCE; (I) OLD TOWN GENEVA, SWITZERLAND; (J) CUENCA, ECUADOR; (K) CHURCH OF ST. AUGUSTIN, MANILA, PHILIPPINES; (L) CHURCH OF ST. AUGUSTIN, MANILA, PHILIPPINES; (M) ROME, ITALY; (N) PANTHEON, PARIS; (O) PANTHEON, PARIS; (P) ABU DHABI, UAE; (Q) PARIS, FRANCE; (R) NOTRE DAME, PARIS; (S) ABU DHABI UAE; (T) PANTHEON, PARIS, FRANCE

norms. Some patterns, such as face reaction-to-emotional state, appear to be inborn (Jain & Li, 2011).

Evidence for the pillar of patterns exist in all disciplines but it is interesting to note that some of the more intriguing studies come from brain detection of *broken* patterns, for example, musical dissonance, cognitive dissonance or

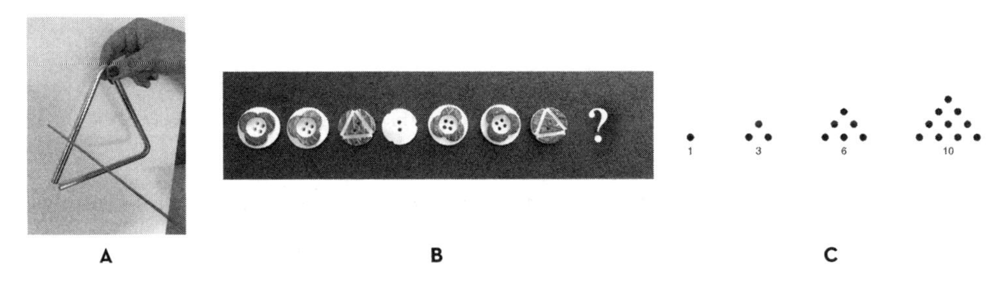

Figure 24. Rhythmic, Shape, and Numerical Patterns. SOURCES: (A) TOKUHAMA-ESPINOSA, 2018; (B) TOKUHAMA-ESPINOSA, 2018; (C) PUBLIC DOMAIN; RIIAN, 2005

detection of incorrect word use. Neuroconstructivism depends on evidence from many fields, including neuroscience, psychology and education. Some studies that support the pattern of pillar can be found in Table 8.

How the Pillar of Patterns Economizes Learning

Experiencing the world through the pillar of patterns economizes learning because all configurations (leaves, clouds, computer programming, urban planning, music), series (events, mathematics, textiles), rules (grammatical, mathematics, government, behavior) and regularity (bodily health, ocean tides, cultural festivities) can reinforce one another. If a child learns about sound patterns by clapping his hands and then immediately is asked to draw or visualize that same rhythm, he will reinforce both his memory and his understanding through multi-modal learning (Xu et al., 2015). Visual object pattern recognition will help rhythmic pattern detection; grammatical rules can reinforce mathematical rules; seasonal patterns reinforce an understanding of cultural patterns; overlapping pathways economize learning. Analogically speaking, identification of one kind of pattern creates the bases for understanding future patterns. Children who are explicitly taught to look for patterns in their world will be more adept at identifying future patterns.

Implications for Student Learning

Observing the world through the pillar of patterns will change the way we see objects, people, customs, math formulas, foreign language rules, the weather and even how and why we sleep, eat and interact. It can also be argued that pillars thinking is not only complementary to our current view of the world but may actually be the natural way the brain takes in and divides information for storage. As there are patterns all around us, children can learn from the earliest years how to observe their world and explore the landscape with this additional lens by seeking out patterns in the clouds, their own bodies, housing structures, and art. Kids can easily identify patterns in configurations, regularity, sequences, series, and in their natural surroundings.

Curriculum design can be enhanced by reminding students to look for patterns in and out of school. Some of the best teachers and textbooks already make sure that patterns are expressed in multiple forms both in formal and informal learning environments. Parents can teach patterns with the simplest of materials, and even the songs they sing (the melody serves as a pattern), and braiding hair serve to rehearse patterns in different sensory modalities. The current curriculum focuses on subject-area knowledge, all but ignoring what could be an additional support structure in natural neuroconstructivist lesson design.

Look up from your book. What patterns are in your midst? How does the fence pattern in the neighbor's yard compare with the curtain pattern in your window? What is similar about the pattern of the news cycle today, or with the pattern of the weekly work schedule? What is the difference between animal fur patterns and plant leaf patterns? How did a break in a pattern improve or deteriorate your mood today? Use of the pillar of patterns will mean students become more conscious of their own mental schemas by self-questioning the origins of the patterns in their lives, see new dimensions about every topic, object, and process around them, and become more efficient in their learning.

Table 8. Example Studies of Patterns in the Brain

FURTHER READING ON THE SCIENCE OF PATTERNS IN THE BRAIN
Pattern Detection in the Brain
Bishop, C. M. (1995). *Neural networks for pattern recognition*. Oxford, UK: Oxford University Press.
DiCarlo, J. J., Zoccolan, D., & Rust, N. C. (2012). How does the brain solve visual object recognition? *Neuron, 73*(3), 415–434.
Haken, H. (2013). *Principles of brain functioning: A synergetic approach to brain activity, behavior and cognition* (Vol. 67). Berlin, Germany: Springer Science & Business Media.
LeCun, Y., Bengio, Y., & Hinton, G. (2015). Deep learning. *Nature, 521*(7553), 436–444.

Lin, Y. P., Wang, C. H., Jung, T. P., Wu, T. L., Jeng, S. K., Duann, J. R., & Chen, J. H. (2010). EEG-based emotion recognition in music listening. *IEEE Transactions on Biomedical Engineering, 57*(7), 1798-1806.

Oliva, A., & Torralba, A. (2007). The role of context in object recognition. *Trends in Cognitive Sciences, 11*(12), 520-527.

Pavlidis, T. (2013). *Structural pattern recognition* (Vol. 1). New York: Springer.

Petersen, S. E., & Posner, M. I. (2012). The attention system of the human brain: 20 years after. *Annual Review of Neuroscience, 35*, 73-89.

Ripley, B. D. (2007). *Pattern recognition and neural networks.* Cambridge, UK: Cambridge University Press.

Samarasinghe, S. (2016). *Neural networks for applied sciences and engineering: From fundamentals to complex pattern recognition.* Boca Raton, FL: CRC Press.

Szegedy, C., Toshev, A., & Erhan, D. (2003). Deep neural networks for object detection. In P. Baldi, J. Cheng & A. Vullo's *Advances in neural information processing systems* (pp. 2553-2561). Cambridge, MA: MIT Press.

Yonelinas, A. P., Otten, L. J., Shaw, K. N., & Rugg, M. D. (2005). Separating the brain regions involved in recollection and familiarity in recognition memory. *Journal of Neuroscience, 25*(11), 3002-3008.

Rule Detection

Ferman, S., & Karni, A. (2010). No childhood advantage in the acquisition of skill in using an artificial language rule. *PloS one, 5*(10), e13648.

Friederici, A. D. (2012). Language development and the ontogeny of the dorsal pathway. *Frontiers in Evolutionary Neuroscience, 4*(3), 1-7 . https://doi.org/10.3389/fnevo.2012.00003

Osterhout, L., Kim, A., & Kuperberg, G. R. (2012). The neurobiology of sentence comprehension. In M. Spivey, M. Joanisse, & K. McRae's *The Cambridge handbook of psycholinguistics*, (pp.365-389.) London, UK: Cambridge University Press.

Pulvermüller, F. (2010). Brain embodiment of syntax and grammar: Discrete combinatorial mechanisms spelt out in neural circuits. *Brain and Language, 112*(3), 167-179.

Musical Patterns and Dissonance

Abrams, D. A., Bhatara, A., Ryali, S., Balaban, E., Levitin, D. J., & Menon, V. (2010). Decoding temporal structure in music and speech relies on shared brain resources but elicits different fine-scale spatial patterns. *Cerebral Cortex, 21*(7), 1507-1518.

Alluri, V., Toiviainen, P., Jääskeläinen, I. P., Glerean, E., Sams, M., & Brattico, E. (2012). Large-scale brain networks emerge from dynamic processing of musical timbre, key and rhythm. *NeuroImage, 59*(4), 3677-3689.

Dellacherie, D., Roy, M., Hugueville, L., Peretz, I., & Samson, S. (2011). The effect of musical experience on emotional self-reports and psychophysiological responses to dissonance. *Psychophysiology, 48*(3), 337-349.

Fritz, T. H., Renders, W., Müller, K., Schmude, P., Leman, M., Turner, R., & Villringer, A. (2013). Anatomical differences in the human inferior colliculus relate to the perceived valence of musical consonance and dissonance. *European Journal of Neuroscience, 38*(7), 3099-3105.

Salimpoor, V. N., Zald, D. H., Zatorre, R. J., Dagher, A., & McIntosh, A. R. (2015). Predictions and the brain: how musical sounds become rewarding. *Trends in Cognitive Sciences, 19*(2), 86-91.

Word and Nonword Pattern Detection

Cappa, S. F. (2012). Imaging semantics and syntax. *NeuroImage*, *61*(2), 427–431.

Strauß, A., Kotz, S. A., Scharinger, M., & Obleser, J. (2014). Alpha and theta brain oscillations index dissociable processes in spoken word recognition. *NeuroImage*, *97*, 387–395.

Taylor, J. S. H., Rastle, K., & Davis, M. H. (2013). Can cognitive models explain brain activation during word and pseudo word reading? A meta-analysis of 36 neuroimaging studies. *Psychological Bulletin*, *139*(4), 766.

Woollams, A. M., Silani, G., Okada, K., Patterson, K., & Price, C. J. (2011). Word or word-like? Dissociating orthographic typicality from lexicality in the left occipito-temporal cortex. *Journal of Cognitive Neuroscience*, *23*(4), 992–1002.

Yoo, S., Chung, J. Y., Jeon, H. A., Lee, K. M., Kim, Y. B., & Cho, Z. H. (2012). Dual routes for verbal repetition: Articulation-based and acoustic–phonetic codes for pseudoword and word repetition, respectively. *Brain and Language*, *122*(1), 1–10.

We now turn to the pillar of order.

3. Order

What is Order?

Order is the organization or disposition of things or people in relation to each other based on a specific arrangement, method, direction, or structure. Order can imply the position of items in space or time in a succession or sequence expressing a formal array. Order can also represent the nature of something (*the presentation was of the highest order*), or the harmonious conditions in which things are aligned to give meaning based on their appropriate places (*after meditating he felt he had ordered his world*). Order also represents a set of laws and rules to regulate behavior, as in society, classroom, work, or other public spaces, and can represent an authoritative command or instruction, expressed verbally or in written form. As a verb or an expression of processes, *to order* can mean to prescribe something, to direct, manage, supply, furnish, regulate, conduct, or arrange suitably or methodologically. Many expressions of order are identified as sequences.

Sequence

Order can be expressed in sequence. A sequence is a particular order in objects, events, or movements for a purpose. Alphabetical order sequences items in the order of the letters (A, B, C, not C, A, B). Children can stand in order of height, or troops in order of rank. The harmonious alignment of items or conditions (*a fortunate sequence of events*) creates the circumstances for balance and "perfect order" in the universe. A sequence is a continuous or connected series, such as found in a sonnet, or a set of elements or scenes in a film, play, or movie. Sequence can also show an order of succession, as in word order in a sentence, world order on earth, or hierarchical order for monarchic succession. Sequences can be based on an infinite number of qualities, including order in time, location, or size. In academia, sequences are often taught to explain structure as in curriculum design. In math, a sequence is a list of numbers or objects in a special order.

A sequence is an infinite series and most (but not all) are part of a pattern. Not all order sequences have patterns, however: A chain of events that expresses a sequence dependent on human behavior can have order but no easily predictable pattern. For example, observe these possible options for the following scenario. You stop your car abruptly. The driver behind you bumps into your car, you get out and . . . [he apologizes] . . . [yells at you] . . . [embraces you] . . . [hands you a card with his insurance provider's contact] . . . [picks up his phone and calls his wife] . . . [you call him an idiot] . . . [you apologize to him] . . . [you laugh, embarrassed]. Humans are more unpredictable than nature. Sequences in science usually follow predictable patterns, such as the way H_2O changes when it is a solid, a liquid, or a gas. Math patterns are almost always predictable and conserve a consistent order. For example, "2, 4, 6, 8 . . ." has an easily anticipated pattern and it can go on infinitely, thus ordering the "even number sequence." The seasonal sequence is a series in time that also repeats itself in a special order. The hands of a clock follow a predictable sequence, as do the manmade "seasons" for sports (basketball, football, baseball, and so on) and shopping (back-to-school, holiday, and so on). Other expressions of order are formulas.

Formulas

Mathematical sequences order elements of a set to structure a way to resolve problems. The order of operations, PEMDAS or "Please Excuse My Dear Aunt Sally" explains the correct sequence in which to approach a math problem. If faced with a math formula with multiple steps, the correct way to approach it would be first to do "**P**arentheses," (work from left to right and simplify what is inside the parentheses) followed by calculating the "**E**xponents," then "**M**ultiplication" followed by "**D**ivision" (from left to right), and lastly "**A**ddition followed by **S**ubtraction" (from left to right).

Math formulas themselves are also expressions of order. A formula is a way of expressing information symbolically, which depends on a precise order. If

Table 9. Mathematical Order of Operations

Problem	Step 1	Step 2	Step 3	Step 4	Step 5	Step 6
$3 + 6 \times (5 + 4)^2 \div 3 - 7$	$3 + 6 \times \mathbf{9}^2 \div 3 - 7$	$3 + 6 \times \mathbf{81} \div 3 - 7$	$3 + \mathbf{486} \div 3 - 7$	$3 + \mathbf{162} - 7$	$\mathbf{165} - 7$	**158**
	Parenthesis	Exponents	Multiplication	Division	Addition	Subtraction

SOURCE: TOKUHAMA-ESPINOSA, 2018

you want to calculate the circumference of a circle, the order of the symbols is vital to preserve the properties. Order matters.

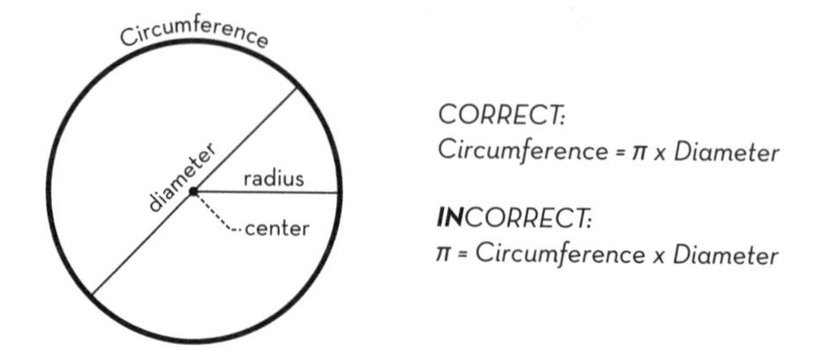

Figure 26. Order of Properties of a Circle. SOURCE: TOKUHAMA-ESPINOSA, 2018

Grammar

The process of writing a correct sentence requires order that depends on a clear sequence of words. All sentences in all languages have a subject, an object, and a verb. Depending on the language, this order is different.

Table 10. Language Typological Ensembles

VSO (verb-subject-object)	SVO (subject-verb-object)	SOV (subject-object-verb)
Arabic (ancient), Berger, Gaelic, Hawaiian, Hebrew, Irish, Maori, Masai, Swedish, Tagalog, Tongan, Welsh	Arabic (modern), Chinese, English, Finnish, French, German (and SOV in past tense), Greek, Guarani, Khmer, Indonesian, Malay, Russian, Spanish, Swahili, Thai, Vietnamese, Yoruba	Armenian, Basque, Korean, German (and SVO in present tense), Hindi, Japanese, Manchu, Mongolian, Navajo, Persian, Quechua and Turkish

SOURCE: TOKUHAMA-ESPINOSA, 2008B, BASED ON GREENBERG, 1966

English is a subject-verb-object language: *John* (subject) *threw* (verb) *the ball* (object). The order of the words is vital to understanding. *John loves Tammy* does not mean the same thing as *Tammy loves John*, for example. This means that the order of the words is important to convey a desired meaning. In addition to words in a sentence, there are also different types of sentences, which are influenced by word order and punctuation.

Sentences are made up of clauses (a group of words that explains a single idea). There are two types of clauses, independent and dependent. Independent clauses can stand on their own, but dependent clauses need an independent clause to complete their meaning. *Simple sentences* have just one independent clause and require a single punctuation mark (for example, *The rent was late*). *Compound sentences* join several simple sentences and can be linked by conjunctions (and, but, so, yet). (For example, *The rent was late, so he lost his lease*). *Complex sentences* combine independent and dependent clauses (for example, *Because his rent was late, he lost his lease*). *Compound-complex* sentences have one central independent clause, surrounded by two dependent clauses (for example, *When signing a housing contract, you must budget your money well, or you might lose your lease*). Change of word order in any of these cases significantly alters the meaning of the sentence.

The sequence of words (or syntax, how words are arranged) is the key to correct language usage. Math formulas and language grammar are expressions of order that are taught to kids throughout schooling. Unfortunately, many students can learn to memorize order without understanding the reasoning behind it, which leads to gaps in basic notions. For example, children can memorize the multiplication tables without any understanding of the math behind them or conjugate verbs in a foreign language without understanding their meaning. This means that every expression of order should be accompanied by the question "*Why*?" or "*Why* does this order count?" "*Why* does the order here make a difference?" Asking the "why" questions related to core notions, and then filling in any gaps that are identified, is key to great teaching.

Cycles

Cycles are other expressions of order. A cycle is similar to a sequence, except it has cyclical repetition. A complete set in a series can be considered a cycle (as in a sonic wave). Cycles often come from nature, such as the cycle of the moon, tides, and seasons or biology, as in menstrual to menopause cycles. Cycles are usually bound by time—such as the 24 hours in a day or the 12 months of a year—and return to their starting point. An unending cycle is infinity: ∞, it does not matter from whence you begin, you will always return to that point. In physics, a cycle is a sequence of states that returns back to its original position and is self-defined (i.e., a cycle per second is one hertz). History is often said to evolve in cycles of war and peace, prosperity and poverty, liberalism and conservatism, as well as social cycles (embrace technology/hate technology, open borders/close borders, globalization/isolationism). Thinking about the order of things through cycles is more common and natural than one would think and is already a part of schooling at all levels. In biology, cycles can be seen in the life cycles of all living things, and in ecology there can be recycling processes and the water cycle. In agriculture, there is a planting cycle and a harvesting cycle. Arguments can be cyclical, so debate and oratory skills are also dependent on cycles. Cycles are very different from "purpose," though they are both expressions of order.

Purpose

Order is often expressed as purpose. People often do things in order to achieve something else. That is, the purpose of their actions is to lead to a specific consequence (*She studies in order to get a good grade*; *He stayed late in order to make a good impression on the boss*; *She ordered a sandwich because she was hungry*). Order expressed as purpose requires an understanding and expectation of cause and effect, which is seen clearly in school examples: *Read the chapter in order to be prepared for class* or *spread out your homework to avoid last-minute cramming.*

Structure

Order can also be considered a structure, as when someone devises a curriculum, or the playbill of songs in a concert, or prioritizes projects or decisions based on their importance. Structures are helpful in arranging and explaining the relations among elements of something complex. Structures are arrangements designed according to a clear plan (order) that often help organize things. Structures necessarily apply a logic or common knowledge that is shared by the users. For example, the structure of a Japanese *ofuro* or "honorable bath" requires a different order for bathing than in Western societies in which one actually bathes *outside* the tub, and then steps into the bath once clean. This order might seem illogical to Westerners because they do not share the same *sense* of order.

Structures can be built by humans or they can be made up in nature, as in the arrangements of molecular structures of atoms or soil components. Structures explain the characteristics of the whole, as in the economic structure or society, the personality structure of an individual or the structure of a language. Structures also imply organization, as in giving structure to a child's life or structuring a legal code. Structure as order in school contexts is often used to share a way of thinking or common format, such as in structuring blocks of classes the same number of minutes. Structure is closely related to organization, another form of order.

Organization

Organization is similar to structure in that both imply a shared definition of order by users, but they differ in that structures are states of something, whereas organization can offer a hierarchy (i.e., *the school organization gave top responsibility to the principal and less to teachers*). Organization also means orderly steps toward a clear end (i.e., *the man put his affairs in order before his anticipated death*). Other examples in which organization is based on specific order (of events, people, or objects) include: *He ordered the papers on his desk before going away on vacation*; *Put your own house in order before giving advice*; *We have to order the office responsibilities better to be fairer*; *The teacher couldn't keep order in the class.* Order can also be expressed in systems thinking.

Systems Thinking

Orders can represent political, economic, or other social systems. Social classes are an example of orders in systems, as are ranks in jobs like the military, the clergy, business, or diplomacy. Hierarchies of any kind represent order, including institutional hierarchies (such as Freemasonry or Templar orders; religious orders; ranks for professors in universities, police department orders, and so on), scholastic hierarchies (*the upperclassmen bossed the younger kids around*), species hierarchies (the higher order of insects as in *the two suborders of spiders*), architectural styles (Corinthian, Ionic, Doris, Tuscan, and Composite orders for designing light, space, column width, and general design), and political divisions (*he is bucking the natural order of the political process*). Systems thinking is harder to conceptualize due to its intangible and macro nature, but is modeled throughout society and in the world order.

There is a growing body of literature on **order** in the brain, including a better understanding of how different learning processes occur. The articles in Table 11 show the developing literature in support of the neuronal underpinnings for the pillar of order in the brain. Some of the literature related to order concerns the brain's ability to predict. For example, the literature suggests that order and predictability are so strong for word anticipation that the brain has to override its natural inclination to predict a word due to its context (Kuperberg et al., 2017). This means that the order of the phonemes and the prediction of a specific word based on those phonemes can be stronger than the prediction of what word should naturally be used in the context of the sentence. This means, in essence, that multiple "orders" have to be managed at the same time in the brain, necessarily creating a hierarchy of processing. The "order of orders" in the brain is a rich area for continued research.

Important recent literature supporting the neuroconstructivist foundations of **order** in the brain includes articles in Table 11.

How the Order Pillar Economizes Learning

Looking at the world through the pillar of order economizes learning because neuronal circuits for future prediction and decision making used in one domain can potentially be used in other domains. For example, someone who has habituated thinking through the pillar of order will easily recognize the order of different governmental systems and can use this understanding to think of the orderly way a hospital, university, or post office might also be organized. Similarly, someone who understands the order of social networks can take advantage of this to understand the pecking order in an office. Overlapping pathways economize learning hierarchies in memory processing and appear similar for math formula recall, semantic structure recall, and likely for other subject areas as well, though this has not yet been proven decisively. In school, we can use the pillar of order to understand the cycles of war and peace from an historical angle to appreciate the cycle of poverty and socioeconomic inequality; an appreciation of hierarchies in the animal kingdom to help facilitate an understanding about hierarchies in human social institutions; and the importance of word order to clarify the vital role of order in mathematical formula sequences. The order of problem solving in engineering can be extrapolated to problem solving in social science (*how does the order of planning city transportation map onto the order of housing districts and socioeconomic status?*). The order of approaching essay writing can facilitate the understanding of approaching meal planning: *an introduction* (*entrée*), *body* (*main course*), *and conclusion* (*dessert*). Knowing one conceptual order improves the likelihood of learning others.

Implications for Student Learning

Learning through the pillar of order changes the way we look at everyday events, phenomena, objects, communication tactics, and social structures, and permeates all aspects of our lives. As order organizes everything we do, from human interactions to institutional design—including schooling—children can see multiple examples in their every action. The order in which they put their clothes on in the morning (socks before shoes), makes a difference. The word order used to get things (*pass me the milk* vs. *me pass the milk*) makes a difference. Parenting also follows orderly commands that create habits that last a lifetime: *First read, then TV*; *First be sure you will get enough sleep before wedging in social media*; *First eat your meal, then have dessert.* Kids of all ages can observe the order of a day and the constant advancement of time, and the wake-eat-school-play-eat-sleep cycle of their day, or the Monday-to-Friday work cycle vs. the Saturday-Sunday weekend cycle in Western countries. Social customs, such as the order of greetings (who approaches who and how) have a clear structure visible in daily life, as do the systems thinking design of cybernetics, public health, schools, or business.

Look up from your book. What order is within eyesight? Is the TV calling out the order of the athletes on the court or reminding us of the constitutional division of powers and order of decision making on a national level? Is the music on your phone ordered by genre or alphabetically (or not at all)? Is your desk ordered in such a way that things are easy to find (and only for you, or is the order obvious to all?). Did your day follow a regular order, or did something out of the ordinary happen? People can learn a great deal by viewing the world through the pillar of **order** and habituating mental processes of transdisciplinary thinking.

Table 11. Example Studies of Order in the Brain

FURTHER READING ON THE SCIENCE OF ORDER IN THE BRAIN

Math Order

Avancini, C., Soltész, F., & Szűcs, D. (2015). Separating stages of arithmetic verification: An ERP study with a novel paradigm. *Neuropsychologia, 75*, 322-329.

Byrge, L., Sporns, O., & Smith, L. B. (2014). Developmental process emerges from extended brain-body-behavior networks. *Trends in Cognitive Sciences, 18*(8), 395-403.

Friedrich, R. M. & Friederici, A. D. (2013). Mathematical logic in the human brain: Semantics. *PlosOne, 8*(1), e53699.

Gullick, M. M. & Wolford, G. (2014). Brain systems involved in arithmetic with positive versus negative numbers. *Human Brain Mapping, 35*(2), 539-551.

Hasson, U., Chen, J., & Honey, C. J. (2015). Hierarchical process memory: Memory as an integral component of information processing. *Trends in Cognitive Sciences, 19*(6), 304-313.

Price, G. R., Mazzocco, M. M., & Ansari, D. (2013). Why mental arithmetic counts: Brain activation during single digit arithmetic predicts high school math scores. *Journal of Neuroscience, 33*(1), 156-163.

Rugg, M. D., & Vilberg, K. L. (2013). Brain networks underlying episodic memory retrieval. *Current Opinion in Neurobiology, 23*(2), 255-260.

Tschentscher, N. & Hauk, O. (2014). How are things adding up? Neural differences between arithmetic operations are due to general problem solving strategies. *NeuroImage, 92*, 369-380.

Language Order

Fengler, A., Meyer, L., & Friederici, A. D. (2016). How the brain attunes to sentence processing: Relating behavior, structure, and function. *NeuroImage, 129*, 268-278.

Golestani, N. (2014). Brain structural correlates of individual differences at low- to high-levels of the language processing hierarchy: A review of new approaches to imaging research. *International Journal of Bilingualism, 18*(1), 6-34.

Hubers, F., Snijders, T. M., & De Hoop, H. (2016). How the brain processes violations of the grammatical norm: An fMRI study. *Brain and Language, 163*, 22-31.

Kepinska, O., de Rover, M., Caspers, J., & Schiller, N. O. (2017). Whole-brain functional connectivity during acquisition of novel grammar: Distinct functional networks depend on language learning abilities. *Behavioural Brain Research, 320*, 333-346.

Krishnan, S., Watkins, K. E., & Bishop, D. V. (2016). Neurobiological basis of language learning difficulties. *Trends in Cognitive Sciences, 20*(9), 701-714.

Pattamadilok, C., Dehaene, S., & Pallier, C. (2016). A role for left inferior frontal and posterior superior temporal cortex in extracting a syntactic tree from a sentence. *Cortex, 75*, 44-55.

Wang, J., Cherkassky, V. L., & Just, M. A. (2017). Predicting the brain activation pattern associated with the propositional content of a sentence: Modeling neural representations of events and states. *Human Brain Mapping, 38*(10), 4865-4881.

Wehbe, L., Murphy, B., Talukdar, P., Fyshe, A., Ramdas, A., & Mitchell, T. (2014). Simultaneously uncovering the patterns of brain regions involved in different story reading subprocesses. *PlosOne, 9*(11), e112575

Westermann, G. (2016). Experience-dependent brain development as a key to understanding the language system. *Topics in Cognitive Science, 8*(2), 446-458.

Event Ordering

Beaty, R. E., Christensen, A. P., Benedek, M., Silvia, P. J., & Schacter, D. L. (2017). Creative constraints: Brain activity and network dynamics underlying semantic interference during idea production. *NeuroImage, 148*, 189-196.

Demblon, J., Bahri, M. A., & D'Argembeau, A. (2016). Neural correlates of event clusters in past and future thoughts: How the brain integrates specific episodes with autobiographical knowledge. *NeuroImage, 127*, 257-266.

Hsieh, L. T. & Ranganath, C. (2015). Cortical and subcortical contributions to sequence retrieval: Schematic coding of temporal context in the neocortical recollection network. *NeuroImage, 121*, 78-90.

Lieberman, J. S., Kyle, C. T., Schedlbauer, A., Stokes, J., & Ekstrom, A. D. (2017). A tale of two temporal coding strategies: Common and dissociable brain regions involved in recency versus associative temporal order retrieval strategies. *Journal of Cognitive Neuroscience, 29*(4),739-754.

Mullally, S. L. & Maguire, E. A. (2014). Memory, imagination, and predicting the future: a common brain mechanism? *The Neuroscientist, 20*(3), 220-234.

Sheldon, S., Farb, N., Palombo, D. J., & Levine, B. (2016). Intrinsic medial temporal lobe connectivity relates to individual differences in episodic autobiographical remembering. *Cortex, 74*, 206-216.

Tylén, K., Christensen, P., Roepstorff, A., Lund, T., Østergaard, S., & Donald, M. (2015). Brains striving for coherence: Long-term cumulative plot formation in the default mode network. *NeuroImage, 121*, 106-114.

Hierarchies and Order

Balaguer, J., Spiers, H., Hassabis, D., & Summerfield, C. (2016). Neural mechanisms of hierarchical planning in a virtual subway network. *Neuron, 90*(4), 893-903.

Dennett, D. C. (2013). Expecting ourselves to expect: The Bayesian brain as a projector. *Behavioral and Brain Sciences, 36*(3), 209-210.

Holm, L., & Madison, G. (2013). Whenever next: Hierarchical timing of perception and action. *Behavioral and Brain Sciences, 36*(3), 217-218.

Horikawa, T. & Kamitani, Y. (2017). Generic decoding of seen and imagined objects using hierarchical visual features. *Nature Communications, 8*, 15037.

Jaber, M. Y. (Ed.). (2016). *Learning curves: Theory, models, and applications.* Boca Raton, FL: CRC Press.

Muckli, L., Petro, L. S., & Smith, F. W. (2013). Backwards is the way forward: feedback in the cortical hierarchy predicts the expected future. *Behavioral and Brain Sciences, 36*(3), 221-221.

Varona, P. & Rabinovich, M. I. (2016, June). Hierarchical dynamics of informational patterns and decision-making. In *Proceeding of the Royal Society Biology, 283*(1832), 20160475.

We turn now to the pillar of categories.

4. Categories

What are Categories?

Categories are divisions and classifications of things that share qualities. Categories are formed based on the qualities and equivalencies of objects, people, places, times, genres, format, style, types, concepts, or schema, that are determined by characteristics or appearances that show how things are similar. Most things in the world can be grouped into multiple categories. For example, an apple can be categorized as a type of food (fruit) or by its color (red, green, yellow), size (small, fits in my fist), being edible, by its sweet smell, or by any number of other classifications based on the learner's experience. Things that are categorized together share at least one common characteristics. In verb form, *to categorize* means to put things or people into groups, and divide or classify them based on the similarities of their features.

At a macro, philosophical level, categories have been used to refer to the primary ways in which the world is divided. One example of categories is by philosophical beliefs about categories themselves.

Table 12. Philosophical Categories

PHILOSOPHICAL CATEGORIES: HOW WE SEE THE WORLD				
ARISTOTLE	**Substance**	**Quantity**	**Qualification**	**Relative or Relation**
	Where, When	Being in a position	Condition	Doing/Action
KANT	**Unity**	**Plurality**	**Totality**	**Reality**
	Negation	Limitation	Inherence and Subsistence	Causality and Dependence
	Community			
PIERCE	**Quality of feeling**	**Ideas**	**Chance**	**Possibility (vagueness, "some")**
	Reaction, resistance, relation	Brute facts	Representation, mediation	Actuality (singularity, discreteness, "this")
		Habits	Laws	Necessity (generality, continuity, "all")
HINDU PADRTHA	**Substance**	**Quality**	**Motion or Action**	**Universal**
		Particularity or Differentiator	Inherence	Absence

SOURCE: TOKUHAMA-ESPINOSA, 2017

These philosophies show us that the way we understand our world can be categorized into groupings of how we see and understand our surroundings. A type of category structure relates to the qualities of an object, person, concept, belief, or other thing that can be assigned at least one characteristic. Categories are often decided by their qualities.

Qualities

All things in the world, living or inanimate, can be categorized by their qualities, and this normally occurs in multiple ways. For example, a young woman can fit the categories of *female*, *teenager*, *student*, *athlete*, *math whiz*, and also be typed by race, religion, nationality, or physical traits (tall, brown, boisterous, intelligent), and so on. Individual mental schema are personal ways that each person's mind categorizes experiences, meaning not everyone will group the same objects in the same ways. For example, we all have a mental schema for "dogs," but depending on what kinds of dogs we have come across in our lives, we will think of dogs differently from the person next to us.

Genres can be grouped together forming multiple categories of movies, literature, academic disciplines, art styles, cuisine, and so on. Categories in nature can be used to divide plants in different ecosystems, minerals in caves, dirt in our gardens, and animals into classifications; all based on qualities. In the animal kingdom, we can have subsets of animals. For example, within the category of mammals, we can have *farm animals*, *animals with short hair*, or *meat eating animals*. Categories can be used to group grammatical and syntactic categories in language, and in linguistics there are lexical, syntactic, and grammatical categories. We can have sub-categories of words, such as nouns, verbs, and adjectives, by which the parts of speech are used to categorize language concepts.

In math, there are different types of classifications, including associative and identity categories. Some sets in math are equivalent, though they need not always be so. Mathematical qualities can be used to categorize sets and subsets. For example, the numbers 1 to 100 can be divided into the subsets of even numbers (2, 4, 6, 8, 10 . . .) and odd numbers (1, 3, 5, 7, 9. . .). Academia itself can be divided into categories. For example, a person can be a psychologist and also belong to a subcategory of cognitive psychologists, developmental psychologists, or neuropsychologists (among others). Restaurant types, cereals, businesses, music, schools, teachers, students, detergents, retailers, politicians, literary genres, cell types, cars, financial markets, genders, philosophies, theories, styles . . . everything in the world can be categorized by its qualities, and usually in many sub-categories as well. Breakfast cereals have sub-categories, such as those made from oats, those with fruits, those that are served hot, and even those that come with a toy in the box, for example.

Similarities and Differences

One of the first skill sets we teach young children in preschool is to identify how things are similar to and different from one another. How is your pet the same as your best friend's pet? How is it different? How is your sister like your little brother, and how are they different? How is your house the same as my house, and how is it different? How is soccer the same as basketball, and how is it different? How are mommy's clothes the same as grandma's, and how are they different? Identifying similarities and differences serves as prerequisite knowledge for category building.

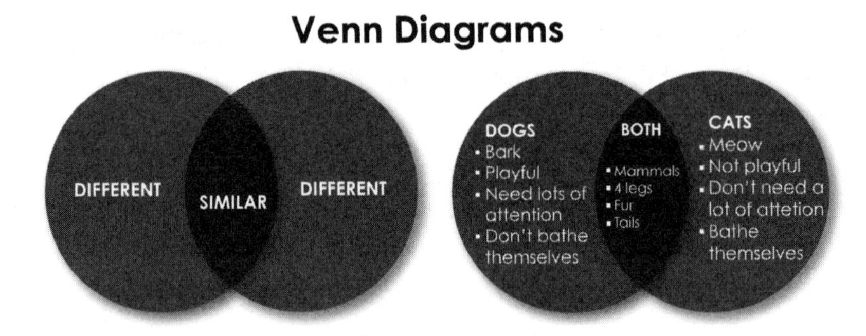

Figure 28. Venn Diagrams of Similarities and Differences. SOURCE: TOKUHAMA-ESPINOSA, 2017

When kids are slightly older, we can encourage them to use visual diagrams of similarities and differences to help them "see" how things can be alike and unlike one another at the same time. Venn diagrams, such as those in Figure 28, neatly show the parameters of similarity and differences and where the "gray" area in the middle comes in to share characteristics or qualities. *Quality* expressions of categories are different from *equivalencies*, which are explained below.

Equivalencies

Equivalencies show parity and (near) equality, and by that definition, they are interchangeable (in value, force, significance, weight, and so on). If two things are equivalent, they are parallel, match, show a high degree of likeness, or can be used synonymously with each other.

Circular definitions are examples of categories that are equivalencies. In logic, propositions that are equivalent are relationships where both statements are true or both false (and when this is not so, the result is a "contradiction"). If "a" is equal to "b," and "b" is equal to "c," then "a is equal to c" is an expression of equivalence in mathematics that satisfies this logical rule. Other examples of equivalencies include: *Human and machine production ran "neck and neck" and are considered equal in output; The two competitors ran at the exact same pace and ended up in a tie; There was parity in arrival time, independent of whether he took his bike or his skateboard; The crowd's attendance was the same whether or not the star player played or not; Cabify and Uber had the same prices as the local cab company, making them equivalent in cost.*

Classifications

Categories require classifications. A classification is a grouping based on shared qualities which are often used in science to sort creatures in the animal kingdom, plant species, and microorganisms into taxonomies. Classifications can also imply rank, not just organization of content. Classification is also often used synonymously with codification or typing.

In 1990, Woese, Kandler, and Wheelis suggested that the highest rank within the taxonomy of living creatures is called "domain," which can be animals, bacteria, or archaea (single-cell organisms with no nucleus).

After "domain," living things can then be classified into one of six "kingdoms" (in the U.S. version—the UK suggests seven): (a) *Animalia* (animals); (b) *Plantae* (plants); (c) *Fungi* (yeasts, molds, and mushrooms); (d) *Protista* (everything else that is not an animal, plant, or fungi), (e) *Archaea/Archaeabacteria* (single-cell microbes including plankton); and (f) *Bacteria/Eubacteria.* Once classified into a "kingdom," next comes "division" (phylum), followed by "class," "order," "family," "genus," and "species."

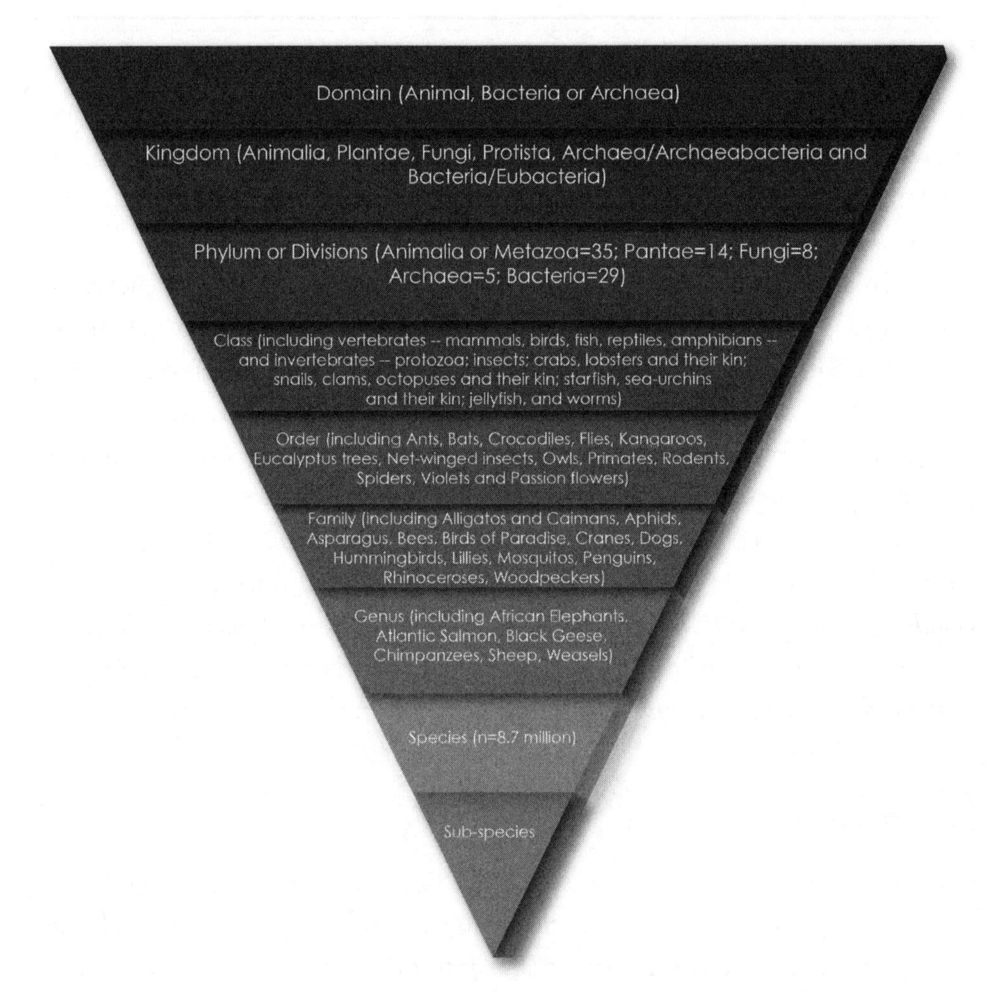

Figure 29. Taxonomy of Living Beings. SOURCE: TOKUHAMA-ESPINOSA, 2017, BASED ON WOESE, KANDLER, & WHEELIS, 1990

Another classification scheme comes from universities. We can classify academic fields in different ways. Perhaps the most thorough division comes from the World Library's *World Heritage Encyclopedia* entry on *academic disciplines*, which lists 46 larger groupings (e.g., engineering, law, economics, and so on), and more than 900 academic fields (an abbreviated version is seen in Figure 30).

If you compare this classification scheme with Wikipedia's *Academic Discipline Categories*, you will see slight differences (Figure 31).

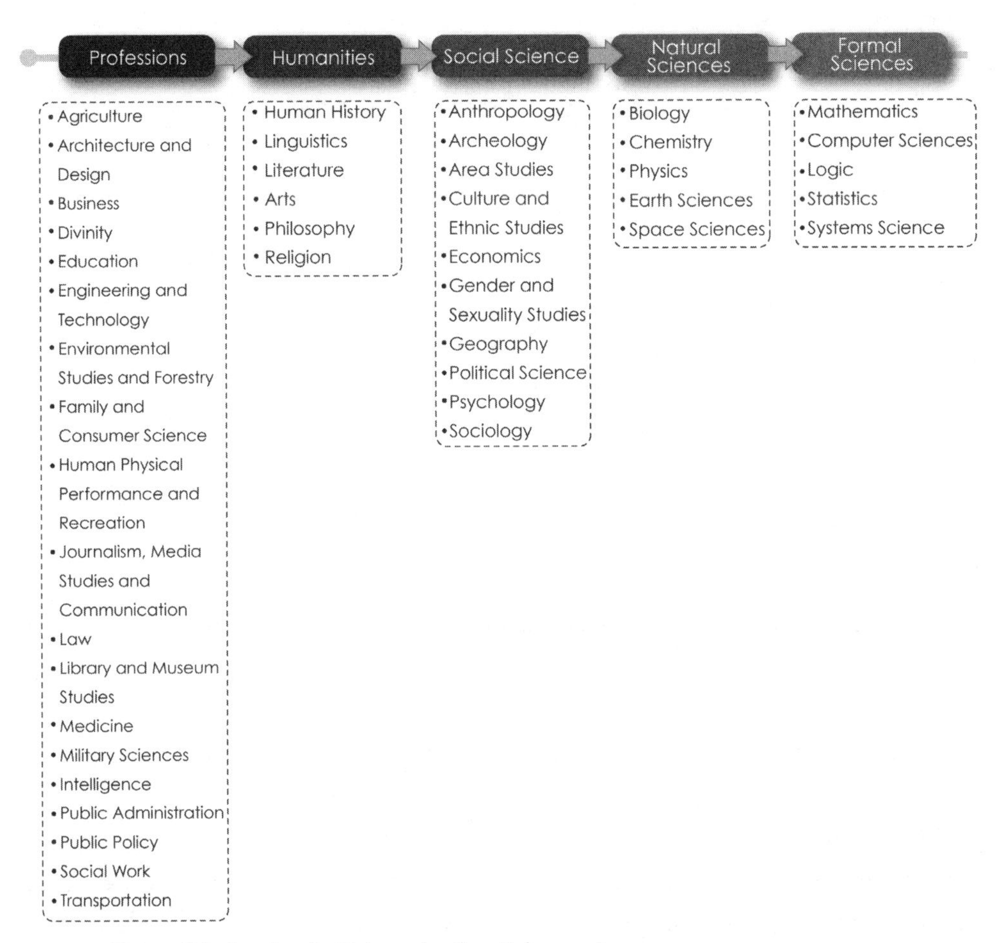

Figure 30. Academic Categorization Scheme A. SOURCE: TOKUHAMA-ESPINOSA, 2018 BASED ON WORLD HERITAGE ENCYCLOPEDIA 2017

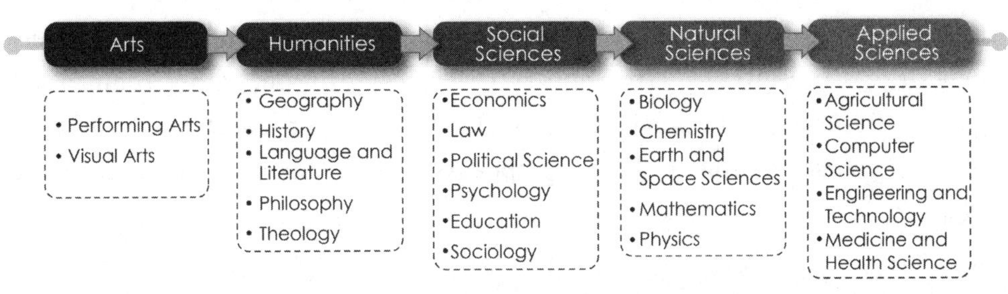

Figure 31. Academic Categorization Scheme B. SOURCE: TOKUHAMA-ESPINOSA, 2017 BASED ON WIKIPEDIA CLASSIFICATION OF ACADEMIC DISCIPLINES, 2017

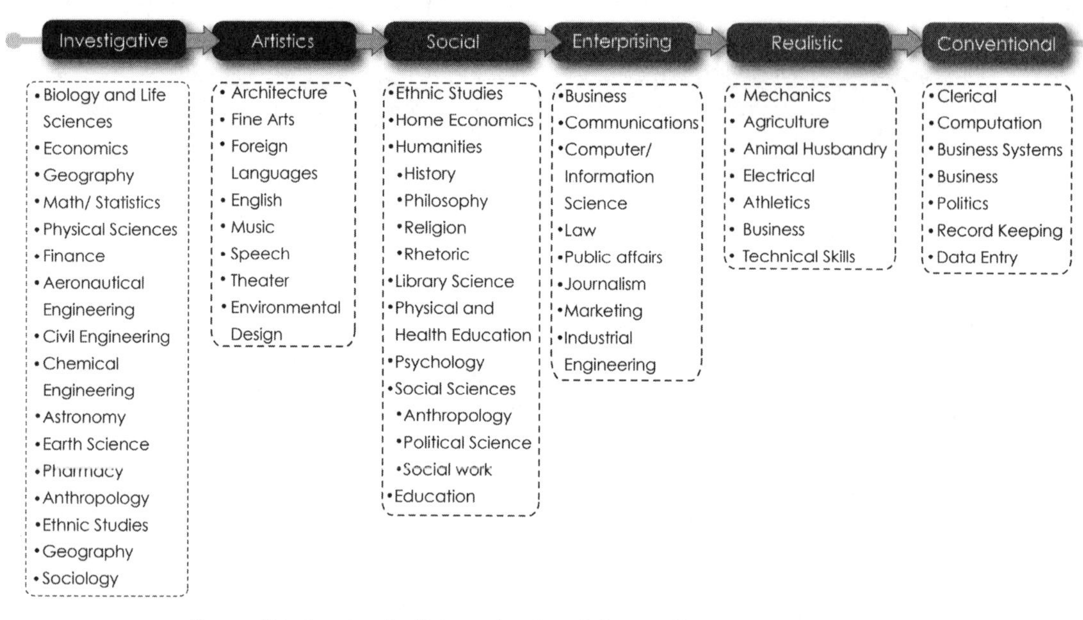

Figure 32. Academic Categorization Scheme C. SOURCE: HOLLAND, 1973

The view of academic classification is further changed if looked at through the lens of a psychological theorist, as seen in Figure 32.

This means that classifications are subject to value choices and different criteria. Furthermore, each academic field can further be broken down and classified into distinct subtypes. For example, educators can be divided into teachers, administrators, researchers, curriculum specialists, special education, preschool, primary, middle school or high school, by subject areas (math, language, science, and so on), or any number of other sub-classifications.

The "Universal Man," who knew a little about everything, was praised in the 16th century. Academic classifications and specializations are relatively new. It was only in the 17th century that specialization, rather than broad general knowledge, became desirable. However, the cyclical return toward broader transdisciplinary thinking appears to have taken hold again in the 21st century.

How the Categories Pillar Economizes Learning

The brain innately recognizes some categories—for example, emotions and faces—and types them together (*sad face=sadness*; *happy face=happiness*) (Ekman & Friesen, 2003). Other categories must be learned, such as mathematical premises (e.g., whole numbers vs. imaginary numbers). If students are taught how to identify categories, starting first with similarities and differences, then building up to explicit categories, they will economize learning throughout life. For example, "representations of shape and category independently coexist [in the dorsal and ventral visual pathways], but at the same time they are closely related throughout the visual hierarchy," (Bracci & de Beeck, 2016, p. 432). When objects have similar spatial properties, they travel similar pathways in the brain during recognition (Watson et al., 2016). Category learning isn't just important in schools; survival can hinge on it.

Human survival depends in part on efficient visual mechanism, so speed and accuracy in identifying target objects is a beneficial trait. Humans identify categories unconsciously and almost involuntarily every day. The ability of the brain to find a specific object is directly related to the speed with which the brain recognizes categories of objects (Cohen et al., 2017). This means that the better the brain is at quickly categorizing information, the faster a person will be able to spot target items in a group. Category identification is biased, however, as the brain adapts to what it is exposed to most. This means each one of us identifies the categories that we are most familiar with before those that are unfamiliar.

Chess has multiple moves (of **order**), which can be categorized into types (or **patterns**). The more a person rehearses the chess moves, the quicker she will be able to anticipate the correct countermoves, which is true of most types of expertise (Nakatani & Yamaguchi, 2014). The ability to predict the order of the opponent's moves is a beneficial trait for survival as well as for any strategy game. Teachers can employ categories to help their students learn. If teachers take the time to go over incorrect answers and categorize the reasons for wrong responses, they can speed up students' future learning. If teachers identify categories of errors, students themselves soon begin to recognize their own errors. If a child has trouble multiplying but can understand what types of errors he is making, he will be able to correct himself in the future, once familiarized

Table 13. Categories of Math Errors

SOME CATEGORIES OF 4th GRADE MATH ERRORS		
Misunderstandings of unit multiplication	Problems with the order of operations (multiplying 9 x 25 first)	Dependence on estimation of rounding up (50 x 20, but added rather than subtracted 25)
(a) 49 × 25 40 × 20 = 800 20 × 9 = 180 5 × 40 = 200 980 1180	(b) 49 × 25 225→(245) 100 325	(c) 49 × 25 1250 25 1275

SOURCE: TOKUHAMA-ESPINOSA, 2017 BASED ON DEBORAH LOWENBERG BALL'S EXPLANATION TO THE MICHIGAN SENATE, 2014.

with typical error categories. The former President of the American Education Research Association, Deborah Lowenberg Ball, neatly explained this phenomenon to the Michigan Senate in 2014 as she showed that specialized pedagogical content knowledge (about math in this case) was much more complex than many politicians believe (her point being that not everyone can be a great teacher because it requires specialized knowledge). She used problems similar to those in Table 13 to show that great teaching is not only a matter of being able to explain the correct way of doing a math problem, but also the expertise of understanding how to explain the **categories of errors** that might occur with different children as they think mathematically.

Category learning in one realm also improves future category learning in other realms (Fera et al., 2014); that is, the more you know, the more you can know (Tokuhama-Espinosa, 2014). The more ways one has to conceive of categories, the easier it gets to recognize categories. Habituated cognition can prime the brain to look for categories, and the more categories one knows, the easier it gets to find them in future learning.

There are several studies that explain how categories are developed in the human brain that lend support to the neuroscientific underpinnings of the categories pillar. Some examples can be found in Table 14.

Implications for Student Learning

Student learning can also be improved by sharing successful models (categories) of correct work. One of the best ways to learn is with a worked model, that is, seeing what the final product should look like (Hattie, 2012). For example, if you tell students they have an essay due shortly, their initial panic can be dissuaded by showing them what the categories of "bad," "good," and "excellent" essays actually look like. Similarly, if you tell students there is a test coming up and they will be "just fine if they can do problems similar to the one on the board," their test anxiety will be reduced. Bad as well as good models help; understanding categories of error types also helps students speed up their learning because the habituated exposure to categories of answers (good and bad) improves the likelihood of independent successful problem solving in the future. Rehearsal of math errors, such as those found in Table 13, improves the likelihood of self-correction and autonomous learning.

Learning throughout the life span, not just as a student, can be enhanced by thinking about the world in a more transdisciplinary way through the pillar of categories. Metacognition means thinking about thinking and is a desirable outcome of education (Chipman & Segal, 2013). One of the first steps in reflective thinking is to ask yourself, *"What do I already know about this new information?"* and the brain does this best by comparing, categorically, how the new information is similar to (as well as different from) what is already known. The simple beginnings of categorization are to gain an understanding of the similarities and differences that exist among objects, concepts, theories, people, places, and anything in the surroundings that can be described with characteristics. Once children begin to view the world in categories, their eyes are opened to a special way of thinking. Even though it might seem overly simplistic to say that categorization begins with an understanding of similarities and differences, this is actually a skill set that is valuable throughout academic life (even doctoral students have to do this!), and into real-world applications.

One of the most important traits of categories is that most things can fit into more than just one, which is also something small children understand, but which must be refined over a lifetime of exposure to different ways of classifying information. Your mother and father (or mother and mother, or father and father) are "parents" but they are also part of "women" and "men," and fall into a specific age group, and socioeconomic status. It is a brilliant lesson to learn that an object, concept, person, problem, process, theory . . . (anything!) can always be viewed in more than one way and, therefore, fits into more than one category. This mental flexibility helps problem-solving skills at all levels. Additionally, categories are also important because they relate to self-described characteristics that we use to identify ourselves that can influence learning outcomes. If I am an Asian woman and I take a math test and think of myself as an Asian, I am more likely to be successful than taking the test and categorizing myself as a woman (see Jennifer Steele's research on stereotype bias in academic performance at Stanford for additional examples [2002, 2003, 2006]). This means that understanding the multiple characteristics we have—and the many categories we can fit into—can be leveraged in both positive and negative ways in school contexts. As teachers, we need to help students identify themselves and their world not only with the greatest number of physical characteristics possible, but also with important attitudinal attributes. Do your students feel they are resilient? Do they think they have a growth mindset? Are they opportunistic, hardworking, and positive? Attitude goes a long way in determining outcome.

Look up from your book. Now think, what categories do you fit into? Male or female or neither? Tall or short or medium height? Smart or average or genius? Are you in the category of "go getter" or more passive? Are you a type A-proactive-intense person, or a type B-laid-back personality? Do you see yourself the same way others see you? How does your categorization of yourself affect the profession you have chosen, where you live, how happy you are, who you consider friends, what you think about your life? Now look around you. What categories of objects surround you? Are there objects you could categorize by colors? Sizes? Shapes? Can you think of unconventional categorizations of the things around you (that is, maybe the chair isn't just a chair, it is also an object bought in the past ten years, a color you love, or a style). Can you place the things in your immediate view into multiple categories, or group them in different ways to create any hierarchical classifications or invent equivalencies? For example, perhaps the basket and the candle are not immediately categorized together in your mind, but could they be if you think about equivalencies in size or price or where they were bought?

Viewing the world through the pillar of categories stretches our imaginations and adds a new dimension to thinking and learning.

Table 14. Example Studies of Categories in the Brain

FURTHER READING ON THE SCIENCE OF CATEGORIES IN THE BRAIN

Category Recognition in the Brain

Adams, R. B. & Janata, P. (2002). A comparison of neural circuits underlying auditory and visual object categorization. *NeuroImage*, *16*(2), 361-377.

Antzoulatos, E. G., & Miller, E. K. (2014). Increases in functional connectivity between prefrontal cortex and striatum during category learning. *Neuron*, *83*(1), 216-225.

Aviv, V. (2014). What does the brain tell us about abstract art?. *Frontiers in Human Neuroscience*, *8*, 85.

Bergamo, A., & Torresani, L. (2014). Classemes and other classifier-based features for efficient object categorization. *IEEE Transactions on Pattern Analysis and Machine Intelligence*, *36*(10), 1988-2001.

Bracci, S., & de Beeck, H. O. (2016). Dissociations and associations between shape and category representations in the two visual pathways. *Journal of Neuroscience*, *36*(2), 432-444.

Brattico, E., Bogert, B., Alluri, V., Tervaniemi, M., Eerola, T., & Jacobsen, T. (2015). It's sad but I like it: The neural dissociation between musical emotions and liking in experts and laypersons. *Frontiers in Human Neuroscience*, *9*, 676.

Carlson, T. A., Ritchie, J. B., Kriegeskorte, N., Durvasula, S., & Ma, J. (2014). Reaction time for object categorization is predicted by representational distance. *Journal of Cognitive Neuroscience*, *26*(1), 132-142.

Chang, H. C., Grossberg, S., & Cao, Y. (2014). Where's Waldo? How perceptual, cognitive, and emotional brain processes cooperate during learning to categorize and find desired objects in a cluttered scene. *Frontiers in Integrative Neuroscience*, *8*, 1–46. DOI: https://doi.org/10.3389/fnint.2014.00043

Cichy, R. M., Pantazis, D., & Oliva, A. (2014). Resolving human object recognition in space and time. *Nature Neuroscience*, *17*(3), 455-462.

Gerlach, C., & Marques, J. F. (2014). Visual complexity exerts opposing effects on object categorization and identification. *Visual Cognition*, *22*(6), 751-769.

Güçlü, U., Thielen, J., Hanke, M., van Gerven, M., & van Gerven, M. A. (2016). Brains on beats. In D. Schweizer (Ed.), *Advances in neural information processing systems* (pp. 2101-2109). Cambridge, MA: MIT Press.

Hadjikhani, N., Zürcher, N. R., Rogier, O., Ruest, T., Hippolyte, L., Ben-Ari, Y., & Lemonnier, E. (2015). Improving emotional face perception in autism with diuretic bumetanide: A proof-of-concept behavioral and functional brain imaging pilot study. *Autism*, *19*(2), 149-157.

Handjaras, G., Bernardi, G., Benuzzi, F., Nichelli, P. F., Pietrini, P., & Ricciardi, E. (2015). A topographical organization for action representation in the human brain. *Human Brain Mapping*, *36*(10), 3832-3844.

Istók, E., Brattico, E., Jacobsen, T., Ritter, A., & Tervaniemi, M. (2013). 'I love Rock 'n' Roll'—Music genre preference modulates brain responses to music. *Biological Psychology*, *92*(2), 142-151.

Kalénine, S., Shapiro, A. D., Flumini, A., Borghi, A. M., & Buxbaum, L. J. (2014). Visual context modulates potentiation of grasp types during semantic object categorization. *Psychonomic Bulletin & Review*, *21*(3), 645-651.

Kemmerer, D. (2017). Categories of object concepts across languages and brains: The relevance of nominal classification systems to cognitive neuroscience. *Language, Cognition and Neuroscience, 32*(4), 401–424.

Khaligh-Razavi, S. M., Henriksson, L., Kay, K., & Kriegeskorte, N. (2014). Explaining the hierarchy of visual representational geometries by remixing of features from many computational vision models. *BioRxiv*, 009936.

Martin, A., Wiggs, C. L., Ungerleider, L. G., & Haxby, J. V. (1996). Neural correlates of category-specific knowledge. *Nature, 379*(6566), 649.

Murre, J. M. (2014). *Learning and categorization in modular neural networks.* East Sussex, UK: Psychology Press.

Perrodin, C., Kayser, C., Abel, T. J., Logothetis, N. K., & Petkov, C. I. (2015). Who is that? Brain networks and mechanisms for identifying individuals. *Trends in Cognitive Sciences, 19*(12), 783-796.

Stansbury, D. E., Naselaris, T., & Gallant, J. L. (2013). Natural scene statistics account for the representation of scene categories in human visual cortex. *Neuron, 79*(5), 1025–1034.

Terasawa, Y., Kurosaki, Y., Ibata, Y., Moriguchi, Y., & Umeda, S. (2015). Attenuated sensitivity to the emotions of others by insular lesion. *Frontiers in Psychology, 6*(1314), 1–10. DOI: https://doi.org/10.3389/fpsyg.2015.01314

Villagrasa, F., Baladron, J., & Hamker, F. H. (2016, September). Fast and slow learning in a neuro-computational model of category acquisition. In *International Conference on Artificial Neuronal Networks* (pp. 248–255). New York: Springer International Publishing.

Vuust, P., Gebauer, L. K., & Witek, M. A. (2014). Neuronal underpinnings of music: The polyrhythmic brain. In *Neurobiology of interval timing* (pp. 339–356). Springer New York.

Wei, W., Liu, J., Dai, R., Feng, L., Li, L., & Tian, J. (2014, March). Different brain activations between own- and other-race face categorization: An fMRI study using group independent component analysis. In *SPIE Medical Imaging* (Vol. 9038, p.903807). Bellingham WA: International Society for Optics and Photonics.

We now turn to the final pillar of relationships.

5. Relationships

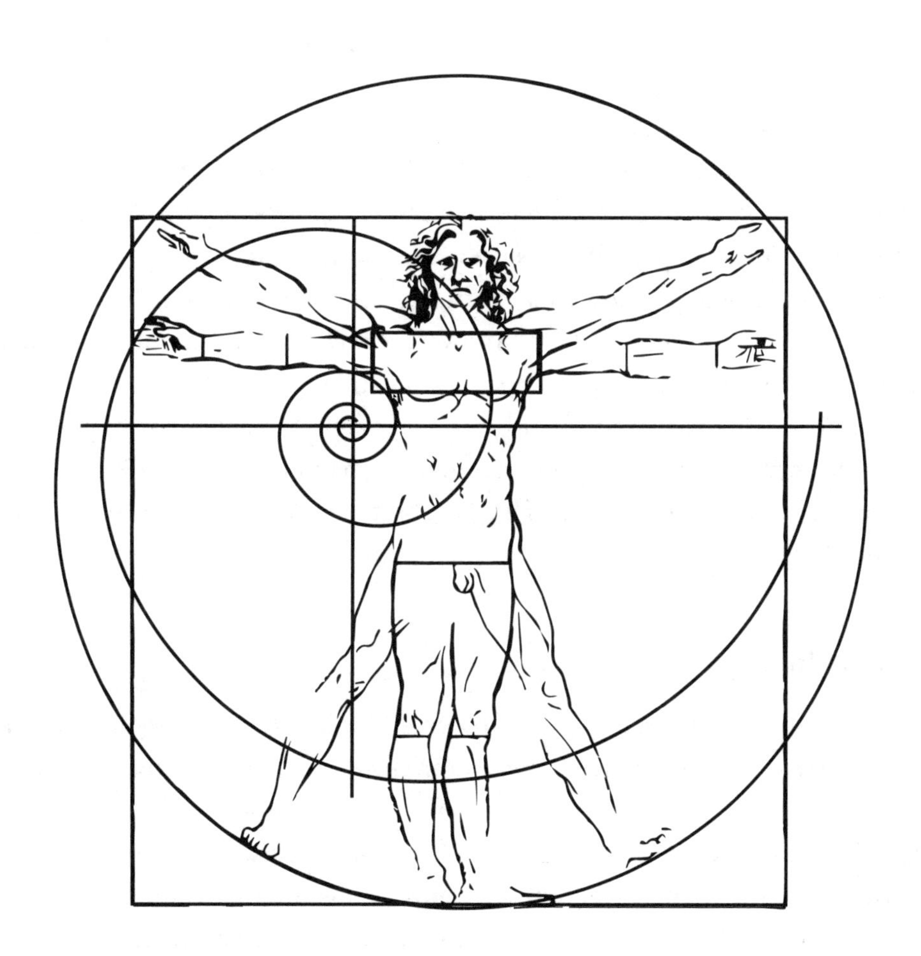

What are Relationships?

A relationship is the way two or more objects, people, or concepts are connected, related, linked, or associated, or the status of how two or more things are connected. Relationships are important because to comprehend them, a person must understand all the objects (concepts, people) being compared before understanding their association. Relationships can also imply dependences, kinships, and affinities among concepts or people, which can often be mutually dependent.

When relationships are between people, they define the way they feel and behave toward one another. When relationships are between entities, they often explain hierarchies, associations, or working arrangements. Relationships can be natural (such as *"breathing" is to "life"*) or contrived and devised (as *the coach worked hard to construct a good relationship between the players*). Relationships can also explain links, such as the connection between poverty and crime; climate change and global warming; and how wars destroy cities and refugees leave for other countries. As a verb, *to relate* means to make, show, or connect two or more things, or to be causally linked.

Relationships is the pillar with the most subsets, including proportions, correspondence, approximation, estimation, magnitude, measure, quantity, space, and context. Examples of each subset are given below, starting with proportions.

Proportions

A proportion is a share, or a part explained in relation to a whole (*Please split the pie into equal proportions; He got a much bigger proportion of the inheritance than his sisters; The politician spent proportionately more time in Washington, DC than in his home state*). Proportions can also be used in math problems, to conceive art, and in social division and sharing. Ratios are among the most common examples of proportions in the math curriculum (*there are 25 students for every teacher, so the ratio is 25:1, or twenty-five to one; your class has 25 students total, and 10 are boys and 15 are girls, so the ratio of boys to girls is 10:15 or 2:3*). You can also teach kids how to double or halve a cooking recipe using proportions. In school, ratios are key to understanding addition, multiplication, and division and can use whole numbers, fractions, and decimals. Without the key conceptual understanding of proportions, many kids can fail at math. Statistical reasoning is directly linked to the core concept of proportions. Since we can never poll 100 percent of a population, for example, we need to sample a proportion, but choosing a proportion that is "significant" means selecting a smaller group that is identical to the whole population.

Art and design rely heavily on proportion, which is often expressed as measures of scale. The accuracy of "true scale" relies on understanding the anatomically correct proportions of humans to their space and other objects in their surroundings. *Dis*proportions can be used as ironic artistic expression, such as in Jeff Jordan's comical imaging of the baby chick that measures twice as tall as a man, or to send messages about how smoking can be "larger than life" as it takes life itself. Such clashes with established mental schema make our brains pay attention to the absurd suggestions made by purposefully distorting correct proportions.

The Golden Ratio explains proportions in balance, and presumably what is considered beautiful or aesthetically pleasing (Livio, 2008). To be "golden" or ideal, the ratio is the same as the ratio of the sum of the larger of the two quantities, as expressed in the formula below in Figure 34. A face that complies with this formula, in which the width of the face has a 1:1.618 ratio to the length gives way to the joke that beauty is in the "Pi" (not eye) of the beholder (Pallett et al., 2010).

Euclid (300 BCE) is credited with the common use of Golden Ratio proportions, but there are records back to Phidias (490–430 BCE), who made the Parthenon statues based on this calculation. The Fibonacci (ca. 1170–1250 AD) sequence of numbers is also based on the Golden Ratio, and Leonardo da Vinci's *De divina proportione* (On the Divine Proportion) is said to have drawn *The Vitruvian Man* (1490 AD) using this formula.

It is particularly interesting that the Golden Ratio is, like most pillar ideas, grounded in nature. Fractals are simple, repeated shapes that duplicate in smaller and smaller (or larger and larger) proportional patterns. They are found in ferns, flowers, vegetables, snowflakes, and pine cones. Fractals are "patterns" but they also represent proportion in terms of the relationships of the parts.

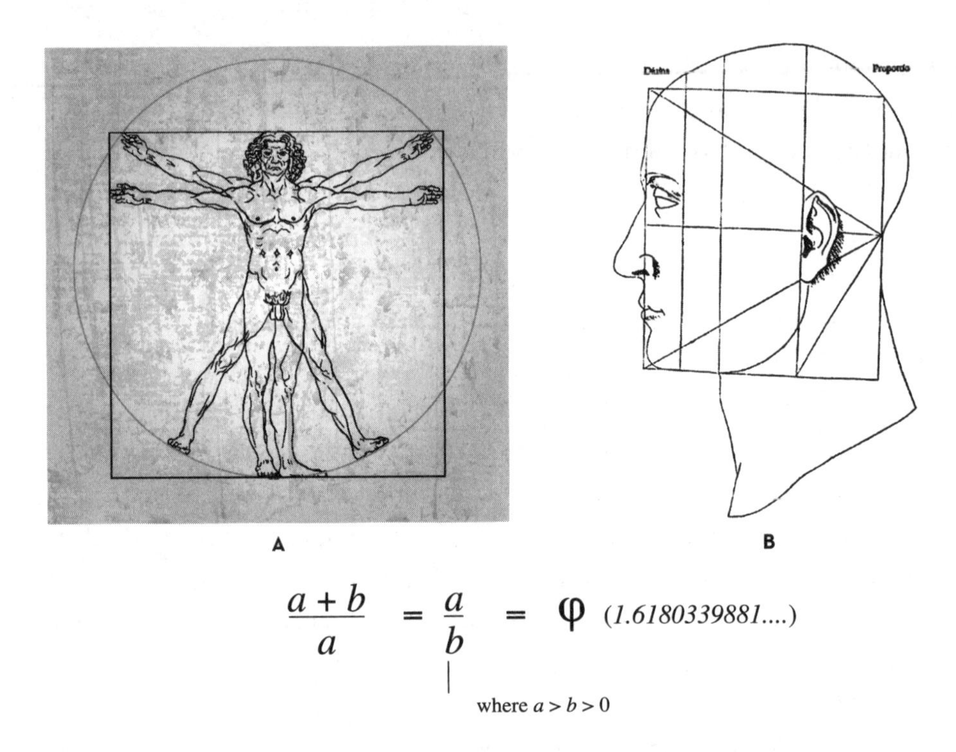

Figure 34. The Golden Ratio. SOURCES: (A) LEONARDO DA VINCI, 1490, GALLERIE DELL'ACCADEMIA, VENICE LEONARDO DA VINCI [PUBLIC DOMAIN], VIA WIKIMEDIA COMMONS; (B) WOODCUT FROM THE "DIVINA PROPORTIONE'" LUCA PACIOLI 1509, VENICE, DEPICTING THE GOLDEN PROPORTION AS IT APPLIES TO THE HUMAN FACE. PUBLIC DOMAIN.

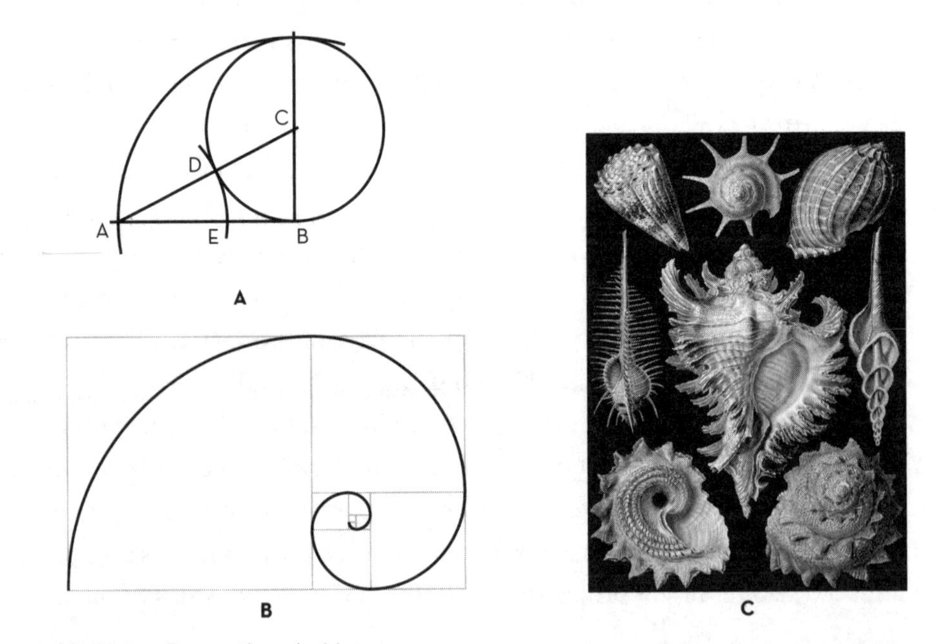

Figure 35. Divine Proportions in Nature. SOURCE: (A) BY MIRACETI, 2010, PUBLIC DOMAIN VIA WIKIMEDIA COMMONS; (B) BY USER: DICKLYON, PUBLIC DOMAIN VIA WIKIMEDIA COMMONS; (C) BY ERNST HAECKEL, KUNSTFORMEN DER NATUR, 1904, PLATE 53: PROSOBRANCHIA, PUBLIC DOMAIN VIA WIKIMEDIA COMMONS

Figure 36. Fractal Patterns and Proportions. SOURCES: (A) TOKUHAMA-ESPINOSA, 2018. (B) TOKUHAMA-ESPINOSA, 2018. (C) BY WILSON BENTLEY, PUBLIC DOMAIN VIA WIKIMEDIA COMMONS (D) TOKUHAMA-ESPINOSA, 2018.

Correspondence

Correspondence is another kind of relation. Correspondence identifies the similarities, equivalences, and connections between concepts. For example, the letter "t" has a particular sound and is used to begin the words "tiger" and "tree," so the symbol "t" corresponds to the sound /t/. Magnitude can be represented as a correspondence, such as in math. The symbols "3," "three," and "***" all correspond to similar magnitudes, despite the differences in the representations. Many physics formulas show correspondence as well (e.g., distance=speed x time). There can also be correspondence between subjects and verbs in a sentence structure, and correspondence between foreign languages and translations.

In school, correspondence is used to teach children the sound-to-symbol connection as they learn the alphabet, or the connections that exist between primary and secondary levels of education. These are purposeful connections that show the relations between two things. Hitting a key on a piano should correspond to a specific sound. The amount of junk food a person eats and the level of obesity of that person are interconnected and correspond. Certain gene combinations correspond to racial phenotypes. There is also a conceptual correspondence between multiplication and division, as there is between addition and subtraction. Some mythical gods in Greek literature correspond to Roman mythology because they try to explain the same phenomena.

Cause and ***effect*** are key examples of correspondence, such as the successful growth of the plant and the amount of sun, water, and good soil received. When one element, action, or event—or their combination—causes another,

Table 15. Correspondence of Greek and Roman Gods

GREEK AND ROMAN GODS		
Role	**Greek**	**Roman**
wisdom	Athena	Minerva
love	Aphrodite	Venus
war	Ares	Mars
water	Poseidon	Neptune

SOURCE: TOKUHAMA-ESPINOSA, 2017

there is correspondence. Cause-and-effect relationships describe dependency correspondence. Some examples of cause and effect include the following: *The man smoked two packs of cigarettes a day and died of lung cancer; I flipped the light switch and the lamp turned on; There was an unexpected oil spill and lots of fish and birds suffered the consequences; The road was icy, and the car could not brake in time; Press the gas and the car goes faster; Drop the egg and it breaks on the floor.*

Analogies are comparisons between two things used to clarify or explain their **relationships**. Use of analogies is one of the best ways to teach when the learner has little or no prior knowledge related to the learning concept. As mentioned earlier, pillars are the analogies of the mind. Analogies permit the use of something known to explain something unknown and can come in many forms. On an interesting note, the symbol for analogies (":") is the same as for ratios or equivalencies.

There are analogies that relate to time (December: winter as April: ____), or measurement (thermometer: temperature as odometer: ____), and others that explain part-to-whole relationships (wing: airplane as ____ : ship), person to situation (teacher: student as a coach: ____), cause to effect (drought: famine as good irrigation: ____), as well as synonymous constructs (basil: herb as oak: ____), or antonymous relations (appalling: pleasing as interesting: ____). Examples of analogical or metaphorical sayings include, *life is like a race*, or *a doctor is like a detective*, or that *genome assembly is like a puzzle.*

While analogies look for direct relationships, relationships can also depend on interpretation or definitions. Some of the best comedians display the most developed sense of relationships, and by extension, they are some of the most intelligent people around. Clever comedians draw parallels and correspondance where others miss the relationships. (From Steve Martin: "*Some people just have a way with words, and other people . . . oh . . . not have way.*" "*Q: Why do the French like to eat snails so much? A. They can't stand fast food.*")

Word roots. While not analogies per se, word roots can explain relationships as well. For example, both neurons and trees have roots—*dendrites* (meaning branching, treelike figures) in the case of neurons. One of the arguments for learning Latin is that so many English vocabulary words are unmasked once their roots are clear. That is, and understanding of how the prefix definition relates to the meaning of the word helps reveal the meaning of the word itself.

Table 16. Relationship of Latin Roots to Common Vocabulary

RELATIONSHIPS OF LATIN ROOTS TO COMMON VOCABULARY			
Latin root	**Meaning**	**Examples**	**Definition**
aqua	water	aquamarine	color of the ocean
pre	before	prehistoric	before history
bio	life	biology	study of life
alter	other	alternative	available as another possibility
bi	two	bilingual	two languages
aud	to hear	auditory	hearing
spec	see, watch	spectacle	striking performance
anti	against	antithesis	exact opposite
uni	one	unicycle	one-wheeled cycle

SOURCE: TOKUHAMA-ESPINOSA, 2017

Magnitude

Magnitude is the size or extent of something. Magnitude explains the relationship to spatial qualities or to weight, height, length, quality, or general numerical comparison of one thing to the whole. *The earthquake was of great magnitude* (relative to the average size of earthquakes). *Venus's brightness has a magnitude greater than other planets* (relative to the other planets). Magnitude can be applied to anything in relation to other like items, for example, *the magnitude of the issue was of historical importance* (relative to other moments in history). Magnitude can be used to describe dimensions, as well as the extent of something relative to another and to express important moments, as in *this is a situation of great magnitude*, or to important personalities, as in *he showed great magnitude in a tough situation.*

Magnitude is most visible in math, but can also be seen in design, finance, history, art, health, and astronomy, and is mainly used to show the relative size of things. For example, "visual magnitude" in astronomy is the apparent brightness of celestial bodies compared to each other.

Measure

Measure is used to determine the size, degree, amount, or quantity of something using an instrument with a scale. Measurement is normally very precise but can vary depending on the tool being used. Measurement tools establish the relative nearness to a standard for use in comparison. More broadly, a measure is the dimension, amount, or capacity of an object or concept, real or imagined. For example, a person from Latin America might perceive temperature differently than a person from Iceland, even if the measure of the temperature itself is the same, indicating their relative sense of hot and cold.

Scale

Measurement usually suggests a perceptible scale, as in how something is compared to another, or to the measurement tool itself. Scales can be things like rulers, thermometers, measuring tapes, weight scales, speedometers, clocks, straightedges, damp meters, and angle finders. All these devices show the relative degree, height, or weight, among others. Scales can measure mass, area, volume, length, area, speed, momentum, force, pressure, torque, acceleration, electrical charge, temperature, density, hardness, shape and surface, humidity, loudness, brightness, pungent smell, distance, granularity, opacity, and more. All scales show the relative measure to a standard.

Approximation

Approximations and estimations are also part of relationships and express a quantity or value that is not exactly correct or the same, but is nearly so. Approximation is the state of being near to or close to something else, for

Table 17. Tools and What They Measure

RELATIONSHIP BETWEEN TOOLS AND WHAT THEY MEASURE		
Tool	**Image**	**What it Measures**
clock		time (seconds, minutes, hours)
thermometer		temperature
speedometer		velocity
caliper		external diameter or width of an object
protractor		angles
measuring tape		inches, millimeters, centimeters

SOURCE: PUBLIC DOMAIN VIA WIKIMEDIA COMMONS

example, *the teacher gave the student an approximate grade after the midterm.* The verb *to approximate* draws elements together (*the arrow approximated the target but did not hit it*).

Approximations can be used in math to quickly calculate large numbers by rounding up or down. For example, 49 x 2 is harder to calculate quickly than the approximation of 50 x 2 (-2), which has a close relationship to the problem. Approximations are often used in science when the exact measurement tool is costly or difficult to use. For example, with a good telescope, you can approximate the distance between planets, as traveling to them for a precise measurement is not really an option (yet). Approximations can also be used to describe physical traits. (*His second wife approximated the physical attributes of his first wife, but their personalities were very different.*) Approximations are likenesses, and while some of the mental processes are similar, they are different from estimations.

Estimation

Estimations are based on less precise data than are approximations. Estimations differ from approximations in that approximations are often based on calculations of something, whereas estimations are rough calculations based on experience rather than process. An approximation resembles the original, whereas an estimation is more like an appraisal based on past experience. For example, a person can look at an approaching airplane and estimate its arrival time, or actually approximate its timing by calculating speed and rate. Estimations are good guesses, while approximations are closer to the original. You estimate when a ballpark figure is good enough and precision is not required. Estimations are often based on opinions or judgment. We can estimate the cost of the dinner by "guesstimating" the amount of each item ordered and the tax and tip.

Quantity

Quantity measures how much there is of something. Quantity is fascinating because it can express a particular or an indefinite amount of anything. Quantity is the total amount or number used to identify the magnitude of an object, and is always determined relative to a scale. It is normally precise, though it can also be estimated. Quantities can be large or small, relative to the aspect of what is being measured. For example, 100 is a relatively *small* quantity if you think of the distance to Mars, but a *big* quantity relative to a human's age.

Quantity can be measured as a multitude or as a magnitude. Quantity is relative ("equal," "more," "less") and measured as mass, time, distance, weight, or anything else that can be expressed as a real number. Quantity is often compared and contrasted with quality. Sometimes these two characteristics are considered competitive, rather than complementary (i.e., *he was after quantity, not quality*) and both are relative to the point of reference.

Quantity is the subject of mathematical operations and compares magnitudes (size, volume, area, length, and so on) and is situationally dependent. Quantity structure and the relationships between quantities is the cornerstone of modern physical sciences, which depend on measuring length, breadth, depth, time, mass, force, temperature, energy and quantum, volume, and mass.

Quantity in music is used to measure the length of a note (Marzilli, 2016). In logic, quantity is the character of a proposition as being universal, particular, singular, or mixed (Sommers & Englebretsen, 2017). In phonetics, quantity is the perceived length of a syllable or vowel sound (Kuuluvainen et al., 2014). In mathematics and physics, quantity is a component that is expressed in numbers (Twomey, 2013). Quantity can be measured in terms of space and time.

Space and Time

A spatial relation is how objects are related to one another in space (Bahr et al., 2016). Relationships can be conducted in space, as in how close or how far away something is relative to something else. Relationships can be conducted in time, as in temporally how near or far something is to something else (Block, 2014), such as the idea that 1:00 p.m. is closer to 2:00 p.m. than it is to 3:00 p.m. Space and time relationships explain much of the basis for the field of physics.

Context

Relationships can be expressed in terms of context, or the circumstances of an event or place. Context can be the environment, the culture, or the circumstance that surrounds an individual. Context is shaped by social and emotional constructs and influences all human interaction (Algoe & Zhaoyang, 2016). In language, this can mean the discourse that surrounds a situation that explains elements, or the interrelated contexts or outlying circumstances. Context can explain why one brand of soap sells better in one city or another due to local perceptions and values (MacInnis et al., 2014). Context is important in teaching-learning processes (Hoffman, 2014), without which the relative location, standing, culture, or "reality" would be missing (Grusec & Hastings, 2014).

There are multiple journal writings that show the role of relationships, including relative quantity, *dis*proportion, the Golden Ratio, approximation, and estimation that lend evidence to the pillar's neuroconstructivist design regarding relationships. Some examples are found in Table 18.

How the Relationships Pillar Economizes Learning

The pillar of relationships can economize learning by taking advantage of similar neuronal pathways. For example, there appear to be similar neuronal tracts for intuitive approximation and number sense (e.g., Libertus, 2015); for numerical estimation and symbolic magnitude calculation (e.g., De Smedt et al., 2013); the Golden Ratio and proportions (e.g., Di Dio et al., 2007) and facial evaluation (Noguchi & Murota, 2013). Consciousness and body perception (e.g., Blanke, 2012); and time and space mechanisms (e.g., Burr et al., 2010; Srinivasan & Carey, 2010) also seem to rely on one another and share similar pathways (as measured by common hubs in the brain) for these relationships. Additionally, we are beginning to understand the relationship between emotion and cognition and the mutually influential role they play in contextualizing human interaction (Dolcos et al., 2011). These examples of neuronal pathways related to the pillar of relationships suggest that learning at least some subsets economizes learning.

Implications for Student Learning

Relationships come in all sizes and shapes, and snowball with each new member: *The more you know, the more you can know.* Relationships are at the core of mental flexibility. The ability to see how two or more things are related in ways that others before may not have seen requires an openness to make connections. Mental flexibility is developed by stretching the imagination about the many ways a thing can be related to others and is a desirable trait sought after in many schools. This broadens conceptual understanding and equips minds for future learning. This is something like playing an infinite game of "Six Degrees of Separation" (Guare, 1990; Karinthy, 1929) in hopes of finding the most direct route to connect two things that initially seemed unlinked.

Looking at the world through the lens of the relationship pillar improves one's transdisciplinary understanding. If we can cultivate a habituated mentality of always questioning what other relationships exist (concept, theory, perspective, object, person, policy, and so on), then our views of the world and our studies will be broadened.

Table 18. Example Studies of Relationships in the Brain

FURTHER READING ON THE SCIENCE OF RELATIONSHIPS IN THE BRAIN
Human Relationships
Cozolino, L. (2014). *The neuroscience of human relationships: Attachment and the developing social brain* (Norton series on interpersonal neurobiology). New York, NY: WW Norton & Company. Immordino-Yang, M. H. (2015). *Emotions, learning, and the brain: Exploring the educational implications of affective neuroscience* (The Norton series on the social neuroscience of education). New York, NY: WW Norton & Company. Immordino-Yang, M. H. (2016). Embodied brains, social minds: Toward a cultural neuroscience of social emotion. In *Oxford handbook of cultural neuroscience, Part II: Cultural neuroscience of emotion* (pp. 129–142). Oxford, UK: Oxford University Press. Israel, S. (2016). Toward a mechanistic understanding of how variation in the oxytocin receptor gene shapes individual differences in brain and social behavior. *Biological Psychiatry, 80*(2), e7-e9. Siegel, D. J. (2015). *The developing mind: How relationships and the brain interact to shape who we are.* New York, NY: Guilford Publications. Tavares, R. M., Mendelsohn, A., Grossman, Y., Williams, C. H., Shapiro, M., Trope, Y., & Schiller, D. (2015). A map for social navigation in the human brain. *Neuron, 87*(1), 231–243.
Relationships in Time or Space
Burr, D., & Morrone, C. (2006). Time perception: space–time in the brain. *Current Biology, 16*(5), R171-R173. Casasanto, D. (2014). Bodily relativity. In *Routledge handbook of embodied cognition* (pp. 108–117). London, UK: Routledge. Cheng, R. K., Tipples, J., Narayanan, N. S., & Meck, W. H. (2016). Clock speed as a window into dopaminergic control of emotion and time perception. *Timing & Time Perception, 4*(1), 99–122. Fingelkurts, A. A., Fingelkurts, A. A., & Neves, C. F. (2010). Natural world physical, brain operational, and mind phenomenal space–time. *Physics of Life Reviews, 7*(2), 195–249. Kononowicz, T. W., Van Rijn, H., & Meck, W. H. (2016). Timing and time perception: A critical review of neural timing signatures before, during, and after the to-be-timed interval. *Sensation, Perception and Attention, 2*, 1–35. Lenay, C., & Steiner, P. (2010). Beyond the internalism/externalism debate: the constitution of the space of perception. *Consciousness and Cognition, 19*(4), 938–952. Matthews, W. J. (2015). Time perception: the surprising effects of surprising stimuli. *Journal of Experimental Psychology: General, 144*(1), 172.

Nyberg, L., Kim, A. S., Habib, R., Levine, B., & Tulving, E. (2010). Consciousness of subjective time in the brain. *Proceedings of the National Academy of Sciences, 107*(51), 22356–22359.
Robbins, S. E. (2010). Special relativity and perception: The singular time of psychology and physics. *Journal of Consciousness Exploration & Research, 1*(5).
Sterzer, P. (2004). Constructive brain processes in motion perception. *Klinische Neurophysiologie, 35*(03), 271.
Van Rijn, H., Gu, B. M., & Meck, W. H. (2014). Dedicated clock/timing-circuit theories of time perception and timed performance. In *Neurobiology of interval timing* (pp. 75–99). New York, NY: Springer.

Relative Consciousness and Embodied Cognition

Chemero, A. (2011). *Radical embodied cognitive science.* Cambridge, MA: MIT press.
Koziol, L. F., Budding, D. E., & Chidekel, D. (2012). From movement to thought: executive function, embodied cognition, and the cerebellum. *Cerebellum, 11*(2), 505–525.
Shanahan, M. (2010). *Embodiment and the inner life: Cognition and consciousness in the space of possible minds.* New York, NY: Oxford University Press.
Thierry, G. (2016). Neurolinguistic relativity: How language flexes human perception and cognition. *Language Learning, 66*(3), 690–713.

Disproportions and Proportions

Di Dio, C. (2012). *Neural correlates of aesthetic experience in art* (Doctoral dissertation). Parma, Italy: Università degli Studi di Parma. Dipartimento di Neuroscienze.
Ishai, A. (2011). Art compositions elicit distributed activation in the human brain. In A.P. Shimamura and S.E. Palmer (Eds.) *Aesthetic science: Connecting minds, brains, and experience,* (pp.337–355). New York, NY: Oxford University Press.
Vessel, E. A., Starr, G. G., & Rubin, N. (2012). The brain on art: intense aesthetic experience activates the default mode network. *Frontiers in Human Neuroscience,* 6.

The Golden Ratio

Conway, B. R., & Rehding, A. (2013). Neuroaesthetics and the trouble with beauty. *PLoS Biology, 11*(3), e1001504.
Elliott, M. A., Kelly, J., Friedel, J., Brodsky, J., & Mulcahy, P. (2015). The golden section as optical limitation. *PlosOne, 10*(7), e0131045.
Ho, M. W. (2014). Golden music of the brain. *Science in Society, 62.*
Shen, H., Chau, D. K., Su, J., Zeng, L. L., Jiang, W., He, J., . . . & Hu, D. (2016). Brain responses to facial attractiveness induced by facial proportions: evidence from an fMRI study. *Scientific Reports, 6.*

Approximation, Estimation

Barth, H. C., & Paladino, A. M. (2011). The development of numerical estimation: Evidence against a representational shift. *Developmental Science, 14*(1), 125–135.
De Smedt, B., Noël, M. P., Gilmore, C., & Ansari, D. (2013). How do symbolic and non-symbolic numerical magnitude processing skills relate to individual differences in children's mathematical skills? A review of evidence from brain and behavior. *Trends in Neuroscience and Education, 2*(2), 48–55.
Leibovich, T., & Henik, A. (2013). Magnitude processing in non-symbolic stimuli. *Frontiers in Psychology, 4.*

Leibovich, T., Katzin, N., Harel, M., & Henik, A. (2017). From "sense of number" to "sense of magnitude": The role of continuous magnitudes in numerical cognition. *Behavioral and Brain Sciences, 40.*
Libertus, M. E. (2015). The role of intuitive approximation skills for school math abilities. *Mind, Brain, and Education, 9*(2), 112–120.
Petzschner, F. H., Glasauer, S ., & Stephan, K. E. (2015). A Bayesian perspective on magnitude estimation. *Trends in Cognitive Sciences, 19*(5), 285–293.
Schneider, M., Beeres, K., Coban, L., Merz, S., Susan Schmidt, S., Stricker, J., & De Smedt, B. (2017). Associations of non–symbolic and symbolic numerical magnitude processing with mathematical competence: A meta–analysis. *Developmental Science, 20*(3).
Slusser, E. B., Santiago, R. T., & Barth, H. C. (2013). Developmental change in numerical estimation. *Journal of Experimental Psychology: General, 142*(1), 193.
Xenidou-Dervou, I., Molenaar, D., Ansari, D., van der Schoot, M., & van Lieshout, E. C. (2017). Nonsymbolic and symbolic magnitude comparison skills as longitudinal predictors of mathematical achievement. *Learning and Instruction, 50,* 1–13.

Look up from your book. What relationships can you see? Are there relationships between form and function (*the way casual clothes in your closet relate to their use for exercise, or how the books fit into the shelf)* or between people *(the photo of your family members on the wall*), or your stomach's growling to the time of day and your need to eat? Are you conscious of the level of the volume button on your computer and its relationship to the noise? Are you aware that the car in the distance is about a half block away related to the sound of the horn? Do you understand the analogous relationship being made on the television program or the book you are reading? Relationships, like the other four pillars, structure the world around us as well as the thoughts within our minds. The more we develop an ability to see the relationships around us, the easier it becomes to identify future ones, as well as to hypothesize relationships in the world of ideas. Some of the best inventions are thanks to the simple ability to see relationships between ideas others thought of as unrelated.

Each of the five pillars stands on its own as an explanation of how to view the world, and taken collectively they are also a new model of human learning. To better understand not only examples of the pillars but also the science behind them, we now turn to the theoretical underpinnings of the five pillars, from Piaget's ideas in the 1950s to our current understandings of the brain.

6. Theoretical Underpinnings: From Piaget to Neurons

The pillars have the potential to make learning more efficient by economizing effort and to make learning more interesting by adding a new dimension to all topics. By applying the five pillars to existing studies, we can map out human learning over a wide range of traditional school subjects as well as consider their intersections, reducing the need for additional teaching time in those areas. This will be explained in more detail with an example in the Appendices. First, we turn to the theoretical underpinnings and science behind the pillars.

Overlapping Networks

Network overlap is an exciting area of research related to "the economy of brain network organization" (Bullmore & Sporns, 2012), which has grown exponentially just over the last few years thanks in part to the Connectome Project. The Connectome Project combines findings from a variety of imaging tools and behavioral and genetic data to render a more thorough understanding of learning.

> The central idea of this Review is that the brain's connectome is not optimized either to minimize connection costs or to maximize advantageous topological properties (such as efficiency or robustness). Instead, we argue that *brain network organization is the result of an economical trade-off between the*

> *physical cost of the network and the adaptive value of its topology.* (Bullmore & Sporns, 2012, p. 347, emphasis added by author)

This means that we as teachers have the potential of economizing student learning as the same neuronal networks can often serve distinct academic goals. For example, as mentioned in the Introduction, Stanislas Dehaene found that many of the neuronal mechanisms required for reading are similar to neuronal mechanisms needed for numeracy skills (Dehaene, 2007, 2009). These overlapping areas provide great insight about how we should actually teach by emphasizing *the similarities* between language and math rather than separating them and highlighting differences, as normally occurs in schools today. Such an approach would lead to a more efficient use of teaching time and stimulate multiple subject-area networks in the brain simultaneously. Instead of teaching math symbols alone, for example, teachers could complement math symbols (or patterns, order, relations, and categories) with symbols from language, science, natural surroundings, art, and so on, which may help children relate to the symbols better and/or remember them more easily. This leads to a more natural transdisciplinary way to think about the world and can make learning more efficient. The fact that symbolic representations overlap in the brain leads to speculation that other pillar networks could do the same. The economizing of learning means that core concepts in school may be mastered faster, providing more time to go into depth in the subject areas. As all teachers know, time is of the essence in our classrooms and many areas of the curriculum are shortchanged in terms of "coverage" due to the few hours dedicated to each subject. The pillars would allow for greater time in distinct domains by economizing areas of overlap.

It is thought-provoking to note that there are overlapping neuronal circuitry for physical pain and social rejection (Eisenberger & Lieberman, 2004); visual attention and eye movement (Striemer et al., 2015); social connection and physical warmth (Inagaki, 2014); self and other perspective taking based on facial expressions (Lamm et al., 2007); social support and stress (e.g., Eisenberger et al., 2007); and facial expressions and emotions (decades of research including Sprengelmeyer et al., 1998). These studies point to the likelihood of finding even further documentation of overlap in pattern, order, categories, and relations networks though the actual search for information along pillar lines has not yet been undertaken. The existence of overlapping neuronal mechanisms coupled with the pillars points to the need for a dramatic restructuring of teacher training, which will be discussed in the next chapter. First, we turn to the theoretical underpinnings of the pillars.

Constructivism and Hierarchical Complexities

At the start of this book I wrote, "The exciting conclusion drawn from this new information is that we teachers can improve student learning outcomes by taking advantage of a better understanding of these neuronal networks, followed by the use of methodologies that correctly stimulate them in an orderly way." And then I lamented that the "orderly way" hadn't yet been found. This isn't *entirely* true.

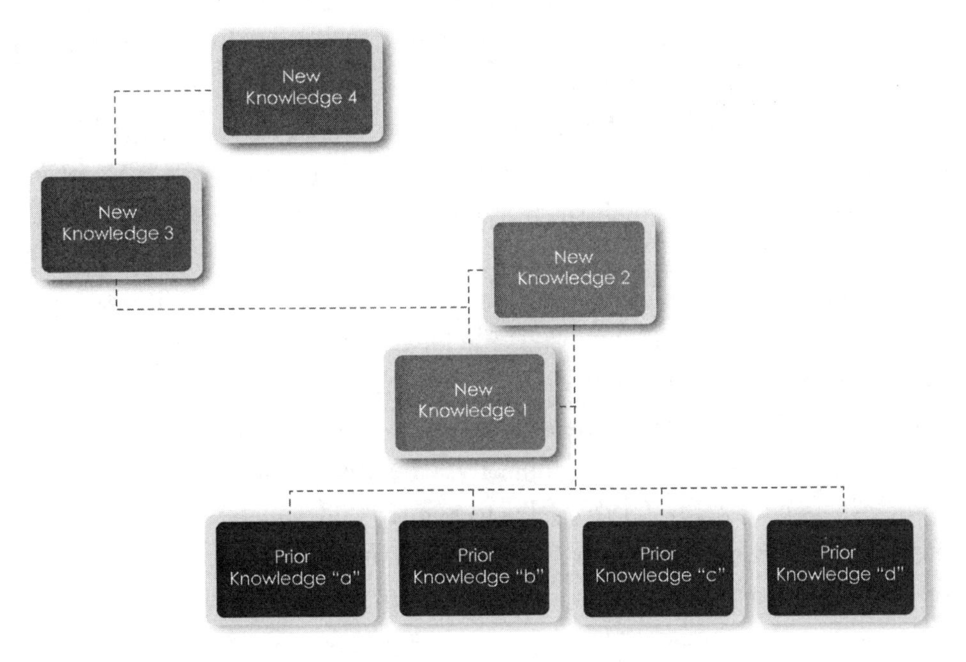

Figure 37. Basic Educational Constructivism. SOURCE: TOKUHAMA-ESPINOSA, 2015

Seeds were planted for better teaching and learning processes based on a constructivist design using a hierarchical model as early as the early 1900s starting with Dewey's, Montessori's, and Piaget's work (Ultanir, 2012). Constructivism means that "basic" elements are taught before "advanced" ones and that this is done through a hierarchy of skills revealed by stripping down subject areas into their "lower" to "higher" elements. The result of introducing learning concepts this way is improved positive transfer for each new higher-order learning stage, as can be seen in Figure 37.

Constructivism also explains why some learning goals are not met. For example, a child cannot learn subtraction (learning goal) if he does not understand addition (prerequisite knowledge). To be successful, he will first need to understand everything behind the concept of addition, and then make his way to the higher-order skill of subtraction. If any one of the prerequisite skills laid out in the hierarchy is not developed properly, the child will be unable to easily master the new knowledge upon which it is based. And even those who appear to master perquisite constructs may not really have done so. It is important to acknowledge that some children will appear to dominate that skill, but in reality, they are simply using extended working memory and an understanding of patterns to feign knowledge—true understanding means they can comprehend, identify, explain, use, and transfer knowledge as evidenced by creating their own problems in subtraction correctly.

In the 1930s and 1940s Luria and Vygotsky helped catalyze the debate on constructivism through contributions on the learning mind (Luria & Vygotsky, 1930; Vygotsky, 1934), which set the stage for the most recognized leader of constructivist design, Jean Piaget, who is well known to educators and psychologists alike for his careful observation and documentation of child learning through constructivist stages (1952). The idea of mastery learning, made popular by Benjamin Bloom in 1956, suggests that students should be helped to master each learning unit before proceeding to a more advanced learning task (Bloom, 1968). Mastery learning objectives are among the greatest benefits of applying the pillars. Mastery's goal is to assure children learn knowledge in a hierarchical fashion, improving the chances that no gaps exist in fundamental notions. Unfortunately, the vision of mastering the curriculum is currently compromised in many classrooms in favor of getting *through* the curriculum, despite decades of research showing the superior efficiency of mastery for both individual and group benefits (Emery et al., 2017; Guskey, 2007; Guskey, 2010; Guskey & Pigott, 1988; McGaghie et al., 2014; McGaghie et al., 2017).

Subsequently, Robert Gagné (former President of the American Psychological Association's Division 15) developed a "hierarchy of knowledge" concept leading to specific curriculum recommendations of basic to advanced learning tasks (Gagné, 1962, 1965, 1968, 1973). Jerome Bruner contributed positively to this important discussion (1960) by complementing a spiral review of hierarchically presented information while preserving Bloom's mastery concept. Bruner declared that when learning was designed in an ever-iterative spiral upward, "[t]he end stage of this process was eventual mastery of the connexity [sic] and structure of a large body of knowledge," (pp. 3-4). That is, the declared goal of education, as stated for the past several decades, is mastery learning achieved through ever-more-complex thinking. Unfortunately, learning goals and educational goals are not always the same, as can be seen by the current educational models found in many countries around the world, which are aimed at standards or minimum acceptable levels in content knowledge through subject-centered curriculum design rather than higher-order thinking skills or mastery.

In the 1970s, many thinkers converged on the idea of hierarchical designs to improve learning outcomes. However, it wasn't until the late 1970s and early 1980s that real curriculum reform measures were launched that capitalized on the concept. White (1973) joined Gagné and elevated the discussion (White & Gagné, 1974) about learning hierarchies, while Phillips and Kelly (1975) summarized the various hierarchical theories of development and educational instruction, propelling the concept of hierarchical complexities into the educational spotlight. Jones and Russell (1979) helped subject-specific queries take hold by looking into the specific hierarchical learning paradigm in science instruction.

The depth and complexity of hierarchical design in learning was also improved upon by Harvard's Kurt Fischer (1980), who began some of the first work stretching hierarchies to consider neuronal networks and the constant change experienced by learners, rather than just discipline or domain-area content. Fischer's original theory of cognitive development related to "the control and construction of hierarchies of skills" (1980) and has since grown into his Dynamic System Theory (2008; Fischer & Rose, 2001; Fischer & Yan, 2002, 2003; Rose & Fischer, 2009; Fischer, Rose, & Rose, 2007). Dynamic System Theory is rooted in two guiding concepts: "(1) Multiple characteristics of person and context collaborate to produce all aspects of behavior; and (2) variability in performance provides important information for understanding behavior and development" (Rose & Fischer, 2009, p. 264). Fischer embellished the basic traits of hierarchical complexity by returning to a more humanistic focus of learning design that involves the "messiness" of individual change, independent of the content area of learning. While others focused on structuring a hierarchical representation of content information, Fischer, Yan, and Stewart (2003) were concerned with how to explain "webs" of knowledge and how thinking processes became more accurate, efficient, and elaborate over time and due to experience (including classroom contexts). Fischer's web of skills describes how learning advances and retreats, similar to "two steps forward and one step back" as a norm, which parallels new synaptic proliferation followed by pruning before more synaptic proliferation.

A new model joining content-based hierarchies and thinking skills was finally achieved in the late 1980s. In Commons and colleagues' *Hierarchical Complexity of Tasks Shows the Existence of Developmental Stages* (1998), the effort to join the domain-vs.-thinking hierarchies became a reality. Fischer and Commons collaborated with other colleagues to unite their theories on the shape of conceptual developmental throughout the lifespan based on complexity levels of moral reasoning (Dawson-Tunik et al., 2005). This merging of the minds expanded the developmental aspect of the constructivist and hierarchical models to include lifelong aspects of learning.

Reigeluth and colleagues summarized the body of work on hierarchy of skills in *The Elaboration Theory of Instruction* (1980), in which they stated what many excellent teachers already knew instinctually as the art in the science of teaching: The best learning moments are organized from (a) simple to complex, (b) general to detailed, and (c) intangible to concrete to abstract. Based on our slightly better understanding of learning gleaned since the 1980s, we can add to these three core hierarchical measures two bookends: prerequisite knowledge at the start and the consolidation the learning through transfer as a closing step as is illustrated in Figure 38.

Learning requires reinforcement. Few things are learned after only a single exposure (and those are only life-threatening situations); all academic learning requires rehearsal. How much rehearsal depends on the learner's past experiences related to the new learning (the greater the prior experience, the less rehearsal required for new learning). The speed of recall depends in part on the myelin sheath surrounding axonal connections that speeds the communication between neurons.

If we combine Bruner's spiral learning with Piaget's constructivism and

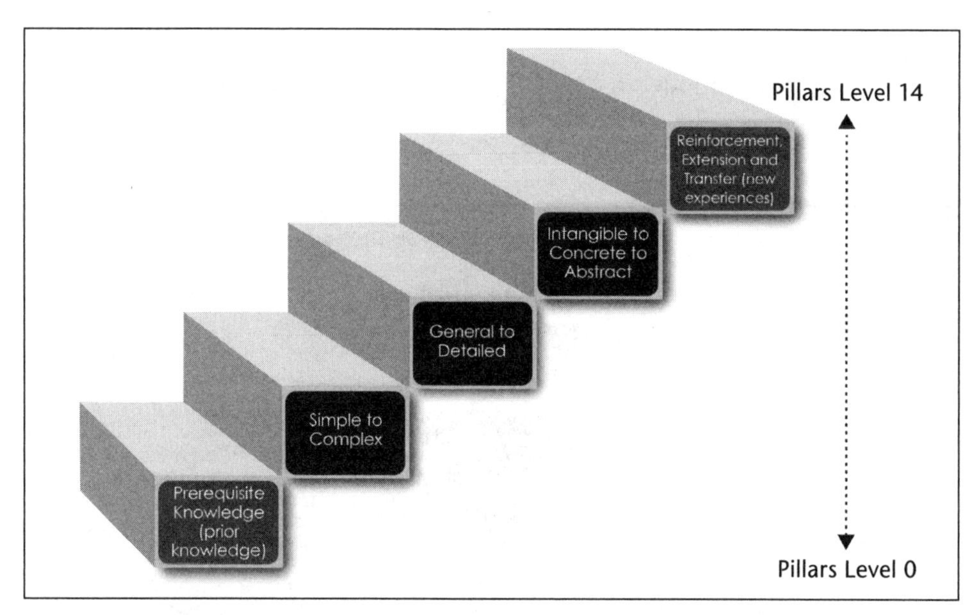

Figure 38. An Embellished Elaboration Theory of Instruction.
SOURCE: TOKUHAMA-ESPINOSA, 2015

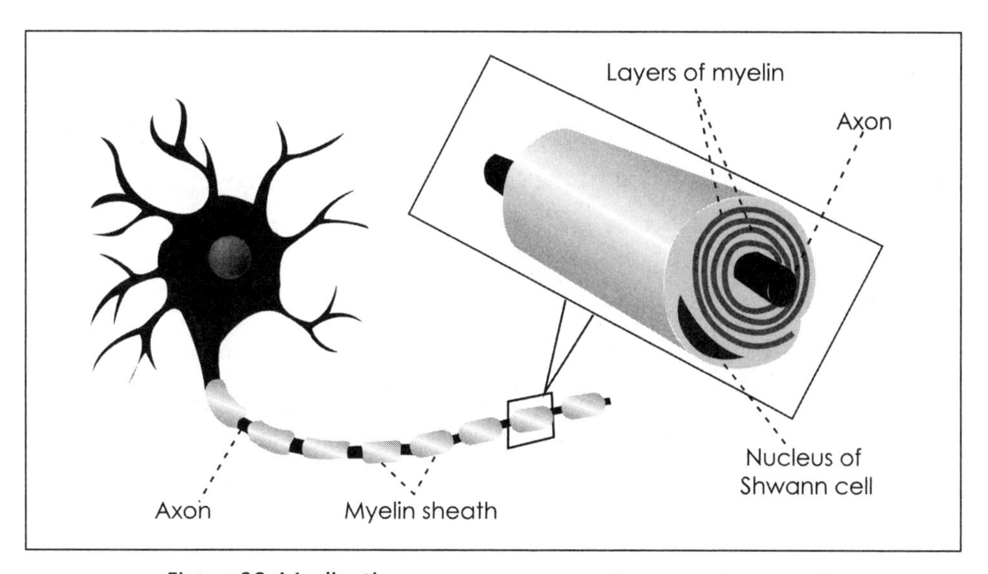

Figure 39. Myelination. SOURCE: RESTREPO FOR TOKUHAMA-ESPINOSA, 2017

add on knowledge about the way the brain's speed of recall is influenced by rehearsal, we have a model that might look something like the following:

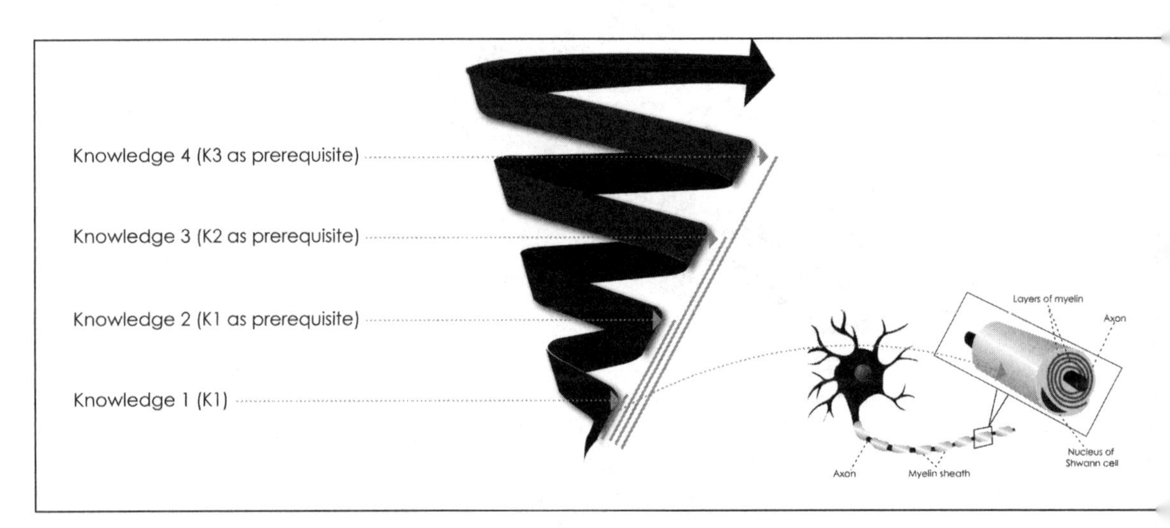

Figure 40. Rehearsal Reinforcement. SOURCE: RESTREPO FOR TOKUHAMA-ESPINOSA, 2015

Transfer of Learning

The greater number of roles a piece of knowledge plays in an individual's life, the more connections related to that information, and therefore, the faster the recall due to multiple rehearsals. This is the basis of the development of mental schemas in psychology. For example, if I know of *cats* in only one way—let's say my aunt's tabby—I have a rather limited understanding of *cat*, and therefore, a rather simple neuronal connection for semantic recall of cat=tabby. But if I am exposed to multiple cats over time—different breeds, cartoon, stuffed, animated, and toy cats, as well as the way they smelled, sounded, and felt, I would then have multiple neuronal pathways reinforcing my mental schema and broadening my understanding of *cat*. This is why something in math that is also learned as a pattern (or symbol or order or relation or category) will be easier to recall than something in math that is learned simply as a "cluster," "set," or "strand," "formula," and so on, because the schema for "patterns" would cover a broader range of concepts from a variety of fields, not math alone.

Context helps learning. Things learned in a vacuum with little context are hard to remember. Unfortunately, many scientific concepts are necessarily taught without authentic context because of their ultra-micro or ultra-macro structures. "Germs," "cells," "celestial bodies," and "black holes," are concepts that few kids learn about in context, due to their intangible nature. Authentic learning contexts, in which the student easily relates new learning to something he is already familiar with, are more memorable, and therefore learned faster with better recall than information without context (Herrington et al., 2014). The lack of authentic context might explain, in part, why so many kids appear to misunderstand basic notions in science.

Neuroscience is beginning to explain the story of observational accounts of cognition hierarchies (e.g., Westermann et al., 2007) and leads to a clear path toward a unifying theory using the pillars' constructivist design. Constructivism (Piaget, 1952, 1954), hierarchies (Bloom, 1956; Commons et al., 1998; Commons & Chen, 2014), spiral learning design (Bruner, 1960), and webs of skills (Fischer & Rose, 2001) are different ideas but coincide in the mapping of learning processes. These foundational theories confirm that learning involves both general cognitive functions (memory and attention) and domain area constructs (e.g., math, language, and so on). The pillars build off of these earlier works.

Where Do Subject Hierarchies Come From?

Over the past 100 years of interest in the idea of complex hierarchies, there has been growing precision in identifying the exact skill sets of domain areas. There are different ways of identifying content hierarchies found in education, which come from different actor perspectives. For example, if I am a curriculum designer, then I see one type of hierarchical structure. A publishing company typically has a "1st grade reader" a "2nd grade reader," a "3rd grade reader," and so on, with content that builds from one level to another. If you compare multiple publishing companies' texts, you gain a vision of one way to view conceptual hierarchies. The U.S. Common Core State Standards, the International Baccalaureate, the German Abitur, the French Baccalaureate, the British International General Certificate of Secondary Education (IGCSE), among others, also have similar hierarchy structures of conceptual knowledge. Educators and publishers have spent many years and hundreds of thousands of dollars researching the correct order of content introduction. Different curriculum structures and their corresponding textbooks tend to align pretty closely, because they have a symbiotic relationship.

Another actor view that has tried to contribute to accurate hierarchies comes from cognitive neuroscience, or the study of how the nervous system changes and learns. Educational neuroscientists and Mind, Brain, and Education (MBE) practitioners research the ways that stimuli in classrooms and other learning contexts change the brain and determine whether or not learning occurs. If curriculum studies are compared with research in educational neuroscience, neuropsychology, and cognitive psychology, a slightly different hierarchy appears, which can serve to confirm or correct the order of introduction of subjects in schools. For example, studies from the learning sciences show that children comprehend and can manage concepts of division earlier (3–5 years) than typical curriculum and textbook introduction (8–9 years) (e.g., Correa et al., 1998; Kornilaki & Nunes, 2005; Mulligan, 1992; Mulligan & Mitchelmore, 1997; Siegler et al., 2013; Squire & Bryant, 2002). In another example, conventional wisdom and many good early childhood programs avoid explicitly introducing concepts of numeracy or literacy until late childhood (six to eight years of age), despite evidence that children actually have a heightened interest in symbol systems starting around two to four years old. If parents and teachers responded to this natural interest at this earlier age, this could lead to prolonged exposure and improved motivation for future numeracy and literacy (Anthony & Walshaw, 2009; Elkind, 2007; Platt, 1977; Strickland & Morrow, 1989; Whitebread & Coltman, 2015).

Comparisons between curriculum hierarchies and educational neuroscience perspectives help, but these are just two actor views. The more comparisons that are made, the greater the level of precision in the hierarchy. An additional view comes from subject area specialists' opinions. For example, once math or language hierarchies have been mapped based on educational textbooks, existing curricula, and studies from the learning science studies, the cumulative hierarchy can be confirmed by math teachers, who can use their real-life student contact to add other perspectives into the successful learning model (see Chapter 8). The consensus from these different actors—researchers and practitioners—is probably the closest and most accurate hierarchy of learning competencies we can achieve until neuroscience confirms the neuroconstructivist design of each subject area. Combined, the general and domain area hierarchies provide a powerful structure for organizing learning, one that is arguably superior to the current subject-specific models. Redesigning curriculum to reflect this pillars hierarchy would order content introduction in a way that human brains would find even more logical and orderly than current textbooks.

Radical Constructivism

The concept of radical constructivism coined by Von Glasersfeld (1995) extends the concept of regular or "trivial" constructivism by adding the element of subjectivity. In radical constructivism, an individual's understanding and his actions are circularly conjoined; an individual's subjective interpretation of his experience also influences the learning cycle. This personalizes the idea of constructivism and shows that not only is the body of unique, individual experiences influential in learning, but the *interpretations* of those experiences change

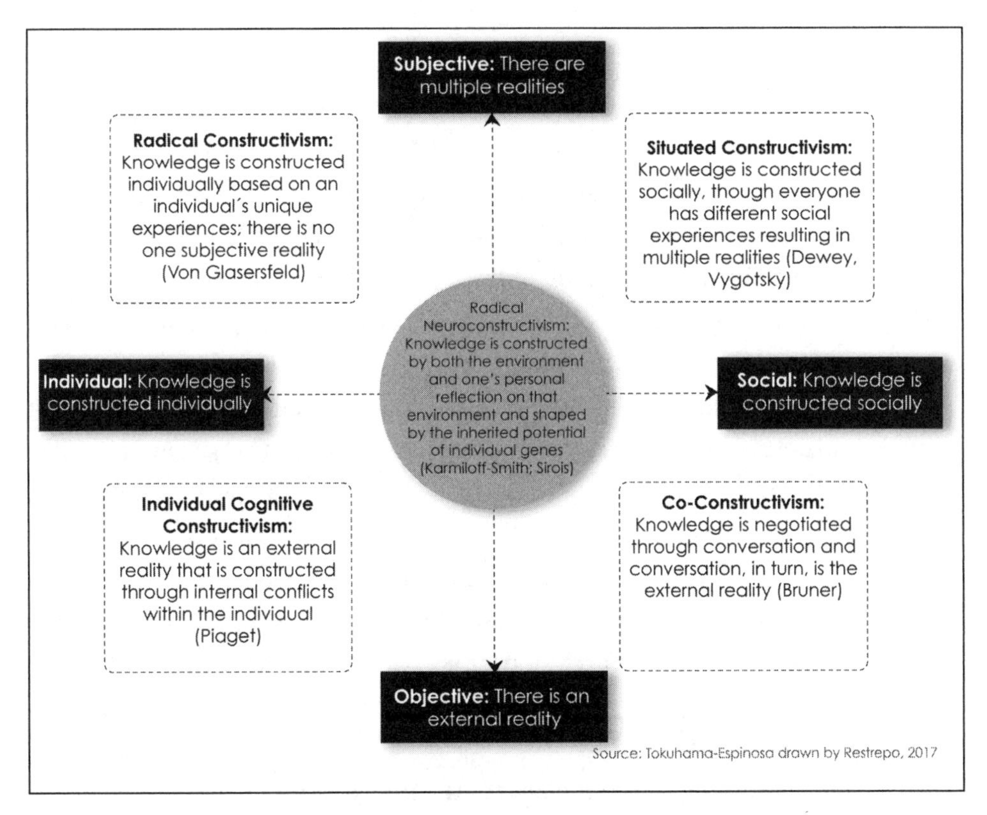

Figure 41. From Constructivism to Radical Neuroconstructivism.
SOURCE: TOKUHAMA-ESPINOSA, 2018

learning outcomes as well. This individualist radical view of constructivism gives weight to the idea that while there are similar configurations for learning mechanisms and neuronal networks in the brain for similar experiences in all humans, there is also a heavy dose of individual interpretation about that learning. This means neural pathways extending from the networks will always vary, which is why there are no two brains that are identical in their neuronal structures (Society For Neuroscience, 2018; Tokuhama-Espinosa, 2017).

Radical constructivism can serve as an explanation for Fischer's web of skills mentioned earlier, which show pulsating advances in knowledge gains rather than a direct line from A to B. These gains could be, as Fischer claims, natural highs and lows in the learning process, or alternatively (or complementarily), they could be the brain's need to consolidate information over time (synaptogenesis and pruning). More likely, however, it is a combination of these ideas: the individual nature of the learner's interpretation of his own experiences, or radical neuroconstructivism.

Neuroconstructivism

Both the hierarchical model of learning and the idea of constructivism are linked by the very important and relatively recent area of study of *neuroconstructivism* (Ansari & Karmiloff-Smith, 2002; Dekker & Karmiloff-Smith, 2011; Karmiloff-Smith, 2006, 2009, 2012a, 2012b; Karmiloff-Smith & Farran, 2011; Mareschal, 2011; Mareschal et al., 2007; Sirois, et al., 2008; Westermann et al, 2010). Neuroconstructivism explores "the construction of representations in the developing brain" based on "the experience-dependent development of neuronal structures supporting mental representations" (Westermann et al., 2007, p. 75). These are identifiable networks that are created or strengthened through new experiences. Similar to the more familiar "educational constructivism," neuroconstructivism considers how new knowledge in the brain is structured through networks in which simple circuits must be laid down before more complex ones can take hold, a process which usually parallels "typical" growth stages.

> Neuroconstructivism emphasizes the interrelation between brain development and cognitive development. We see constructivist

> development as a progressive increase in the complexity of representations, with the consequence that new competences can develop based on earlier, simpler ones. This increase in representational complexity is realized in the brain by a progressive elaboration of cortical structures. (Sirois et al., 2008, p. 322)

Some of the most respected authors in neuroconstructivism argue for learning's "middle ground," in which the basic architecture for learning is not purely inborn—as nativists would argue—nor it is completely externally and experience-driven—as cognitivists would argue—but rather somewhere in the center, in which "cascades of interactions across multiple levels of causation from genes to environments" influence learning outcomes (Karmiloff-Smith, 2009, p. 99). I see this as an argument in favor of the pillars. General neuronal networks for learning are documented in neuroscience as having typical or atypical development in all humans, but it is clear that individual experiences (including classroom instruction) also alter these global configurations, as does human variance that comes from genetic differences. ***What is clear is that the brain's efficiency groups similar types of learning along more predictable pathways than once thought.*** Whereas just a few years ago it was common to talk about the possibility of each neuron connecting to millions or billions of other neurons, it is now clear that there is a more organized and greatly reduced possibility of connections.

> Neuronal circuitry is often considered a clean slate that can be dynamically and arbitrarily molded by experience. However, when we investigated synaptic connectivity in groups of pyramidal neurons in the neocortex, we found that both connectivity and synaptic weights were surprisingly predictable. (Perin et al., 2011, p. 5419)

Perin and colleagues (2011) discovered that neuronal connections were highly influenced by their neighbors and that "the neurons cluster into small world networks" (p. 5419) depending on what is happening close by. This means that neuronal connections do not occur haphazardly, without a plan, or from any neuron to any other, but rather within generally predictable areas of the brain and with purpose. While there are no two brains that are identical, due to unique experiences, the general structure of learning domain area skills (such as language and math), as well as non-academic learning (how to walk, cook, or garden), follow clear patterns. Perin and colleagues (2011) discovered "a simple clustering rule where connectivity is directly proportional to the number of common neighbors, which accounts for these small world networks and accurately predicts the connection probability between any two neurons" (p. 5419). The small world networks described allow us to identify and observe the general structures in the brain for learning, which appear to be designed in a hierarchical fashion.

> We speculate that these elementary neuronal groups are prescribed Lego-like building blocks of perception and that acquired memory relies more on combining these elementary assemblies into higher-order constructs. (Perin et al., 2011, p. 5419)

This elegant finding explains why neuronal networks for specific skills gather along similar tracts and are not randomly located throughout the brain in an indiscriminate way. Work is still underway in the exciting area of neuro-constructivism, but an even more radical idea is underfoot.

Radical Neuroconstructivism

Most teachers understand that there are no two identical brains because the connections between synapses and the resulting neuronal pathways rely, to an extent, on individual experiences (and no two individuals have identical experiences). This "uniqueness" is counterbalanced by the fact that there is a general design to how the brain "typically" learns different skills through general network patterns as we can see in several Connectome Project studies explained earlier, such as how it manages the multiple sub-elements of reading or math (e.g. Berninger et al., 2017). That is, certain areas and networks within the brain tend to function in similar ways in all humans, though there are differences based on experience and important exceptions as well as differences due to culture, and/or atypical development.

There seems to be more consistency in networks, as seen by "hubs" or "nodes," which are the well trafficked areas of the brain, than for pathways. For example, Broca's area and Wernicke's area are key "hubs" for language in the brain. This does not mean that language *resides* in these areas, but rather that network signals crisscross these hubs with great frequency in order to *process* language. While the specific neuronal tracts might vary, the hubs seem consistent across humans. That is, networks for reading—identified by their key hubs—are the same across most humans who live in the same cultural contexts. For some people, like those with dyslexia, the normal networks might be blocked, have missing elements, or be inaccessible. This means the brain alters pathways to reach the hubs. For example, most humans use pathways outlined by Dehaene and others (2009) to learn to read, but some people who have dyslexia are forced to use distinct networks (Ozernov-Palchik & Gaab, 2016; Shaywitz et al., 1998). Others who live in cultures with different conceptual schemas from the West due to distinct cultural artifacts for written language also vary in networks for reading (e.g., Tan et al., 2000). This means that there appear to be similar networks that all humans use to do tasks like reading or math, but the pathways that create them differ by individual (see the Appendices for more details about networks and pathways).

Neuroplasticity means that we can never say "X" pathway or neuronal network is responsible for "Y" function in all humans (Pessoa, 2014); there will always be exceptions, due both to the uniqueness of individual human experiences, capacities, and cultures. This means that while there are typical pathways that can be documented in studies with large numbers of participants to indicate a "norm," it will be impossible to prescribe teaching methodologies that will *always* work on *all* subjects.

Just as radical constructivism introduced the subjectivity of experience and perception into the original constructivist design, I suggest that there is such a thing as radical neuroconstructivism, which is also due to the influence of individual experience and perception. I suggest that radical neuroconstructivism explains why there are differences in human brains, specifically the ways that pathways vary between people, most likely due to individualized experiences.

Figure 42 illustrates my initial attempt to lay out the hierarchy of math in young children 0–6 years based on the pillars. For an explanation of this neuroconstructivist design and an explanation of the proposed pillar curriculum mapping process, please see the Appendices.

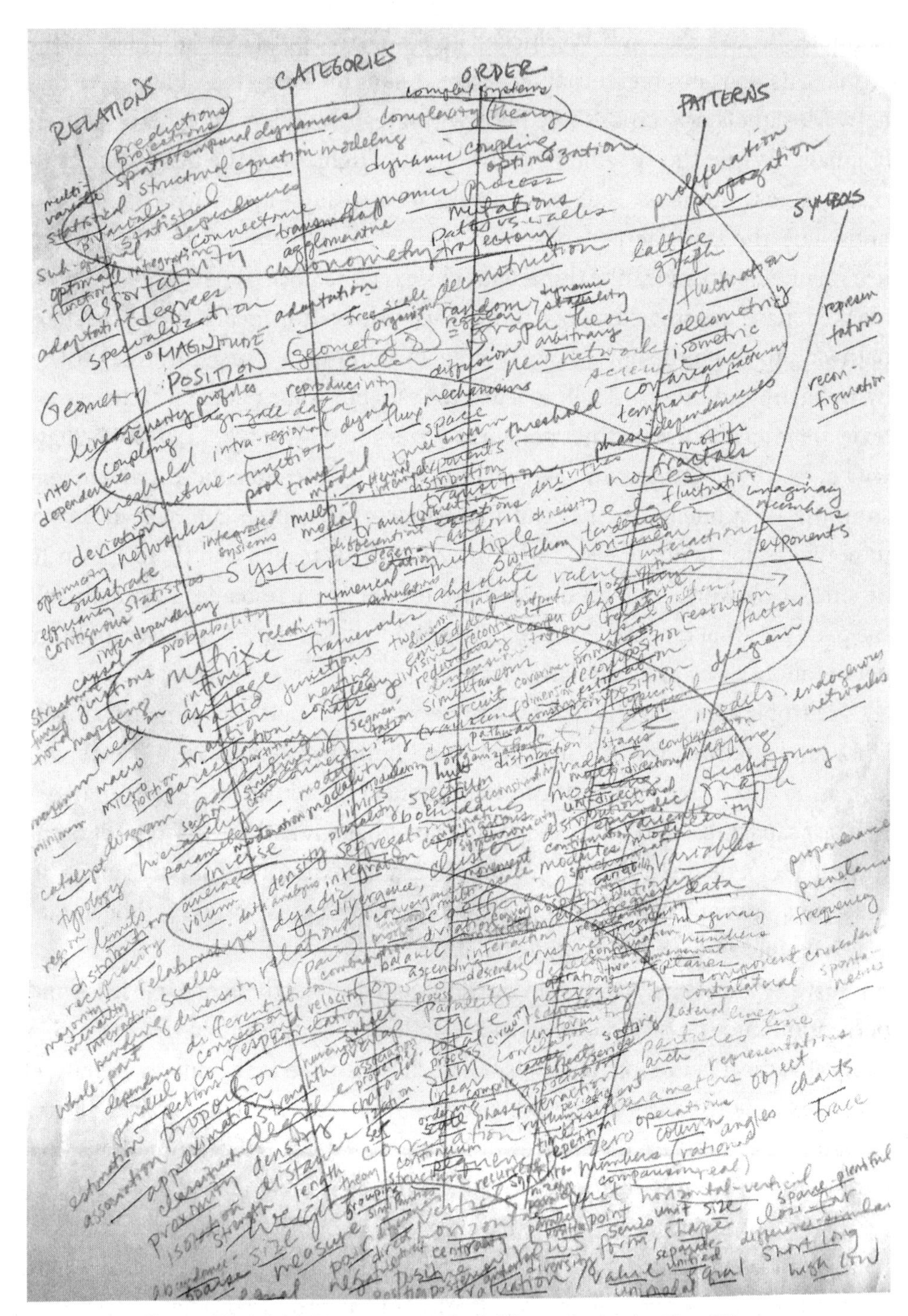

Figure 42. Initial Attempt at a Math Hierarchy in the Five Pillars.

SOURCE: TOKUHAMA-ESPINOSA, 2015

Radical Neuroconstructivism Meets Curriculum Design

Curriculum debates are usually limited to impassioned pleas for a few more hours of physical education class or more space for the arts course (e.g., Kirk, 2014). Radical neuroconstructivism may point to a new justification to trigger change in current curriculum design. The evidence for a hierarchy of complexities in the brain based on the five pillars seems strong and logical, given the limited understanding of the brain so far. Unfortunately, teachers do not yet learn about the brain in regular training, which may be an obstacle to their implementation.

Many who work in curriculum design have spent their careers perfecting the subject-centered model; it will be hard to let go of something familiar, even if it is deficient. This is akin to giving up the typewriter for the computer, the gas-guzzler for the electric car, or land lines for cell phones. Change is hard, even if we are convinced of the benefits. One way that the five pillars hierarchy can enter mainstream schooling is with the help of early adopters, or those who already know and appreciate information coming from Mind, Brain, and Education science.

Can the pillars move beyond the "interesting idea" stage and into the classroom? It is likely that this is possible only if teachers learn more about the brain, the organ of our profession, and do so at the level of other learning scientists. Such a recommendation was made by the Organisation for Economic and Cultural Development (OECD) expert panel on teachers' new pedagogical knowledge (Guerriero, 2017), and multiple other sources (e.g., Akil, et al., 2016; Edelenbosch, et al., 2015; Horvath, & Donoghue, 2016; Tokuhama-Espinosa, 2015) but it remains to be seen if teachers' education programs adapt to this recommendation in the foreseeable future.

In Chapter 7, we look at the practical application of this information and question whether educational curriculum could be modified by the pillars.

7. What Would the Five Pillars Look Like if Applied to Curriculum Design?

The Theory of the Five Pillars of the Mind is one thing; its actual application is another. While there is convincing evidence of the pillars conceptually, there is little evidence that this way of organizing learning works in practice, as the theory is too new to have been tested. How would the five pillars look if applied in schools? This chapter considers three different ways the pillars could be integrated into current school design, and the Appendices suggest how the curriculum would look in one subject area—math—if it was plotted and applied using the pillars. To help explore whether implementation would really contribute to improved academic success, the second half of this chapter responds to questions posed by experts in education, psychology and cognitive neuroscience about the pillars.

Options in Pillar Use

Below are three different scenarios that allow for different degrees of implementation. Option A is the least disruptive and uses the pillars as **methodology**. Option B uses the pillars hierarchy to reach **mastery**. And Option C uses the pillars in place of traditional **curriculum**. Each scenario would mean different degrees of change, as seen in Table 19.

Table 19. Options in Pillar Application

THREE WAYS THE PILLARS CAN BE APPLIED IN THE CLASSROOM			
	Option A: Subject-Focused Curriculum	**Option B: Mastery-Focused Curriculum**	**Option C: Pillars-Focused Curriculum**
	Low level change: Pillars as methodology	**Medium level change: Pillars as mastery**	**High level change: Pillars as curriculum**
Teacher Training	Coach teachers to use pillars thinking as a methodology in their subject area	Coach teachers to develop mastery designs for their course(s) using the pillars	Coach teachers on how to replace old curriculum with the pillars
Textbooks	No change	Pillars overlay	New texts
Additional resources	No change	Pillars overlay	New curriculum
Arrangement by age or level	Age	Level	Level
Focus on passing grades or mastery learning	Passing grades	Mastery	Mastery
Improved diagnosis of learning problems		X	X
Enhanced transdisciplinarity	X	X	X

SOURCE: TOKUHAMA-ESPINOSA, 2017

Option A: Pillars as Methodology

In the first option, the pillars are simply a change in methodology and mindset; there is little boat rocking as teachers just add mention of the pillars as they teach. For example, the algebra teacher goes about his lesson in the same way he always has, but reminds his students of the symbols, patterns, order, categories, and relationships in the lessons (the history teacher would do the same, as would a 2nd grade teacher). This application of the pillars would merely require keener observation and a flexible mind as the teacher makes explicit and implicit references to the **symbols** (forms, shapes, representations); **patterns** (configurations, series, rules, regularity); **order** (sequences, purpose, formulas, structure, organization, cycles, systems thinking); **categories** (qualities, equivalencies, classifications); and **relationships** (proportions, correspondence, magnitude, measure, approximation, estimation, quantity, context) of the subject being taught.

Once there is a reasonable level of acceptance of the pillars as methodology, teachers could be encouraged to move beyond their grade levels to think about the continuum of content knowledge in their subject areas—eventually, becoming familiar with all grades in all pillars so that they appreciate the complete hierarchical scale within a discipline. For example, a middle school art teacher might begin looking at the pillars uniquely from a 7th grade perspective, then branch out to 6th and 8th grade, and slowly add other grade levels to her repertoire of knowledge. (Once all levels of all pillars across subject areas are mapped, it may be time to consider option B.)

In the following sections, we show how the minimal use of the pillars in option A might look in the subject areas most commonly taught around the world (see Table 1). To utilize the theory of the five pillars as methodology, teachers must themselves become more aware of the pillars and their different iterations, and then habituate the practice of incorporating them into instruction. Many great teachers will recognize how they already identify the pillars in their implicit teaching. They are now encouraged to imagine how they might do so more explicitly in the future. While a full neuroconstructivist hierarchy in all five pillars would require much more extensive descriptions, below is a small sampling of the ways subject area teachers might begin to think of the pillars.

Languages and Literature

In language, literature and foreign languages, the most intuitive understanding of the pillars comes from the knowledge that what a person can *think* can become what a person can *write* (**relationships**). This is developed through the process of literacy, which involves sound-to-symbol equivalencies (**relationships**) between letters (**symbols**) and phonemes. Other important **symbols**, such as question marks, exclamation marks, periods, and commas, can change the meaning of a text and must be explicitly taught to reach language proficiency. (The implications of punctuation errors are sometimes enshrined in jokes, as on a T-shirt that boasts "commas save lives" followed by the example: "Let's eat, Grandma" is not the same as "Let's eat Grandma".) Language teachers at all levels can call attention to the changes of meaning caused by word **order** (for example, *I have to read this book* means something very different than *I have this book to read*). At a more advanced level of literacy, students begin to develop **symbolic** or metaphorical understanding, such as the

relationship between mythical gods and natural phenomena, or how Shakespeare's Juliet "is the sun." Teachers can help students categorize word types to remember correct writing rules (**order**) about nouns, verbs, and adjectives (**categories**), and eventually comprehend distinct genres (**categories**) of literature. When analyzing literature, teachers can ask about the specific sequence of events (**order**) in a novel and delve further into the **symbolic** references in the text.

Language mediates all learning and, therefore, all teachers can be considered language teachers. Debate is a language-driven activity that any subject area teacher can use to reflect on the structure of arguments (**order**), the cyclical nature of deliberation (**order**), norms of courteous behavior and the rules for interaction (**patterns**) during class. Related, but different, are foreign language classes in which a teacher's recognition and reinforcement of the pillars can be relied upon to facilitate learning. For instance, the Spanish language teacher can call out grammatical **patterns** and highlight how they are the same or different (**relationships**) in English.

Mathematics

The conceptualization of mathematical magnitude is innate; even young, preverbal children understand quantity. Children soon learn to incorporate **symbol**-to-magnitude **relationships** as they master basic counting (1, 2, 3…), then see the same relationship represented on a number line. Students' understanding of comparative data can easily be reinforced in classroom exchanges. For example, teachers can call attention to the ratios between groups of individuals in a classroom, such as the number of dark-haired students to blondes, or the total number of students to teachers (**relationships**). Teachers can constantly remind students of the vital role the order of operations plays in successfully completing a math problem by showing students how **patterns** of errors occur when **order** is changed: for example, when a learner violates the PEMDAS rule and performs subtraction as a first rather than last step in a math problem (see Table 9). A 3rd grade teacher could help students **categorize** the kinds of typical errors made when learning how to multiply, which will foster learner autonomy and hone students' metacognitive skills (see Table 13). A high school math teacher could remind students of the different mathematical **symbols** that evolve with math complexity; the **patterns** in statistical analysis found in formulas and outcomes; and the **relationships** between equivalencies or the

categories of mathematical thinking, such as arithmetic, algebra, analysis, geometry, probability, and so on.

Social Studies/History/Civics

Even before children go to school, they begin to learn about the **patterns** of civil behavior, the roles different professionals play in the community (**categories** and **relationships**), and the **order** of events (*Jason waits for the stoplight to turn green before he crosses the street*). The **patterns** in cultures, such as the ways foods in one culture are at once the same and different from students' home eating habits, can be taught explicitly starting early in life. In middle school, teachers could call attention to the **symbols** used to distinguish different human **relationships**: the salutations people use to greet one another, the design of clothing that different sub-cultures dress in (**categories**), or the ways different societies treat their aging populations (**patterns**). High school social studies teachers can ask essential questions, such as *Why do people go to war?* to identify **patterns** of behavior; **categories** of catalysts (for beliefs, for territory, for natural resources, to defend their allies, and so on); the role of **relationships** (*what is an* enemy, *what is an* ally?); **order** of decision-making (*if the enemy does X, I will react with Y*); and what are considered **symbols** of good or bad faith in the local or international arena.

Art, Music, Design

An intuitive use of the pillars in the arts is to identify types or genres (**categories**) of creative expression, such as the similarities and differences between jazz and classical music or realistic vs. modernist painters (**relationships**). Later, teachers can explicitly call out **patterns** in the similarities and differences between these genres, linking them to the time in history and place on the map where they flourished (**patterns, categories,** and **relationships**). The music teacher can query how changing the **order** of notes would change the structure and mood of a song or talk about the way musical instruments are grouped into string, percussion, brass, keyboard, or woodwind **categories**. An art teacher can use proportions to explain core design concepts such as the Golden Ratio, show how parts are related to the whole, and how they can be used to send messages as well as to shape aesthetic appreciation (**relationships**). A less intuitive application of the pillars is through **symbolic** understanding. How did the artist use lighting to convey a specific meaning, or an actor use a certain intonation to convey a specific emotion? The arts are ripe with examples from the five pillars, and many teachers already intuitively apply them in their teaching. For the pillars to be used as a methodology, they would need only to be more explicitly and systematically applied.

Science

Science, like art, easily lends itself to the pillars methodology. Science is full of examples of cyclical **order**, ranging from global phenomena that are easily comprehended by small children (such as the 24 hours in a day), to more complex cyclical structures in physics (such as the hertz unit used to measure frequency). Everything in the physical world can be measured relative to a scale: length to a measuring tape, weight to a balance, and so on (**relationships**). A middle school science teacher could ask students to reflect on **patterns** of crop growth, weather, and agricultural yield to illustrate favorable conditions (**relationships**) for food production. Seismologists, volcanologists, and climatologists can use the pillars to explain the relative magnitudes of different natural phenomena such as earthquakes, volcanos, and hurricanes (**relationships**). Many scientific concepts rely heavily on both math and language. For example, the physics teacher could call attention to the **symbols** in the formulas being used to resolve a problem and explain their math or language roots to aid recall. She could also explain different forms of graphic representations of the formula outcomes (**symbols**). The chemistry teacher can classify the elements in the periodic table (**categories**), while biology teachers can help students understand **categories** such as genetic variations or species types (mammals, vertebrates, amphibians, and so on), and **patterns** of human growth and development.

Physical Education/Health

Health and wellness studies also lend themselves to pillars thinking and provide multiple intuitive examples. A natural connection is how the body impacts the mind and vice versa. Teachers can call out the **relationship** of smoking (or drugs or alcohol) to well-being, for example. Caregivers can remind students that their study and sleep, nutrition and exercise **patterns** can influence learning outcomes as well as quality of life. Physical education teachers can explain signs of good health (**symbols**), such as increased physical strength correlated with exercise, or lack of stamina due to poor nutrition (**relationships**). Many aspects of well-functioning bodily systems are invisible to the naked eye, so teachers might instead begin with analogous examples. To explain digestion, for example, a 1st grade teacher could initially ask how the students' eating, digesting, and bathroom visiting **patterns** are similar to and different from those of their pets. The health of plants can also parallel **relationships** affecting human health, such as the need for nutrients (food), good soil (learning environments), and sunshine (stimulation). In sports, **order** can be highlighted through coordination of players on teams, the rules of games, and the way strategies are developed. The physical education teacher can talk about **categories** of sports (individual vs. team), game types (with or without balls; water vs. mountain, etc.), or informal exercise (gardening, dog walking, and so on) in order to broaden students' appreciation for physical activity.

Social-Emotional Learning and Other Important 21st Century Skills

Just as academic domain areas can be taught using the five pillars, so can social and emotional learning skills (SEL). The pillars are visible in emotional intelligence processes, for example. Emotional intelligence has four steps in its simplest form (Mayer & Salovey, 1997; Mayer et al., 2003): (a) perceiving emotion (understanding the **relationship** between sensation and emotion), (b) using emotion to facilitate thought (**order** of stimuli to response), (c) understanding emotion (including the **categories** we use to classify emotions and feelings), and (d) managing emotion (**patterns** of social interaction).

In another example, counselors, teachers and parents can help students learn about risk and protective factors (**categories**) to health and well-being and how they have the same roots. Your family (or genes, friends, school environment, country, laws) can all either be a risk or a protective factor to general wellbeing, depending on your personal situation. Other skills, such as being able to collaborate, can also be taught using the pillars. What does our society accept as signs (**symbols**) of cooperative behavior? What are indicators (**patterns**) of solidarity? How can we identify steps (**order**) in good collaborative learning? Anything that is learned in school or outside of it can be learned using the pillars as methodology.

In summary, option A is the best choice if the goal is to implement change through the pillars with the least resistance, because it involves only a supplemental methodology. This option would require training teachers to use the pillars as an additional dimension of instruction, first by recognizing the familiar symbols, patterns, order, categories, and relationships that already exist in the subjects they teach, and then by sharing them with students. Most teachers can do this with about a day's worth of reflection. In this application of the five pillars, teachers need only think of examples related to the subjects they teach, and refer to them during instruction explicitly as well as implicitly.

Option B: Pillars as Mastery

In Option B, teachers would apply the pillars hierarchy curriculum *in parallel* with regular subject-area curriculum; that is, the pillars would be neuroconstructivistly plotted and overlaid onto the regular curriculum. This can be seen as "deconstructing" or "backwards engineering" learning. The main goal in option B is **mastery learning**, rather than grade-level achievement for a specific subject area (e.g.,focusing on students passing 9th grade English by the time they are 14 to 15 years old). As a neuroconstructivist design, option B suggests that lower level competencies (knowledge, skills and attitudes) should be mastered before advancing to higher order concepts.

To plot mastery learning goals, each subject would be disaggregated by the hierarchy and pillar (see Appendices A, B and C for an example in mathematics). The mapping of the pillars involves breaking down each subject area from beginner to advanced levels, which I propose to be divided by levels 0 to 14 rather than our current grade levels. The 0–14 level structure presumes starting education, though not necessarily schooling, from birth, with formal education culminating more or less around 18 to 20 years of age, unless students choose to attend university, in which case there would be additional levels. Option B creates more flexible student groupings based on mastery within broader age ranges, potentially benefiting many students. To advance a level in math—such as progressing from addition to subtraction—the student would have to master all pillar elements in a hierarchical trajectory order. For example, the student should master all the pillar elements of addition before moving on to subtraction.

While it is intuitive to think students should master basic concepts before moving on to higher order ones, it can be more difficult to operationalize the concept of mastery learning in the subjects we teach. One of the reasons plotting for mastery is hard is because mastery trajectories are not always exactly the same as "standards" or "learning outcomes" or "achievement criteria" used in textbooks or articulated in state standards; these benchmarks are familiar but often more tradition-bound than scientific. Plotting the hierarchy of learning trajectories based on neuroconstructivist criteria would give a far more precise method of designing mastery criteria that would be transparent to both teachers and learners.

The overlay of the pillars onto current curriculum means more precision in instruction and a confirmed hierarchy of learning trajectories of basic to complex notions: learn the **patterns** of basic tunes in music before trying to improvise; learn the **order** of basic composition before advanced art; learn the fundamentals of physics before considering rocket science (**relationships** and **categories**); comprehend nuclear family **relationships** before expanding to society, country, and international relations.

Once children understand how to determine the ways two things can be different and the same, they can then move up to understanding how the same object can have multiple characteristics and be categorized into many different subsets. Obvious **categories** should be taught before subtle categories. For example, a literature teacher can assist students in understanding about "good guys" and "bad guys" before categorizing nebulous characters who do good but who are bad, or who are forced to do bad things, even if they are good. In biology this means students learn the species type of their household pet before tackling an understanding of genera, families, classes, divisions, and kingdoms (**categories**). They would learn to wash their hands (**order** and **relationships**) to create context for subsequently learning about germs. From germs, they can advance to viruses, healing processes, and eventually the study of unknowns, like cancers (**categories**). This vision of curriculum confirms what we know intuitively: students should study basic human body development (**symbols, patterns, order, relationships,** and **categories**) before artificial insemination, organ replacement, or cloning.

In summary, option B is preferable if the goal is mastery learning of subject area content. Option B would overlay the pillars mapping—a disaggregated hierarchy of all objectives we have—onto traditional subject-area curriculum so that content is organized by levels of knowledge. The pillars hierarchy of complexities is key to making any gaps in learning a child might have visible because each larger learning goal is broken down into its smaller parts and into all of its prerequisite competencies. This creates a transparent road to mastery.

Mastery Through Backward Design and Neuroconstructivism

Many teachers struggle to integrate mastery learning into their schools because as a society we have spent decades perfecting a standards-based model in which we focus on topical competencies rather than on **mastery objectives** that embrace the combination of **knowledge** (dates, facts, formulas, concepts, theories, etc.), **skills** (how and when to apply the knowledge), and **attitudes** (the value-based competencies, including soft skills like collaboration, solidarity, empathy, and compassion). To construct learning in a mastery design, the pillars model suggests combining Backward Design thinking (decide on the objective, determine the evaluation criteria, and then decide activities), with evidence from a neuroconstructivist design for subject specific competencies.

In practice, this means that the first step is that teachers, curriculum designers, and policy makers need to re-examine what it really means to *master learning* at each level of our current education system. If the overall objective of education has grown beyond pure content area knowledge in a limited number of subject areas (Table 1), and if we now also value and expect schools to teach things like social-emotional learning (Figure 46), then it becomes imperative that the tools we have to measure and teach must also grow and evolve. High-stakes multiple choice tests and grade level readers are poor tools to evaluate and teach the complex learning goals of the 21st century.

To evolve towards pillars thinking and mastery, a 4th grade teacher would have to ask herself: "*What are all of the types of knowledge* (content from language, math, science, social-emotional learning, art, physical education, and so on), *skills* (knowing how and when to apply the knowledge), *and attitudes* (the value-based competencies, including soft skills like collaboration, solidarity, empathy and compassion) *a child should have to justify promotion to the 5th grade*?" Moving to the pillars from the current system would require teachers and curriculum specialists to (a) identify each objective of the 4th grade (whether it be knowledge, skills, or attitudes), (b) disaggregate all aspects of each objective into its smallest sub-sets, (c) identify the prerequisite knowledge needed to be able to achieve each objective, and (d) use the neuroconstructivist trajectory of learning available to confirm the learning order hierarchy.

For example, if we agree that one of the learning objectives of 1st grade is *addition*, then addition is part of 1st grade mastery (point "(a)" above). After identifying this objective, we would then have to disaggregate all aspects of *addition* into its smallest parts, (point "(b)" above). Specifically related to the pillars themselves, to add we can see from the pillars that a child needs to understand the **symbols** (e.g., *Arabic numerals*); **patterns** (*that combining two numbers results in a bigger number*); **order** (*order of operations*); **categories** (*that the two or more items being combined are called "addends" and their result is called the "sum"*); and **relationships** (*that the sum is equal to the joining of the addends or parts*) of addition. We know that each of these smaller pieces of addition also has multiple prerequisite competencies underlying their structures (point "(c)" above) that need to be firmly in place before a child can add. For example, to understand the **symbols** of addition (e.g., *Arabic numerals*), a child needs the prerequisite knowledge of symbol-to-magnitude understanding. But to have symbol-to-magnitude understanding, rehearsal of magnitude concepts, such as "more" and "less, "different" "similar" "near" and "far" is necessary to be able to relate specific symbols to an equivalent magnitude (*** equals 3, for example). Finally, a review of the neuroconstructivist understanding of addition would confirm the order of introduction in the pillars curriculum (point "(d)" above). See Appendices A, B and C for more on this topic.

In Backwards Design terms, this means starting with the end in mind (*what does it mean to master addition?*), examine evaluation criteria and the indicators that would help us measure whether or not we are reaching the mastery goal (*has the child mastered all of the smaller sub-elements of addition? If not, which prerequisite competencies is he missing?*), then we can decide on the best resources, activities, methodologies and strategies that scaffold the necessary experiences to reach the objective. Embracing this more detailed understanding of addition (and all the other objectives we hope to achieve in the 1st grade) is an exciting change in education and creates an evidence-based path towards mastery learning.

Option C: Pillars as Curriculum

If radical change is desirable and feasible, option C is the best choice. Option C uses the pillars *in place* of the current curriculum structure; that is, curriculum is mapped by pillar, rather than subject area. In this design, all domain areas

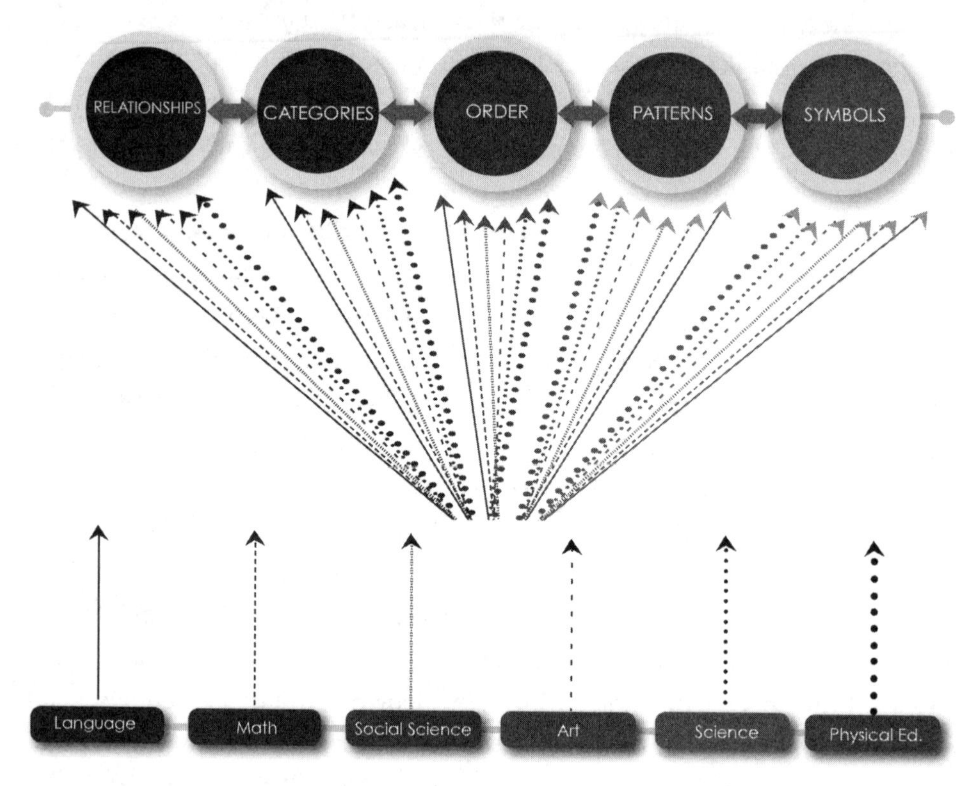

Figure 43. Overlap Mapping of Pillars and Subject Areas. SOURCE: TOKUHAMA-ESPINOSA, 2017

of traditional subjects (math, language, science, art, computer science, physical education, history, social studies, and so on) would be neuroconstructivistly plotted individually in a hierarchical form by pillar. Once all domain areas have been plotted, they would be overlaid, one upon the other. Once all subjects regularly taught in school have been plotted in a pillars-hierarchical-constructivist model, a final curriculum design emerges that not only provides an orderly and efficient structure for school study, but , creates more authentic learning for students in a transdisciplinary design, as shown in Figure 43.

In this completely revamped curricular model, students would have five classes a day, with each class devoted to one pillar across all areas of learning. For example, the class on symbols would explain symbols in every subject area (math symbols, language symbols, art symbols, human relations symbols, historical symbols, graphic symbols, mechanical symbols, programming symbols, and so on), as well as symbols in the surrounding environment and informal learning contexts. Once the global introduction of each pillar has been made at each level of learning (0–14), specialized symbols by domain would be taught. Classes would be structured to help students see how things are alike before exploring how they are different, which takes advantage of the brain's desire to use prior knowledge, identify the known, and then give saliency to the unknown.

Initially, all students would grow in their knowledge of **symbols** as they learn the similarity between musical, chemical, historical, mathematical, literary, biological, and computational symbols, among others, and highlight how they share characteristics. After identifying how symbols are alike, then each level would explore specific symbols for different subject areas (i.e., the unique symbols in chemistry; the unique symbols in art, and so on). Likewise, the class on **patterns** would discuss patterns in all subject areas, as well as those found in the real world, such as weather patterns, sleep patterns, geography patterns, and so on. After the commonality of patterns is clear, then students would delve deeper into the specifi c patterns of different subject areas. The class on **order** would consider expressions of order in academic subjects as well as the real world. Once the basic conceptual understanding of order is clear, then students would learn about the divergent order systems in different subject areas. The class on **categories** would initially define and use categories on a generic level. Once the pillar of categories was understood, then specific domain area categories would be introduced. The class on **relationships** would consider all relationships, from familial contexts to the relationship between ideas. Once the initial introduction, definition, and use of each of the relationships is clear, then students would dive deeper into the specialized relationships of subject area in different domains. Option C means that transdisciplinary thinking is prized, and that all subject areas are used to reinforce each other.

In summary, Option C would cause the greatest disruption of all and would constitute the most radical use of the pillars. This option is the hardest to imagine, as the shift in all known areas of educational planning would be drastic, ranging from adaptations of textbooks and timetabling to teacher training. The imagined benefits are vast: natural transdisciplinary instruction; reduced content load; flexible learning for all students working toward their strengths; better diagnosis of learning problems; higher probability of differentiation; elimination of age as a criterion for grade work; and greatly reduced scheduling problems—no more infighting about which subject teacher gets the early morning slot! But the required changes to reap those benefits would also be far-reaching; option C would require teachers and schools to abandon the past 200 years of structure and adopt a completely new mind frame about what defines "success" in school settings. This makes its immediate use unlikely. Change is hard, and radical change even harder. The debate should begin, however, to rethink whether the curriculum we currently have serves our students in the best way possible.

The pillars can be applied in different degrees by different teachers and institutions, ranging from their use as a methodology (Option A), to a mechanism for mastery (Option B), to a completely reconceptualized curriculum (Option C). All of the options share two main benefits: First, they cater to a more natural way of learning about the world and second, they have the added benefit of improving the diagnosis of where a student might be finding difficulties.

We now turn to questions posed by experts.

Can the Pillars Improve Academic Success? Questions from the Experts

Change for change sake is not a good enough reason to adopt the pillars. To adopt the pillars, teachers must be convinced they would yield better student learning. To help teachers make this decision, a concept paper was sent to experts in education, psychology and neuroscience, and some of the most provocative questions are included here to advance the debate. The first came from Howard Gardner.

"How do the pillars account for valuing differences between the nature of the materials (subjects)?"

"I have to say that I am suspicious of taxonomies that ignore the nature of the materials. For example, patterns are important in poetry and in chemistry, but they are entirely different entities, and to speak of "patterns" in both cases is to erase those differences. How do the pillars account for valuing these differences between the nature of the materials?" (H. Gardner conversation, May 5, 2015).

The five pillars add a new dimension to subject-area knowledge rather

than erasing important differences between them. Poetry will still be explored as poetry, but in addition, it will be explored through its symbols, patterns, order, relationships, and categories. Chemistry will still be chemistry, but in addition, it will be explored through its symbols, patterns, order, relationships, and categories. This means that we can value the nature of each subject area on its own, but also notice that the "science in the poetry and the poetry in the science," to the extent that poetry itself will be richer and chemistry itself will be more complete if they share dimensions of analysis through the pillars. The beauty of the pillars is that they don't presume to replace our appreciation of different academic fields, but rather celebrate them in a new way. The addition of the pillars reminds learners to think more transdisciplinarily about the world and all of the different subjects possible.

"How do the pillars account for the 'competition' that similar stimuli might have in the brain?"

The pillars suggest that learning different subject area symbols at the same time should create a naturally complementary understanding of symbols themselves. That is, learning about letters (language) should complement learning numbers (mathematics) when their similarities can be called out to students. However, there is also an argument that symbols can compete for the brain's energy and therefore, understanding.

An analogous example is related to learning two different foreign languages at the same time. Let's say I speak English and I want to learn French and Chinese and begin to take classes in these languages at the same time. It is likely that the similar symbols used in French and English could, indeed, cause problems and compete for attention in my brain, due to their similarity, whereas the very different Chinese characters would not. Some kinds of symbols (patterns, order, categories, or relationships) are closer than others, and proximity can cause confusion. To resolve this in multilingual classrooms, strategies that contextualize authentic use of the language in real settings are often helpful and recommended. A similar strategy could be used for the pillars. This means going beyond just knowing how math and language symbols are alike and how they are different but to also explain and explore the context for their authentic use. That is, teachers should regularly call out the way the pillars exist in real life contexts as well as in school subjects, especially when a pillar seems too similar to one another.

"Does loss in one domain reflect loss in another?"

Dee Rutgers, a postdoctoral student in bilingualism at the University of Cambridge, asked, "Do you feel you can substantiate the claim that a lack of understanding of symbols in maths (sic) can have implications for symbols in language for example?" Having a weakness in one of the pillars for one subject area does not necessarily mean having the same deficit across all disciplines. However, there is strong evidence that suggests this is true in some cases related to symbols. For example, the comorbidity of dyslexia and dyscalculia is very high, primarily because the interpretation of symbols in general is disrupted, leading to both language and math problems. Wilson and colleagues (2015) found "the developmental learning disabilities dyscalculia and dyslexia have a combined prevalence of 10% or more, and a co-occurrence (comorbidity) rate of around 40%" (p. 118) suggesting that 4 out of 10 sufferers of dyslexia will likely also have dyscalculia and vice-versa. Ulfarsson and colleagues (2017) also identified that a specific gene plays a role in both dyslexia and dyscalculia, suggesting that comorbidity might be related to genetic structure based on its deletion, (which is associated with a smaller left fusiform gyrus). The thinking behind this idea is that regular numerical and lexical symbol processing is affected by this change in networks in the brain. Retraining the brain to bypass this network, or to strengthen contralateral areas of the brain to do this job, might improve people's abilities to cope with dyslexia and dyscalculia.

There are multiple networks responsible for math (and language and likely all other subject areas, see Appendix C). As mentioned in the previous chapter, these networks are defined by key hubs or core areas in the brain through which signals pass with frequency. As each cognitive skill has multiple networks and multiple hubs some may be shared. Coping mechanisms to deal with dyslexia have, in some cases, overlapped with dealing with dyscalculia, namely in increased repetition and speed of symbol to sound (Widmann et al., 2012) or symbol to magnitude references (Price & Ansari, 2013). Other treatments have to do with interventions in attention systems (e.g., Stein, 2014; Wang et al., 2012), central visual perception (e.g., Kucian, 2017), or auditory processing (e.g., Holland, 2014), meaning that dyslexia and dyscalculia are multifaceted disorders that can require a combination of different interventions. Depending on the deficit area, other subject areas can be affected. This shows that while deficits in one area might indicate deficits in another, they do not always do so.

To respond more explicitly to the question then, can lack of math symbol understanding have implications for language symbols? Yes and no. In some cases, lack of symbols understanding in math can parallel a lack of language symbol comprehension and be treated with similar interventions, but this is not always the case. Can improvement in math symbol understanding improve language symbol understanding? Again, while not always the case, there is evidence for spinoff effects of learning math symbols for language understanding and vice-versa, depending on the intervention.

It is not known how and to what extent current teaching methods reinforce fundamental neuronal circuits necessary for development. However, there is evidence that the lack of proper stimulation leads to learning gaps or deficits in the constructivist development of skill sets that impact global achievement. For example, children who do not receive adequate language stimulation at home begin schooling with an estimated "30 million word gap" that translates into lower school achievement throughout their lifespan (Hart & Risley, 2003). Early childhood education training can contribute to reducing the achievement gap based on insufficient stimulation in the early years because attention to one area of deficit can often lead to improvement in various cognitive areas. I suggest that if specific methodologies, activities, and home/classroom strategies were better aligned to strengthen key neuronal circuits for strong neuroconstructivist development in the frequent gaps found in early childhood education that tend to widen and spread throughout the educational experience can be reduced. Identifying the gaps in an individual's pillars' hierarchy in any domain area of knowledge will often, but not always, improve pillar knowledge in other domains.

Accurate diagnosis is half the solution to learning problems. This includes a better understanding of precisely which network is not being rehearsed enough. For example, if the child is struggling with learning how to read, pillar use makes it much easier to see if his problem rests in **symbols** (i.e., sound to phonemes recognition); the **pattern** of syntactic structure; the **order** of letters to make words or words to make sentences; **categories** of word types (nouns, verbs, adjectives); or the **relationship** between subject-noun agreement, or any number of other uses. It is unfortunate that in current practice, when a child begins to fail in math we often globally recommend more rehearsal (i.e., additional worksheets) but such rehearsal may not be in the area of need. This lack of diagnostic accuracy means that we often send the wrong type of remediating work, which is a waste of time and can potentially exacerbate the problem as the child's frustration grows. Teachers do not yet have access to easy diagnostic tools that can help accurately identify problem areas with such precision. Hopefully the new five pillars constructivist hierarchy will change how classroom teachers can react and treat gaps in knowledge. (More about using the pillars hierarchy for evaluation at the end of this chapter.)

"How do the sensitive periods influence the pillars?"

Learning academic topics has no critical periods as agreed upon by an international panel of experts in Mind, Brain, and Education (Tokuhama-Espinosa, 2008a), but there are sensitive periods, and they can be leveraged to make learning more efficient. The hierarchy of learning suggested by mastery level teaching stipulates that lower order concepts are taught before higher order ones. As students aren't bound by age levels in the pillars, they advance at the pace that correlates best with their cognitive stage and prior experiences, meaning the pillars are likely to be more coherent with sensitive periods than the current curriculum.

"How do the pillars account for process and content?"

One of cognitive psychology's finest minds, Michael Posner, asked, "In cognitive psychology, there is a longstanding distinction between process and content. How do the pillars account for process and content?" As the pillars are currently explained, they might appear more content-based and less processes-based, but the vision can and should be understood as being both content and process. The pillars should be seen as "symbols" (content) *and* symbolizing (process); "order" (content) *and* "ordering" (process); "pattern" *and* "patterning" (process); "categories" *and* "categorization" (process);

"relationships" *and* "to relate" (process). Traditionally, psychology explains mental processes (how the brain creates relationships, categorizes, orders, finds patterns, and symbolizes the world), and the pillars should also explain the development of thinking processes, not just content. The evidence from neuroscience suggests that processes, not just content, are as supported as content within the pillar structure. The key difference between content and processes as they relate to the five pillars is that the processes are begun at the earliest moments of education and *never finish* formation, as they can always be continually perfected, whereas content knowledge can often be mastered. An analogy could be that of foreign language learning, where one might master a certain level of language content (vocabulary, sentence structures, grammatical rules, and so on), but never ever really perfects the language. Both content and process are a part of the pillar design.

"How do the pillars relate to social and emotional capacity including self-regulation, persistence, motivation, and mindset?"

Another reviewer and Montessori teacher, Julia Volkman, asked how the evidence for the pillars found in academia carried over into learning in the socioemotional realm. I suggest that all learning, including socioemotional competencies, can be achieved through the pillars. Self-regulation, persistence, motivation, flexible mindsets (grit, resilience, and so on), all have symbols (e.g., thumbs-up, heroes); patterns (e.g., *it doesn't matter how many times you fall, so long as you stand back up*); order (e.g., trial and error; hardship and triumph); categories (e.g., good vs. bad experiences, intrinsic vs. extrinsic motivation); and relationships (e.g., human exchanges, habituated attitudinal reactions). Socioemotional learning and cultural contexts of learning spaces can and should be explained through the pillars, which are not limited to academic content, but rather apply to anything humans can learn. These areas have not yet been developed to the same extent as academic areas, but this an important item on the to-do list.

"How does the need for movement come into play in the pillars?"

All living creatures move, and all learn. Movement is important for learning and central to several learning theories, especially in early childhood. The pillars can be used to learn physical movements. For example, pathways for gross motor skills can be measured through the thickening of white matter tracts in general neuronal networks (e.g., Sampaio-Baptista et al., 2013). As the pillars focus primarily on content and not instructional practices, movement as content falls into the pillar structure, but movement as method has not yet been discussed.

"How are the pillars complementary to Backward Design?"

The use of Backward Design (first identify objectives, then evaluation criteria, and lastly choose activities [Wiggins & McTighe, 2005]) also improves the likelihood of differentiation at the moment the teacher chooses activities (Tomlinson & McTighe, 2006).

Depending on a student's prior knowledge, interests, and needs, the teacher can conduct any number of activities that lead to the achievement of the objective. This pillar model avoids the prescription of activities, and rather encourages teachers' creativity. This means the pillars offer a logical format and structure backed by science, while encouraging teachers to use their own art in their craft of teaching.

The pillars force teachers to think about the ***"optimal" activities that might stimulate all the pillars and their corresponding networks*** introduced at appropriate levels ***in a hierarchical fashion***. This is easier than it sounds. Teachers who participated, for example, in the Berkeley Math Readiness Project prekindergarten program in differentiated math trajectory (Klein & Starkey, 2004) based on National Association for the Education of Young Children/National Council of Teachers of Mathematics (NAEYC/NCTM), and who were given support throughout the year "learned to deliver a conceptually broad mathematics curriculum that significantly enhanced children's informal mathematical knowledge in all areas assessed" (Klein & Starkey, 2004, p. 357). I suggest that successful programs like the Berkeley Math Readiness Project might simply add the pillars to their teacher training. Adding the pillars format has the added benefit that content can become more uniform across regional, state and country boundaries. This also permits schools the freedom to become more creative in their transdisciplinary thinking and gives teachers the space to develop better teaching mechanisms that differentiate the needs of all learners.

Approx level	Approx age	Network	Pillar		Evidence in Neuroscience	Related Brain Hubs	Educational Evaluation Criteria	Classrooms Activities
Preschool	36-48 months	Cognitive (domain specific)	RELATION-SHIPS	Numerosity (sets)	Butterworth, 2005; Dehaene, 2011; Gray & Reeve, 2014; Hannula, & Lehtinen, 2005; Izard, Streri & Spelke, 2014; Mussolin, Nys & Leybaert, 2012; Park, Li, & Brannon, 2014; Passolunghi, Lanfranchi, Altoè & Sollazzo, 2015; Sarama & Clements, 2009; Starkey, & McCandliss, 2014; Xenidou-Dervou, Lieshout & Schoot, 2014; Xenidou-Dervou, van der Schoot & van Lieshout, 2015	"...We identified a strictly right lateralized modality invariant fronto-parietal circuit, comprising intraparietal, pre-motor and dorso-lateral prefrontal cortex, which, given temporal sequences of visual and auditory items, is more activated when subjects estimate the number of items than when they attend to their color or pitch...." (Piazza, Mechelli, Price & Butterworth, 2006, p.181).	"Child can reproduce a set of four or five given a model set; "The next level after counting small numbers is to count out objects up to 5 and produce a group of four objects. When asked to show four of something, for example, this child can give four objects" (Clements, 2011, p.23, level 7).	?

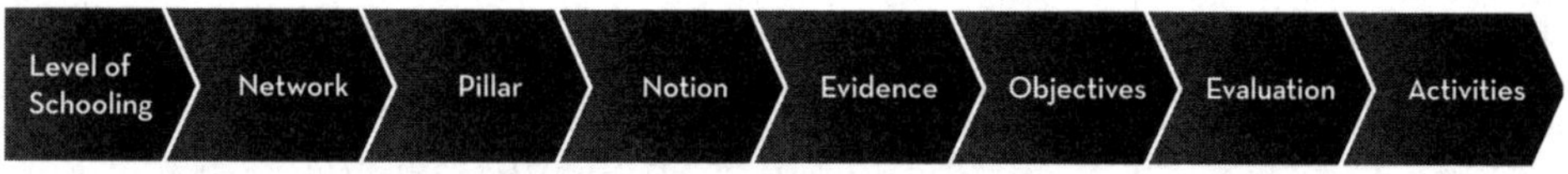

Level of Schooling › Network › Pillar › Notion › Evidence › Objectives › Evaluation › Activities

Figure 44. Backward Design and the Pillars. SOURCE: TOKUHAMA-ESPINOSA, 2017

"Do the pillars help us differentiate learning or to identify learning difficulties?"

I suggest that the precision with which we can identify and correct problems increases by following the five pillars constructivist hierarchy. The use of the pillars would break down the overlap information into manageable and easily understood groupings, improving the probability of application in real classrooms and enhanced diagnostic capability.

Rather than lamenting that a kid "doesn't have the head for language," the pillars permit teachers to diagnose whether he has a breakdown in general sensory perception, socioemotional regulation, cognitive skills, or domain-area skills. Once it's determined which strand of learning is compromised, teachers can then precisely hone in on the areas of need and offer more personalized diagnosis and treatment. This is vital, as different classroom activities improve different aspects of learning. For example, related to language, activities that enhance grammar do not necessarily improve vocabulary; what betters working memory does not necessarily better intonation and prosody; what aids handwriting does not aid semantic memory; what influences attention does not necessarily influence analogic understanding; and so on. The precision with which a teacher can identify a student's struggle will lead to better interventions and hopefully better learning. I firmly believe that half the solution is understanding the problem; a good diagnosis of exactly which aspect of mathematics (which pillar) escapes a child can go a long way to remediating his global math skills. A misdiagnosis can set a child behind, lower self-esteem, and create a downward spiral toward failure, while proper identification of learning needs enhances both the speed and the accuracy with which problems can be remediated.

Many teachers know that children can appear to have math problems when they really have language problems. An additional benefit of applying the pillars is that it would make ***the exact area of deficit more transparent,*** as distinct domains can be analyzed through the similar lens of a single pillar (math and language through the pillar of symbols, for example). Once the maps are overlapped, a teacher would then be able to see if the missing prerequisite knowledge was located in math or in language, and in doing so, be able to provide more accurate remediation to fill that gap. For example, if a child is successful in school up through the concepts of multiplication but begins to show signs of weakness as he starts to divide, a teacher can review the prerequisite skills or area knowledge to better identify how to fill in his gaps, so he can continue to flourish in math. Rather than globally stating "he has problems with math" teachers can ask themselves, *Is he lacking reinforcement on the different types of* ***symbols*** *learned between multiplication and division stages?* Or *has he misunderstood the* **order** *of operations?* Or *how the* **relationship** *of numbers is changed in division when they are positive and negative?* Or *does he simply misunderstand the written directions (a language, not a math problem)?*

"Is this a theory or is it usable knowledge?"

To make the information from neuroscience more usable in real classrooms, we need to translate what is observable through neuro imagery (changes in neuronal networks at a molecular level) into observable classroom behavior. Related to the pillars, this means taking neuroconstructivist data and postulating ways to make it observable to teachers in real classrooms. Whereas most teachers are not aware of how to read brain scans, almost all teachers know how to design and use rubrics. Readers are encouraged to view the example in the Appendices of how this neuroconstructivist design would actually look if applied in schools. Tables 29-31 in the Appendices show how we identified 16 neural networks for early math and preliteracy, then mapped this on to the current curriculum structure using descriptors for existing experts in learning trajectories. This permits us to take the information one step further and convert the evidence from neuroscience into observable classroom behavior as seen in Figure 45, and then make this useable knowledge in rubric form (Table 20).

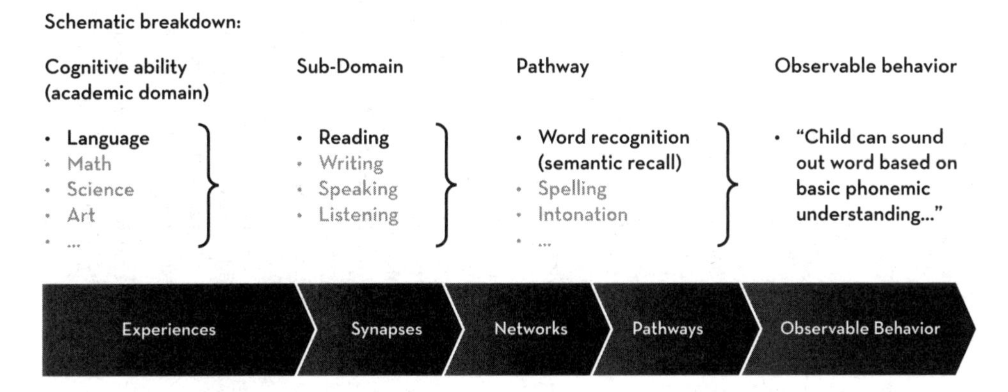

Figure 45. Academic Domain, Subdomains, Pathways, Observable Behavior.
SOURCE: TOKUHAMA-ESPINOSA, 2017

To construct great rubrics, there are a handful of basic guides. For example, when using the pillars, level rubrics are preferable to age rubrics. However, as developmental rankings and typical classrooms use age as a primary criterion for grouping children, I created a rubric based on age as well as level to make them as familiar to teachers as possible. The end result is a teacher-friendly tool based on observable classroom behavior. The rubrics not only include the domain specific behaviors, but the physical, socioemotional, cultural, and general cognitive aspects of learning as well.

This "pillar rubric" simplifies what is known about specific neuronal networks into observable behavior. For example, the concept of "ordinality," which is key to math notions and measured in changes related to the hub of the intraparietal sulcus (among other areas and not mentioned in the rubric), is equated to "child can count to four," which is an observable behavior that any teacher

Table 20. Example of a Rubric Using the Pillars

3 YEAR (36 MONTHS) MATHEMATICS									
Developmental Stage	**Age/Evidence of first testing**	**Network**	**Pillar**	**Description**	**How does this look (observable behavior)**	**1**	**2**	**3**	**4**
Preschool	36 months	Cognitive domain (specific)	Symbol	Analogic quality systems	Child can use tallying to mark value one through ten; "At this level a child can keep one-to-one correspondence between counting words and objects—at least for small groups of objects laid in a line. A corresponder may answer 'how many' by recounting the objects starting over with one each time" (Clements, 2011, p.23 level 5).				
Preschool	36 months	Cognitive domain (specific)	Symbol	Coding (Arabic integers)	Child can identify symbolic number representations in Arabic integers ("1," "2," "3,"); "Child can find sums for joining problems up to 3 by counting all with objects. For example, when asked 'You have 2 balls and get 1 more. How many in all?' counts out 2, then counts out 2 more, then counts all 3: "1, 2, 3, 3!" (Clements, 2011, p.26.Adding and Subtracting level 3)				
Preschool	36 months	Cognitive domain (specific)	Symbol	Forms/ Shapes/ Geometry (beginning shape naming)	Child has informal knowledge of math; he can name shapes (circles, squares, triangles);" child can recognize and name prototypical circle, square, and less often, a typical triangle...Some children may name different sizes, shapes, and orientations of rectangles, but also accept some shapes that look rectangular but are not rectangles...Children name these shapes 'rectangles' (including the nonrectangular parallelogram)" (Clements, 2011, p.31 Geometric Shapes level 2).				

SOURCE: TOKUHAMA-ESPINOSA, 2017

can identify. Such a rubric can help teachers evaluate educational advances in the domain-specific subject areas divided not by approximate age, but by exact mastery levels as expressed by the pillars curriculum. The explicit and quantifiable criteria within the rubric permit teachers to quickly and easily evaluate advancement by children. It is hoped this also permits greater remediation of missing skills and enhanced differentiation among children's needs.

Questions about the complementary nature of the pillars, the way that neuroscientific contributions make their way into education; how areas such as emotions and movement play a role in pillar use, and how they coincide with backward design are all important concerns that help us determine the true utility of the pillars. The pillars are currently just a theory but can potentially become usable knowledge. On the whole, the evidence seems strong enough, at the least, to continue the debate.

We turn now to the Conclusions and a discussion about curriculum reform, as well as the benefits the pillars can bring learners.

Conclusions

Curriculum Overhaul?

One can argue that the pillars are a rejection of subject-area instruction; this is not my intention. The pillars and subject or domain areas are highly complementary forms of structuring teaching and learning. The pillars remind us that there are distinct ways to divide curriculum instruction beyond just thematic (e.g., "Egypt," "Weather," "Human Body and Health"), topical (e.g., "Environment in the News," "Individual vs. Collective Rights"), methodological (project- or problem-based learning, Socratic instruction, case studies, and so on), or modeling structures (e.g., "Makerspace," "ScienceLab,"), and invite a new way to conceptualize learning. The pillars can work in tandem with all existing school designs and can do so in a way that enhances deeper understanding of core notions in education.

It's clear from educational research data from academics such as Lynda Darling-Hammond (2000) that teacher expertise is most evident not through content instruction, but rather when teachers help kids learn to *think* ("think like a biologist," "think like an artist," "think like an historian," and so on) pillars add a new dimension to thinking..

As we saw earlier in the book, it can be argued that it is easier to divide physical spaces, teachers, textbooks, and budgets when they can be separated into subject areas. This is true, and it is definitely comfortable. After all, "that's the way we've always done it," as Ian Jukes likes to say (Jukes et al., 2000, p. 8). It is far easier for publishers to generate textbooks when they deal with a single subject (language arts, math, chemistry, and so on); organize class schedules and physical rooms by subject blocks; and hire teachers by their areas of content knowledge than to consider changing a system that has been in place for nearly two centuries. Likewise, dividing by subjects is easier on the school administrator who can hold staff meetings by department, timetable classes with a balance of subjects, and hire based on the academic title of the teacher. But who benefits from this "easier" way of going about structuring our schools? This is what I like to call the "delivery room" model—it makes sense for the doctor to have a woman lie on her back, but it goes against the very nature of physiology, physics, and a woman's best instincts when she's ready to give birth. That is, the way we have done things in the past may not be the most beneficial to the users: our students.

Where did curriculum subject divisions come from in the first place? If we think back to the oldest "classrooms" in which Socrates seamlessly integrated different domain areas under wider case studies, problem-based learning, or real-world dilemmas, it seems almost comical to imagine him dividing up his day starting off with an hour of pure math (or language arts, or science). In was common for Socrates to delve into a problem or case and elicit reflection from a variety of disciplinary lenses to resolve it, while children in school today are asked to study subjects such as chemistry in a vacuum, often far away from physics, math, history, and biology, though each has multiple overlaps with the other. Socrates is reputed to have run inquiry-based learning, something highly recommended in today's schools (Campbell & Groundwater-Smith, 2013). When education became free and obligatory for all at the end of the 19th century, more children than ever filled our schools, forcing us to "streamline" the educational practice and divide our time by different subjects, children by ages, and faculty by specialty areas.

This leads us to the present, in which the focus on subjects taught in silos for a specific number of minutes a week is largely divorced from the students' understanding of their real-life contexts. One of the failures of the current school structure is its distance from what students consider to be "the important problems," which are rarely resolved with information from a single domain area (Putnam & Borko, 2000). While expertise is desirable, narrowing down one's approach to problem-solving to a single domain area limits the potential answers we can offer. As mentioned in the Introduction, pure subject area studies are rarely superior in problem solving using transdisciplinary approaches. Some enlightened schools are moving away from subject-bound course design and broadening their approach to be based on real-life problems that use subject area knowledge to reach resolution (Søby, 2015) rather than as an end in itself. The textbook dilemma, the physical space distribution question, and teacher formation all hinge on the decision of whether or not to teach curriculum in subject matter divisions or not. The pillars could change all of this in ways that are likely more beneficial to the student, but would likely challenge administrators on an organizational level and society on a conceptual level.

Mastery, Over All

The five basic pillars of human learning take on a new importance for me as I witness the never-ending discussions by schools, universities, and entire governments contemplating "curricular reform". *Should we give more hours to math and fewer to foreign language? Should physical education even have a place in an academic curriculum or be relegated to after school activities? How important are the arts vs. the hard sciences?* Then I asked myself, could the curriculum debate about the different priorities in education (STEM vs. Core Curriculum vs. "the basics" vs. the International Baccalaureate, and dozens of other options) at different times in history based on different convictions become trivial if viewed under the pillars? Can the curriculum debate be resolved by enhancing subject-area instruction with an interdisciplinary look at symbols, patterns, order, relations, and categories in a hierarchical or constructivist fashion?

My belief is that school curriculum can be redesigned around the pillars and delivered in a constructivist way throughout formal schooling, though this is an as-yet unproven hypothesis. A pillars design could introduce student to *all current subject areas* simultaneously, and add on even more subjects that have less priority in traditional curriculum (foreign languages, the arts, physical education), which arguably deserve more space in education. This would surely bring more dynamism to school learning by making every lesson transdisciplinary and authentic, as well as celebrate the way the brain builds these networks naturally.

If adopted, the pillars would mean a paradigm shift. Publishers would have to abandon years of practice in which single-subject texts are the norm. It is not uncommon to find that children's textbooks pose questions that appear single-subject-dependent, but real teachers in real classrooms know that the solutions that students propose are almost always more transdisciplinary because they are more in touch with considerations we can now see in the five pillars. For example, a 4th grader might be asked how much pizza each child gets when the pizza is divided evenly by four kids (answer: 25 percent; ¼; one-quarter). But almost any 4th grader will tell you a mathematical solution is not enough. Some kids are bullies and will take more than their fair share (**patterns** of social dominance). Others dislike the toppings and will take less (**categories** of likes and dislikes). Yet others want hamburgers and hate pizza and will protest and take none (**relationships** of cause and effect). Others have a parent who "shares" the piece with their child, rendering a fraction (**order** of family structure). Depending on the size of the pizza, a fourth might be too much for the average 4th grader to eat (**relationship** of size of stomach to amount of food). And so on. There are multiple angles and considerations in every real-world problem, and most children don't let us forget that as they try to answer the ridiculously simple pizza dilemma in their textbooks. When students offer us all these non-mathematical answers, they are teaching each other and us about different perspectives on the same problem. This is a display of cognitive flexibility as students relate to real-life anecdotes and something we should celebrate in our classrooms.

The brain adapts to what it does most. If children are forced into "siloed" thinking models to complete their workbooks on time, or asked to respond to the pizza question from a purely mathematical angle, this means that when it comes time to face the real-world problems outside their classrooms, they will be at a disadvantage from those who have habituated a transdisciplinary frame of mind. After years of habituating domain-specific responses, it is ironic that in the upper grades we spend a lot of time explicitly telling students they need to think in more interdisciplinary ways. It's not hard to imagine that if children, from the earliest moments of their education, were asked to use the pillars to think of the pizza question in terms of **symbols** (*how many different symbols can be used to express 25 percent?*); **patterns** (*what else looks and divides like a pizza? clocks? cakes?*); **order** (*how many different ways can we order this problem?*); **relationships** (*what is the relation of each piece of pizza to the whole?*); and **categories** (*would one-fourth be the same in a pizza as in a square? are words, fractions, decimals, and percentages the same or different?*); then we could habituate better thinking practices over time. Habits formed early in life lead to automated responses, and integrated transdisciplinary skills lead to better problem resolution.

My belief is that if children are taught in a transdisciplinary manner from the start of their education, they would not have to explicitly learn how to do so later; rather, this approach would come naturally (Ramanathan et al., 2012). Look up from your book. What do you see? What are the symbols jumping out at your trained eye? How many patterns can you identify? Can you find at least two or three category divisions to the things in your surroundings? Hopefully, seeing the pillars around you is becoming easier. Practice makes permanent, so starting early with the pillars is likely to have a stronger effect. The more rehearsal you have with the pillars, the more natural it is to see the world with this added dimension.

Teacher Training: Past, Present, and Future

The history of teaching and learning has evolved slowly but surely towards a more scientific and evidence-based foundation. If we look back at the evolution of teacher education, we can note important changes and a clear direction towards a more "clinical model" in which evidence plays the leading role (Conroy et al., 2013). A hundred years ago, medicine was a profession of ill repute; today it has evolved to being one of the most respected in society. *Why?* Because there was a conscious effort to elevate standards, document practice, and enhance global quality. In education, we have the foundations to launch a similar campaign for a new model of teacher formation. Eisner (1979) pointed to the many ways that curricula could be structured and how learning occurred in explicit ways (through content-area knowledge) and implicit ways (how we think about what we are learning). Shulman (1986) was the first to disaggregate the many elements of "teacher knowledge" into sub-areas of knowledge of the learner and teacher characteristics, general pedagogical knowledge, knowledge of contexts, knowledge of educational objectives, knowledge of curriculum, content knowledge, and pedagogical content knowledge. And he was one of the first to appreciate that each of these pieces was a complex universe, and that the whole of great teaching depends on an understanding of each piece to construct the puzzle of learning.

Lowenberg Ball and colleagues (2008) agree with Shulman's general assertion that being experts in teachers' pedagogical content knowledge (TPCK) is what leads to greater student success. They note that strong TPCK is a better indicator of great teaching than content alone or pedagogy alone (Lowenberg Ball et al., 2008). Knowledge of math does not make you a good math teacher, nor does knowledge of teaching make you a good math teacher, but rather knowledge of math *and* knowledge of teaching math make you a good math teacher. In their studies on math teacher formation, Lowenberg Ball and colleagues make it clear that "the mathematical knowledge for teaching" that is needed to be a successful math teacher also relates to the general hierarchy of math concepts, which no level of good pedagogy can substitute (Lowenberg Ball et al., 2008, p.403). Teachers' new pedagogical knowledge should also include more knowledge about these learning trajectories and the hierarchy of concepts, both provided by the pillars.

In a summary review of the many ways "quality education" can be disaggregated, we identified 218 key indicators divided into 11 categories (access and coverage; equality and equity; retention, completion, staying-rates; standards; academic achievement; teachers and teaching; evaluation; financing; governance; family and community; context [culture, legal system and demographics]) used in different combinations by different governments (Tokuhama-Espinosa, 2015b). The greatest number of indicators fell under the category of Teachers and Teaching. The quality of the teacher— and more specifically, the teacher's pedagogical content knowledge—is what drives educational quality. Teachers who know how to help kids learn to think drive quality education. Ironically for this book, we found one of the least influential indicator in quality education is the choice of curriculum. For this reason, the pillars seek an overhaul in a way that changes thinking about the teaching and learning dynamic; *how* we teach matters more than pure content knowledge. Pillars thinking adds a new sorely needed dimension to quality education.

If a new pillars model were to be implemented, **a strikingly new type of teacher formation** would occur, in which the traditional TPCK would be supplemented with a **disaggregation of concepts** as expressed through the five pillars constructivist hierarchy. **This would mean teachers become more like learning scientists** as they learn the many sub-elements within each topic within each domain or subject area. In some ways, this returns to Schulman's understanding of the various elements that comprise good "teacher knowledge" (1986). Just as he realized there are many aspects to great teaching -- including knowledge of the different actors and their roles and relationships; knowledge of the contexts; knowledge of the subject material; and so on – the pillars add yet one more element to the basics of what makes great teachers and enhances the probability of success in the teaching-learning dynamic.

Teaching teachers about the pillars is an easy way to segway into neuroscientific knowledge as well, which is now recommended as a part of teacher formation (Guerriero, 2017).

Challenges

Adopting the constructivist pillars model for mastery disturbs many traditional approaches to education. The entire discussion on standards will have to rerouted to match levels in symbols, patterns, order, relations, and categories and no longer tied to age and grade levels. Publishing companies will have to complement their product lines will new books and formats that adhere to the pillars. Teacher training will have to be modified to include not only traditional methodology, but a new pedagogy that approaches thinking skills from the pillars angle. Educational researchers will have to embark on a new branch of study as they map and confirm the pillars in every existing domain area and the effectiveness of distinct pedagogies in fulfilling the learning outcomes promised by each level of learning. Neuroscientific researchers and translators in the field of Mind, Brain, and Education will have to diligently document the evidence in neuroconstructivism as it grows and better explains learning hierarchies in the brain to assist in new types of teaching methods. In short, the pillars suggest an overhaul of the educational system.

The greatest challenge to the pillars is its untested structure. Many questions arise here. First, how can we assure that the hierarchical mapping of the learning concepts is correct? Is confirmation from a handful of specialists enough? Probably not, meaning that it will take several years of actual application in classrooms to test for accuracy. In the meantime, changes will have to be made as new data comes in—a risky an unethical venture, some might argue. However, countering this criticism is the fact that the changes the pillars recommend are no more invasive than a change in pedagogical approach, which currently occur with dizzying frequency in schools. Teachers are usually open to anything that might potentially help their students, and so multiple changes are often entertained each school year, meaning new ideas are the norm in many school settings. Teachers have learned to resist fads, however, and so the neuroconstructivist evidence behind the pillars must be shared in a clear and concise way with teachers if they are to accept this addition to their tool box.

This means that integration of the pillars in teacher practice depends on evidence. How much evidence is "enough" to sustain backing for the use of the pillars as an additional teaching tool or as a justification to change curriculum design? Does the educational community feel at ease with the neuroscientific evidence presented so far? Has teacher professional development integrated enough information about the brain and learning to appreciate the pillars? What happens if neuroscientific evidence sustains the pillars, but educators reject it anyway? Is there the political will to attempt such a radical change in the way we have always conducted schooling by teaching through domain areas of study? Do we have, collectively, the intellectual courage to break with the past and comfort of what we know, despite all its imperfections ("better the devil you know than the devil you don't"), and part with curriculum design divided by content area alone? Answers to these questions will be indicative of the pillars integration.

Opportunities

There are at least two main benefits of using the pillars. First and foremost is that the pillars advance the possibility of achieving more learning in more areas that are highly desirable in modern society, but which are not always present in current school curriculum due to the limited timetables in a typical school day. It is clear that the demands on curriculum design, which incorporate 21st century soft skills that develop good communicators; collaborators; culturally sensitive individuals; community contributors; personally responsible individuals who are creative; and critical thinkers who can work well in heterogeneous groups use tools (including technology); and who are autonomous in their actions are not yet met in many traditional models found in schools today (Figure 46). Our educational system is antiquated and the pillars are a viable option. The push for 21st century skills adds to the debate about content and curriculum design, which has been ongoing for more than two decades without resolution. Modern educators are encouraged to reach beyond simplistic delivery of domain content information and to become more creative in how they integrate these life skills into the classroom.

Society expects much more from schools and teachers than it did just a generation ago. Most students believe that in school contexts, "to know is not enough," as most content is *Googleable* and much of what is found in textbooks can be found online. Knowledge is much more readily available to learners outside of school, at their fingertips, via their phones, and mostly for free, making many students question why they should invest resources in a system that does little to extend learning beyond what is already available online. The sheer accessibility of content knowledge means that we educators are expected to go well beyond simple exposure to knowledge, and up our game to include new skill sets and accept responsibility for certain attitudinal mindset changes. This is analogous to a restaurant with a new main dish, an architect's new take on housing design, or a seamstress that imagines a different way to use fabric combinations in a new clothing line; all respect the basic functions of their trades, but also understand that innovating the way they go about their work has benefits for modernizing society. The pillars offer a radical shift in thinking and stretch a student's ways of knowing beyond current structures, which would hopefully be a welcome change for many. The goals of teaching have changed, therefore the way we structure learning must also change.

Studies from innovative researchers—such as Sugata Mitra's "hole in the wall" experiment—offer surprising findings about how humans can learn. Mitra's studies illustrate how small groups of self-organizing children can

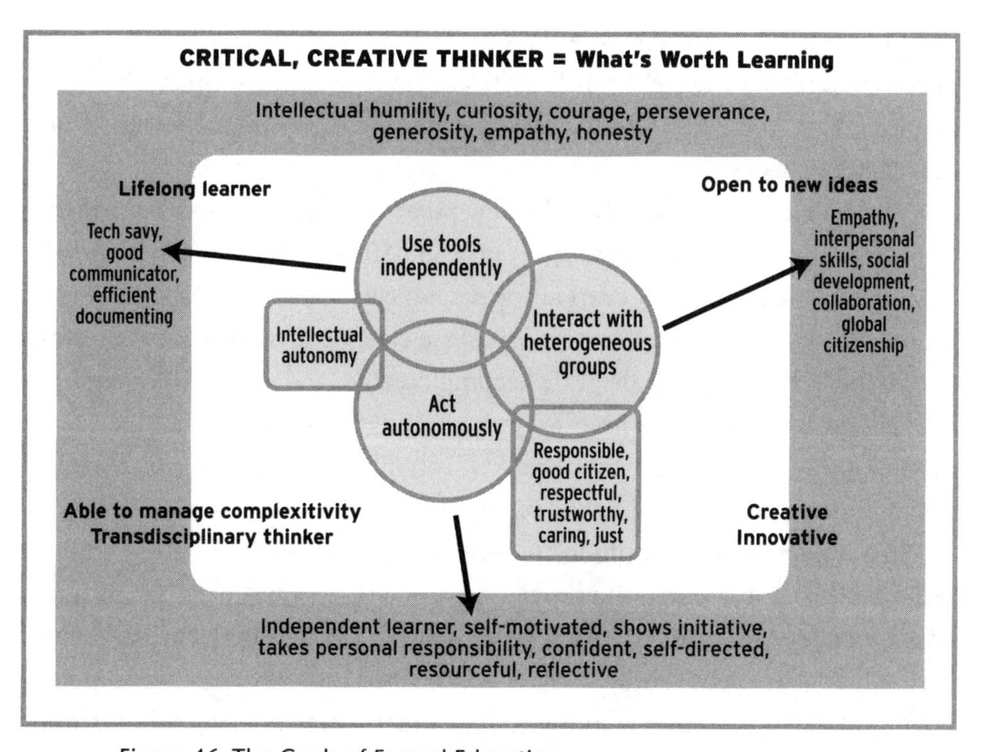

Figure 46. The Goals of Formal Education. SOURCE: TOKUHAMA-ESPINOSA, 2014

teach themselves the content of the entire primary school curriculum in a shorter time than normally achieved in formal school settings (Dolan et al., 2013; Mitra, 2003; Mitra & Crawley, 2014). This means that it is no longer important for teachers to focus solely on math formulas, for example, as the Internet can do that through free apps and usually in a shorter time frame than many classroom teachers, but rather on the *use* of those formulas. We no longer need teachers who simply deliver content, but rather teachers who know how to explain *how* and *why* the content can be used to resolve problems in the real world. This tells us that the way some of us currently teach has to change and use of the pillars can facilitate this.

There is no shortage of knowledge these days, as was once the challenge for previous generations, who had limited access to resources. The difficulty today is that there is often a deficit in good judgment about the quality of information and an understanding of how to evaluate good vs. bad sources using critical thinking skills. Teachers are the new knowledge brokers in the 21st century whose job, in part, is to help students navigate the sea of information that is at their fingertips. Any kid with a smartphone has access to a world of data. What they need is to learn to judge its quality. Our jobs as teachers have gone from information deliverers to guides in judging quality evidence for specific purposes. Shifting the emphasis to critical thinking skills in this way is complemented by the pillars, which constantly reminds learners to view the world through multiple lenses.

While there is no guarantee, the new pillars design lends itself to a higher level of thinking and a more proactive problem-solving mentality that could be habituated throughout the current formal education process. As a result, the more personalized and transparent structure clears a more direct path toward one of the 21st century goals of developing creative and critical thinkers. The new pillars approach lends itself to (though does not guarantee) a higher level of thinking and a more proactive problem-solving mentality based on the additional dimensions provided by the pillars.

In addition to responding to the demands for better 21st century skills, a second important opportunity provided by pillar use is to **replace grade levels based on age with mastery**. The "ages vs. stages vs. prior experience dilemma" highlights the ineffective way we have approached maximizing student potential by prioritizing age over cognitive stages and prior experience as foundations for prerequisite knowledge. We would do well to heed the recommendation to teach toward mastery as opposed to presuming all students born on the same day can perform equally well in our classrooms. The pillars constructivist hierarchy model permits a mastery by level scheme in which all students will be able to achieve in a logical manner, independent of their home conditions, their socio-economic status or zip code.

Because of the mastery layout, the pillars make learning more transparent because each level in the hierarchy is neuroconstructivistly designed. The hierarchical mapping of skills would be visible and tangible, making learning goals clearer to the student himself as well as to teachers and parents, meaning **earlier and more accurate diagnosis of student learning problems**. Furthermore, as children experience multiple corrections based on pillar levels over time, they will begin to become more independent in identifying their own gaps by interpreting the concept hierarchy. This means more independent learners.

Additionally, there are benefits to applying the pillars outside of formal schooling as well. Many parents want to help their kids find success, but most new parents do not know how brains work, nor what they should do to help. The pillars are a simple, easy-to-understand guide. If parents can be convinced to raise their children with the stimuli of the five pillars by calling attention to the symbols, patterns, order, categories, and relationships that surround them, they will help start habituating skills that facilitate transdisciplinary, authentic, and creative thinking. This means that, at least on an individual level, the model can be applied immediately.

Final Thoughts

We began this book by talking about the inspirations that led to the creation of the five pillars model. The pillars approach appears to be complementary to existing educational structures, adding a new dimension to the thinking and learning process without detracting from existing models. This is to say that, while we don't know if the pillars actually enhance learning, we know they can't hurt. The evidence from educational constructivism and neuroconstructivism reinforces thinking about learning in an ever-spiraling hierarchy of complexities, which can be detailed with a high level of accuracy, given the backdrop of nearly 100 years of previous research. This book joins studies that were published in isolation into a new model that integrates their use in a distinct way. I argue that the insights on constructivism and the hierarchies model take on a new vibrancy when combined with the pillars.

We considered the origins of the five pillars and examined them one by one—symbols, patterns, order, categories, and relationships—beginning with their definition, current literature, and potential use. We hypothesized about what the pillars would mean for curriculum change, and suggested three options of how to integrate the pillars: one with little disruption, in which the pillars are used as methodology (Option A), one in which the pillars are used to design mastery curriculum (Option B), and one in which the pillars become the new curriculum (Option C). I personally prefer "the middle way" (Option B), in which the pillars can be used to motivate mastery by levels to improve student learning outcomes by creating a safety net for students, and a more personalized learning experience, but I accept that it would be easier to first apply the pillars as methodology (Option A). We then reviewed the challenges and opportunities the pillars provide, including improved 21st century skills and the elimination of age divisions in school in favor of mastery levels. Finally, in the Appendices, readers can find an example of a hypothetical neuroconstructivism curricular design using the pillars.

Too many changes at once? Perhaps. However, it can also be argued that small educational reforms in the past have done little to move the tide of educational progress toward the needs of the 21st century. Could it be time for a radical paradigm shift in thinking?

Change can be instigated by a small group and does not have to be nationwide from the start. Ian Jukes, an inspirational 21st century thinker, likes to remind teachers that there are many things we do in education simply because we have always done them that way (curriculum structure by subject and grades by age groupings, for example) and we forget to question whether the original reasons are valid in modern times. Jukes encourages us to remember that a handful of educators can turn the tide, similar to the way sardines all move in one direction until a few decide to break with the school and go in the opposite direction—and then the masses follow. He calls for a "committed sardine movement," by a handful of dedicated change agents in education to shift the tide. Only you personally, and we as educators collectively, can make this decision.

On a recent positive note, news from Finland has called attention to that country's decision to emphasize transdisciplinary thinking through an integrated curriculum, rather than single-subject-focused classrooms (Halinen, 2015). Could this be a sign that the world is ready for a radical break from tradition (or at least those countries with a sufficiently forward-looking mentality)? Realistic options include a cautious approach by prudently applying this new curriculum structure on a smaller scale in a Mind, Brain, and Education Lab School or other willing institution before launching it out to the wider world. Will there be willing early adopters to this model? This remains to be seen.

I hope this book serves to stir debate about the state of educational curriculum structures today and begin a tide of change simply by getting teachers to think differently about the way we educate. I suggest we each start by adding the pillars dimension to our review of curriculum, research, and teaching to think through the pillars ourselves. To habituate a behavior, the behavior has to be rehearsed over time. Once more: Look up from your book. What are the symbols calling out to you from your surroundings? What types of patterns are more salient in your senses? What expressions of order structured your day or are out of synch with expectations? What categories can you place objects and concepts into that are natural (and what can be categorized in uncommon ways)? What are the relationships between the ideas and notions you have contemplated today? Hopefully thinking through the pillars has become almost intuitive during the time it has taken you to read this book; teaching our students to do the same is within our reach.

Education has advanced in so many ways over the past decades, yet it has been nearly 200 years since curriculum has undergone a significant reform. Is it possible that using the pillars can help tip the education movement into quality reform, rename teachers "learning scientists," and help kids reach their potential in our schools? That is the hope. What we can say is that becoming more observant of the **symbols** in our midst, the **patterns** in our surroundings, the **order** in our personal contexts, the **categories** of ways we can understand our world, and the **relationships** that all things have to each other broadens our understanding of the world and ourselves.

References

Abrams, D. A., Bhatara, A., Ryali, S., Balaban, E., Levitin, D. J., & Menon, V. (2010). Decoding temporal structure in music and speech relies on shared brain resources but elicits different fine-scale spatial patterns. *Cerebral Cortex, 21*(7), 1507–1518.

Adams, R. B. & Janata, P. (2002). A comparison of neural circuits underlying auditory and visual object categorization. *NeuroImage, 16*(2), 361–377.

Akil, H., Balice-Gordon, R., Cardozo, D. L., Koroshetz, W., Norris, S. M. P., Sherer, T., . . . & Thiels, E. (2016). Neuroscience training for the 21st century. *Neuron, 90*(5), 917-926.

Algoe, S. B. & Zhaoyang, R. (2016). Positive psychology in context: Effects of expressing gratitude in ongoing relationships depend on perceptions of enactor responsiveness. *Journal of Positive Psychology, 11*(4), 399–415.

Alluri, V., Toiviainen, P., Jääskeläinen, I. P., Glerean, E., Sams, M., & Brattico, E. (2012). Large-scale brain networks emerge from dynamic processing of musical timbre, key and rhythm. *Neuro-Image, 59*(4), 3677–3689.

Almeida, D. & Poeppel, D. (2013). Word-specific repetition effects revealed by MEG and the implications for lexical access. *Brain and Language, 127*(3), 497–509.

Altieri, N., Stevenson, R. A., Wallace, M. T., & Wenger, M. J. (2013). Learning to associate auditory and visual stimuli: Behavioral and neural mechanisms. *Brain Topography*, 1–15.

Amalric, M., & Dehaene, S. (2016). Origins of the brain networks for advanced mathematics in expert mathematicians. *Proceedings of the National Academy of Sciences, 113*(18), 4909–4917.

Amedi, A., Stern, W. M., Camprodon, J. A., Bermpohl, F., Merabet, L., Rotman, S., . . . & Pascual-Leone, A. (2007). Shape conveyed by visual-to-auditory sensory substitution activates the lateral occipital complex. *Nature Neuroscience, 10*(6), 687.

Amedi, A., von Kriegstein, K., van Atteveldt, N. M., Beauchamp, M. S., & Naumer, M. J. (2005). Functional imaging of human crossmodal identification and object recognition. *Experimental Brain Research, 166*(3–4), 559–571.

Andres, M., Pelgrims, B., Michaux, N., Olivier, E., & Pesenti, M. (2011). Role of distinct parietal areas in arithmetic: An fMRI-guided TMS study. *NeuroImage, 54*(4), 3048–3056. doi: http://dx.doi.org/10.1016/j.neuroimage.2010.11.009

Andric, M. & Small, S. L. (2012). Gesture's neural language. *Frontiers in Psychology, 3*, 99.

Anobile, G., Stievano, P., & Burr, D. C. (2013). Visual sustained attention and numerosity sensitivity correlate with math achievement in children. *Journal of Experimental Child Psychology, 116*(2), 380–391.

Ansari, D. (2015). Number symbols in the brain. *Mathematical Cognition and Learning, 2*, 27–46.

Ansari, D. & Karmiloff-Smith, A. (2002). Atypical trajectories of number development: A neuroconstructivist perspective. *Trends in Cognitive Sciences, 6*(12), 511–516.

Anthony, G. & Walshaw, M. (2009). Mathematics education in the early years: Building bridges. *Contemporary Issues in Early Childhood, 10*(2), 107–121.

Antzoulatos, E. G. & Miller, E. K. (2014). Increases in functional connectivity between prefrontal cortex and striatum during category learning. *Neuron, 83*(1), 216–225.

Appel, M. & Kronberger, N. (2012). Stereotypes and the achievement gap: Stereotype threat prior to test taking. *Educational Psychology Review, 24*(4), 609–635.

Ardila, A. (2012). Interaction between lexical and grammatical language systems in the brain. *Physics of Life Reviews, 9*(2), 198–214.

Asano, M., Imai, M., Kita, S., Kitajo, K., Okada, H., & Thierry, G. (2015). Sound symbolism scaffolds language development in preverbal infants. *Cortex, 63*, 196–205.

Avancini, C., Soltész, F., & Szűcs, D. (2015). Separating stages of arithmetic verification: an ERP study with a novel paradigm. *Neuropsychologia, 75*, 322–329.

Aviv, V. (2014). What does the brain tell us about abstract art? *Frontiers in Human Neuroscience, 8*, (85), 1-4.

Bahr, B., Lemmer, B., & Piccolo, R. (2016). Relative space and time. In R. Piccolo, B. Lemmer, & B. Bahr (Eds.), *Quirky quarks* (pp. 116–119). Berlin, Germany: Springer.

Balaguer, J., Spiers, H., Hassabis, D., & Summerfield, C. (2016). Neural mechanisms of hierarchical planning in a virtual subway network. *Neuron, 90*(4), 893–903.

Barnhardt, C., Borsting, E., Deland, P., Pham, N., & Vu, T. (2005). Relationship between visual-motor integration and spatial organization of written language and math. *Optometry & Vision Science, 82*(2), 138–143.

Baroody, A. J. (2004). The developmental bases for early childhood number and operations standards. In D.H. Clements, J. Sarama, & A:M. DiBiase's *Engaging young children in mathematics: Standards for early childhood mathematics education*, (pp. 173-219), Abingdon-on-Thames, UK: Routledge.

Barth, H. C. & Paladino, A. M. (2011). The development of numerical estimation: Evidence against a representational shift. *Developmental Science, 14*(1), 125–135

Baumann, O., Chan, E., & Mattingley, J. B. (2012). Distinct neural networks underlie encoding of categorical versus coordinate spatial relations during active navigation. *Neuroimage, 60*(3), 1630–1637.

Beaty, R. E., Christensen, A. P., Benedek, M., Silvia, P. J., & Schacter, D. L. (2017). Creative constraints: Brain activity and network dynamics underlying semantic interference during idea production. *NeuroImage, 148*, 189–196.

Bergamo, A. & Torresani, L. (2014). Classemes and other classifier-based features for efficient object categorization. *IEEE Transactions on Pattern Analysis and Machine Intelligence, 36*(10), 1988–2001.

Bergeson, T. R. & Trehub, S. E. (2006). Infants perception of rhythmic patterns. *Music Perception 23*(4), 345–360.

Berglund, E. V. A., Eriksson, M., & Westerlund, M. (2005). Communicative skills in relation to gender, birth order, childcare and socioeconomic status in 18-month-old children. *Scandinavian Journal of Psychology, 46*(6), 485–491

Berninger, V. W., Richards, T. L., & Abbott, R. D. (2017). Brain and behavioral assessment of executive functions for self-regulating levels of language in reading brain. *Journal of Nature and Science, 3*(11).

Berridge, K. C. & Kringelbach, M. L. (2013). Neuroscience of affect: Brain mechanisms of pleasure and displeasure. *Current Opinion in Neurobiology, 23*(3), 294–303.

Berwick, R. C. & Chomsky, N. (2015). *Why only us: Language and evolution*. Cambridge, MA: MIT Press.

Bialystok, E. & Poarch, G. J. (2014). Language experience changes language and cognitive ability. *Zeitschrift für Erziehungswissenschaft, 17*(3), 433–446.

Binder, J. R., Frost, J. A., Hammeke, T. A., Cox, R. W., Rao, S. M., & Prieto, T. (1997). Human brain language areas identified by functional magnetic resonance imaging. *Journal of Neuroscience, 17*(1), 353–362.

Bishop, C. M. (1995). *Neural networks for pattern recognition*. Oxford, UK: Oxford University Press.

Bishop, J. L. & Verleger, M. A. (2013). The flipped classroom: A survey of the research. *ASEE National Conference Proceedings, 30*(9), 1–18.

Blanke, O. (2012). Multisensory brain mechanisms of bodily self-consciousness. *Nature Reviews Neuroscience, 13*(8), 556.

Block, R. A. (2014). *Cognitive models of psychological time*. London, UK: Psychology Press.

Bloom, B. S. (1956). *Taxonomy of educational objectives, Vol. 1: Cognitive domain*. New York: McKay.

Bloom, B. S. (1968). Learning for mastery. Instruction and curriculum. Regional Education Laboratory for the Carolinas and Virginia, topical papers and reprints. *Evaluation Comment, 1*(2), n2.

Boula, J., Morgan, K., Morrissey, C., & Shore, R. (2017). How do students understand new ideas? In response to the Deans for Impact Report (DFI). *Journal of Applied Educational and Policy Research, 3*(1), 5-11.

Bracci, S. & de Beeck, H. O. (2016). Dissociations and associations between shape and category representations in the two visual pathways. *Journal of Neuroscience, 36*(2), 432–444.

Brattico, E., Bogert, B., Alluri, V., Tervaniemi, M., Eerola, T., & Jacobsen, T. (2015). It's sad but I like it: The neural dissociation between musical emotions and liking in experts and laypersons. *Frontiers in Human Neuroscience, 9*, 676.

Brauer, J., Anwander, A., & Friederici, A. D. (2011). Neuroanatomical prerequisites for language functions in the maturing brain. *Cerebral Cortex, 21*(2), 459–466.

Brooks-Gunn, J., Burchinal, M. R., Espinosa, L. M., Gormley, W. T., Ludwig, J., Magnuson, K. A., . . . & Zaslow, M. J. (2013). *Investing in our future: The evidence base on preschool education* (Vol. 9). Washington, D.C.: Society for Research in Child Development and Foundation for Child Development.

Brooks, L. & Miller, A. (1979). A comparison of explicit and implicit knowledge of an alphabet. In P. A. Kolers, M. E. Wrols , & H. Bouma (Eds.), *Processing of visible language* (pp. 391–401). New York: Springer US.

Brophy, J. E. (2013). *Motivating students to learn*. London, UK: Routledge.

Bruce, C. D., & Hawes, Z. (2015). The role of 2D and 3D mental rotation in mathematics for young children: What is it? Why does it matter? And what can we do about it? *ZDM, 47*(3), 331–343.

Bruner, J. (1960). *The process of education*. Cambridge, MA: Harvard University Press.

Budd, M. J., Paulmann, S., Barry, C., & Clahsen, H. (2013). Brain potentials during language production in children and adults: An ERP study of the English past tense. *Brain and Language, 127*(3), 345–355.

Bueti, D., & Walsh, V. (2009). The parietal cortex and the representation of time, space, number and other magnitudes. *Philosophical Transactions of the Royal Society of London B: Biological Sciences, 364*(1525), 1831-1840.

Bugden, S., Price, G. R., McLean, D. A., & Ansari, D. (2012). The role of the left intraparietal sulcus in the relationship between symbolic number processing and children's arithmetic competence. *Developmental Cognitive Neuroscience, 2*(4), 448–457.

Bullmore, E. & Sporns, O. (2012). The economy of brain network organization. *Nature Reviews Neuroscience, 13*(5), 336–349.

Burr, D. C., Ross, J., Binda, P., & Morrone, M. C. (2010). Saccades compress space, time and number. *Trends in Cognitive Sciences, 14*(12), 528–533.

Burr, D. & Morrone, C. (2006). Time perception: space–time in the brain. *Current Biology, 16*(5), R171–R173.

Bus, A. G., Van Ijzendoorn, M. H., & Pellegrini, A. D. (1995). Joint book reading makes for success in learning to read: A meta-analysis on intergenerational transmission of literacy. *Review of Educational Research, 65*(1), 1–21.

Butterworth, B. (2005). The development of arithmetical abilities. *Journal of Child Psychology and Psychiatry, 46*(1), 3-18.

Butterworth, B., Varma, S., & Laurillard, D. (2011). Dyscalculia: from brain to education. *Science, 332*(6033), 1049–1053.

Byrge, L., Sporns, O., & Smith, L. B. (2014). Developmental process emerges from extended brain–body–behavior networks. *Trends in Cognitive Sciences, 18*(8), 395–403.

Callaghan, B., & Fifer, W. P. (2017). Perinatal attention, memory and learning during sleep. *Enfance*, (3), 349-361.

Campbell, A. & Groundwater-Smith, S. (Eds.). (2013). *Connecting inquiry and professional learning in education: International perspectives and practical solutions.* London, UK: Routledge.

Campbell, J. I. (Ed.). (2005). *Handbook of mathematical cognition.* London, UK: Psychology Press.

Cao, F., Kim, S. Y., Liu, Y., & Liu, L. (2014). Similarities and differences in brain activation and functional connectivity in first and second language reading: Evidence from Chinese learners of English. *Neuropsychologia, 63*, 275–284.

Cappa, S. F. (2012). Imaging semantics and syntax. *NeuroImage, 61*(2), 427–431.

Carlson, T. A., Ritchie, J. B., Kriegeskorte, N., Durvasula, S., & Ma, J. (2014). Reaction time for object categorization is predicted by representational distance. *Journal of Cognitive Neuroscience, 26*(1), 132–142.

Carreiras, M., Monahan, P. J., Lizarazu, M., Duñabeitia, J. A., & Molinaro, N. (2015). Numbers are not like words: different pathways for literacy and numeracy. *Neuroimage, 118*, 79–89.

Carreiras, M., Quiñones, I., Hernández-Cabrera, J. A., & Duñabeitia, J. A. (2014). Orthographic coding: brain activation for letters, symbols, and digits. *Cerebral Cortex, 25*(12), 4748–4760.

Casasanto, D. (2014). Bodily relativity. In L. Shapiro (Ed.), *Routledge handbook of embodied cognition* (pp. 108–117). London, UK: Routledge.

Cassia, V. M., Picozzi, M., Girelli, L., & de Hevia, M. D. (2012). Increasing magnitude counts more: Asymmetrical processing of ordinality in 4-month-old infants. *Cognition, 124*(2), 183–193.

Castelli, D. M., & Hillman, C. H. (2012). Physical activity, cognition, and school performance: from neurons to neighborhoods. In A. L. Meyer & T. P. Gullotta (Eds.), *Physical activity across the lifespan* (pp. 41–63). New York: Springer.

Cavina-Pratesi, C., Kentridge, R. W., Heywood, C. A., & Milner, A. D. (2010). Separate channels for processing form, texture, and color: evidence from fMRI adaptation and visual object agnosia. *Cerebral Cortex, 20*(10), 2319–2332.

Center for the Developing Child. (2018). *Serve and return.* Cambridge, MA: Harvard University. Downloaded 21 June 2018 from https://developingchild.harvard.edu/?s=serve+and+return

Chafee, M. V., & Crowe, D. A. (2017). Implicit and explicit learning mechanisms meet in monkey prefrontal cortex. *Neuron, 96*(2), 256-258.

Chang, H. C., Grossberg, S., & Cao, Y. (2014). Where's Waldo? How perceptual, cognitive, and emotional brain processes cooperate during learning to categorize and find desired objects in a cluttered scene. *Frontiers in Integrative Neuroscience, 8*, 1-46. DOI: https://doi.org/10.3389/fnint.2014.00043

Chemero, A. (2011). *Radical embodied cognitive science.* Cambridge, MA: MIT Press.

Cheng, R. K., Tipples, J., Narayanan, N. S., & Meck, W. H. (2016). Clock speed as a window into dopaminergic control of emotion and time perception. *Timing & Time Perception, 4*(1), 99–122.

Chesney, D. L., McNeil, N. M., Matthews, P. G., Byrd, C. E., Petersen, L. A., Wheeler, M. C., . . . & Dunwiddie, A. E. (2014). Organization matters: Mental organization of addition knowledge relates to understanding math equivalence in symbolic form. *Cognitive Development, 30*, 30–46.

Chevalier, N., Kurth, S., Doucette, M. R., Wiseheart, M., Deoni, S. C., Dean III, D. C., . . . & LeBourgeois, M. K. (2015). Myelination is associated with processing speed in early childhood: Preliminary insights. *PloS One, 10*(10), e0139897.

Chipman, S. F., & Segal, J. W. (2013). Higher cognitive goals for education: An introduction. *Thinking and Learning Skills, 2*, 1–18.

Chomsky, N. (1967). Recent contributions to the theory of innate ideas. In R. S. Cohen & M. W. Wartofsky (Eds.), *A portrait of twenty-five years* (pp. 31–40). Amsterdam, Netherlands: Springer.

Christie, S. & Gentner, D. (2014). Language helps children succeed on a classic analogy task. *Cognitive Science, 38*(2), 383–397.

Cichy, R. M., Pantazis, D., & Oliva, A. (2014). Resolving human object recognition in space and time. *Nature Neuroscience, 17*(3), 455–462.

Ciesielski, T. H., Aldrich, M. C., Marsit, C. J., Hiatt, R. A., & Williams, S. M. (2017). Transdisciplinary approaches enhance the production of translational knowledge. *Translational Research, 182*, 123–134.

Clements, D.H. (2011). Learning trajectories for primary grades mathematics. Pre-publication document for Early childhood mathematics learning. In F. K. Lester, Jr. (Ed.), *Second handbook of research on mathematics teaching and learning.* New York: Information Age Publishing. Downloaded 4 August 2018 from https://eclass.uowm.gr/modules/document/file.php/NURED221/%CE%AC%CE%BB%CE%BB%CE%BF%20%CF%85%CE%BB%CE%B9%CE%BA%CF%8C/building_blocks_learning_trajectories.pdfa

Clements, D. H. & Sarama, J. (2014). *Learning and teaching early math: The learning trajectories approach.* New York: Routledge.

Clements, D. H., Sarama, J., & DiBiase, A. M. (2003). *Engaging young children in mathematics: Standards for early childhood mathematics education.* Abingdon-on-Thames, UK: Routledge.

Cohen, M. A., Alvarez, G. A., Nakayama, K., & Konkle, T. (2017). Visual search for object categories is predicted by the representational architecture of high-level visual cortex. *Journal of Neurophysiology, 117*(1), 388–402.

Common Core State Standards Initiative (CCSI). (2011). *English language arts standards.* Retrieved March 28, 2018 from http://www.corestandards.org/ELA-Literacy/RL/11-12/4/

Commons, M. L., & Chen, S. J. (2014). Advances in the model of hierarchical complexity (MHC). *Behavioral Development Bulletin, 19*(4), 37.

Commons, M. L., Trudeau, E. J., Stein, S. A., Richards, F. A., & Krause, S. R. (1998). Hierarchical complexity of tasks shows the existence of developmental stages. *Developmental Review, 18*(3), 237–278.

Conroy, J., Hulme, M., & Menter, I. (2013). Developing a 'clinical' model for teacher education. *Journal of Education for Teaching, 39*(5), 557-573.

Conway, B. R. & Rehding, A. (2013). Neuroaesthetics and the trouble with beauty. *PLoS Biology, 11*(3), e1001504.

Correa, J., Nunes, T., & Bryant, P. (1998). Young children's understanding of division: The relationship between division terms in a noncomputational task. *Journal of Educational Psychology, 90*, 321–329.

Costa, A. L. & Kallick, B. (2009). *Habits of mind across the curriculum: Practical and creative strategies for teachers.* Alexandria, VA: ASCD.

Cozolino, L. (2014). *The neuroscience of human relationships: Attachment and the developing social brain* (Norton series on interpersonal neurobiology). New York: W. W. Norton & Company.

Curran, T. & Schacter, D. L. (2013). Implicit memory and perceptual brain mechanisms. In D. Herrmann, C. McEvoy, C. Hertzog, C. Hertel, & M. K. Johnson (Eds.), *Basic and applied memory research: Theory in context* (Vol. 1) (pp. 221–240). London, UK: Psychology Press.

Currie, J. & Thomas, D. (2012). Early test scores, school quality and SES: Long run effects on wage and employment outcomes: 35th anniversary retrospective. *Research in Labor Economics, 35*, 185–214.

Cushman, K. (2012). *Fires in the mind: What kids can tell us about motivation and mastery.* Hoboken, NJ: John Wiley & Sons.

d'Avila Garcez, A., Gori, M., Hitzler, P., & Lamb, L. C. (2015). Neural-symbolic learning and reasoning (Dagstuhl seminar 14381). In *Dagstuhl Reports from the* Dagstuhl Seminar 1481 "Neuronal-Symbolic Learning and Reasoning," September 14th to 19th, 2014. (Vol. 4, No. 9). Schloss Dagstuhl-Leibniz-Zentrum fuer Informatik. doi: 10.4230/DagRep.4.9.50

Darling-Hammond, L. (2000). Teacher quality and student achievement. *Education Policy Analysis Archives, 8*, 1.

Darling-Hammond, L. (2016). Research on teaching and teacher education and its influences on policy and practice. *Educational Researcher, 45*(2), 83–91.

Davies, A. (2003). *Nativism*. Hoboken, NJ: Blackwell Publishing Ltd.

Davis, B. G. (2009). *Tools for teaching.* Hoboken, NJ: John Wiley & Sons.

Dawson-Tunik, T. L., Commons, M., Wilson, M., & Fischer, K. W. (2005). The shape of development. *European Journal of Developmental Psychology, 2*(2), 163–195.

DeLoache, J. S. (1995). Early understanding and use of symbols: The model model. *Current Directions in Psychological Science, 4*(4), 109-113.

De Smedt, B., Noël, M. P., Gilmore, C., & Ansari, D. (2013a). How do symbolic and non-symbolic numerical magnitude processing skills relate to individual differences in children's mathematical skills? A review of evidence from brain and behavior. *Trends in Neuroscience and Education, 2*(2), 48–55. https://doi.org/10.1016/j.tine.2013.06.001

Deans For Impact. (2015). *The science of learning.* Austin, TX: Author.

Dehaene S. (1997). *The number sense: How the mind creates mathematics.* New York: Oxford University Press.

Dehaene, S. (2007). Symbols and quantities in parietal cortex: Elements of a mathematical theory of number representation and manipulation. In P. Haggard & Y. Rossetti (Eds.), *Sensorimotor foundations of higher cognition: Attention and performance XXII* (pp. 527–574). Oxford, UK: Oxford University Press.

Dehaene, S. (2009). Origins of mathematical intuitions. *Annals of the New York Academy of Sciences, 1156*(1), 232–259.

Dehaene, S. (2011). *The number sense: How the mind creates mathematics.* New York, NY: Oxford University Press.

Dehaene, S., Bossini, S., & Giraux, P. (1993). The mental representation of parity and number magnitude. *Journal of Experimental Psychology: General, 122*(3), 371.

Dehaene, S. & Cohen, L. (2011). The unique role of the visual word form area in reading. *Trends in Cognitive Sciences, 15*(6), 254–262.

Dehaene, S., Pegado, F., Braga, L. W., Ventura, P., Nunes Filho, G., Jobert, A., . . . & Cohen, L. (2010). How learning to read changes the cortical networks for vision and language. *Science, 330*(6009), 1359–1364.

Dehaene, S., Spelke, E., Pinel, P., Stanescu, R., & Tsivkin, S. (1999). Sources of mathematical thinking: Behavioral and brain-imaging evidence. *Science, 284*(5416), 970–974.

DeKeyser, R. (2008). Implicit and explicit learning. In C. J. Doughty and M. H. Long (Eds.), *The handbook of second language acquisition*, (pp.313-348). Hoboken, NJ: John Wiley & Sons.

Dekker, T. M. & Karmiloff-Smith, A. (2011). The dynamics of ontogeny: A neuroconstructivist perspective on genes, brains, cognition and behavior. *Progress in Brain Research, 189*, 23.

Dellacherie, D., Roy, M., Hugueville, L., Peretz, I., & Samson, S. (2011). The effect of musical experience on emotional self-reports and psychophysiological responses to dissonance. *Psychophysiology, 48*(3), 337–349.

Demblon, J., Bahri, M. A., & D'argembeau, A. (2016). Neural correlates of event clusters in past and future thoughts: How the brain integrates specific episodes with autobiographical knowledge. *NeuroImage, 127*, 257–266.

Dempsey, L. A., Cooper, R. J., Powell, S., Edwards, A., Lee, C. W., Brigadoi, S., . . . & Hebden, J. C. (2015, July). Whole-head functional brain imaging of neonates at cot-side using time-resolved diffuse optical tomography. In *European Conferences on Biomedical Optics* (pp. 953818–953818). Bellingham, WA: International Society for Optics and Photonics.

Dennett, D. C. (2013). Expecting ourselves to expect: The Bayesian brain as a projector. *Behavioral and Brain Sciences, 36*(3), 209–210.

Dennis, N. A., & Cabeza, R. (2011). Age-related differentiation of learning systems: an fMRI study of implicit and explicit learning. *Neurobiology of Aging, 32*(12), 2318.e17–e30.

Deoni, S. C., Mercure, E., Blasi, A., Gasston, D., Thomson, A., Johnson, M., . . . & Murphy, D. G. (2011). Mapping infant brain myelination with magnetic resonance imaging. *The Journal of Neuroscience, 31*(2), 784–791.

Dew, I. T., & Cabeza, R. (2011). The porous boundaries between explicit and implicit memory: Behavioral and neural evidence. *Annals of the New York Academy of Sciences, 1224*(1), 174–190.

Di Dio, C., Macaluso, E., & Rizzolatti, G. (2007). The golden beauty: Brain response to classical and Renaissance sculptures. *PloS One, 2*(11), e1201.

Diamond, A. (2012). Activities and programs that improve children's executive functions. *Current Directions in Psychological Science, 21*(5), 335–341.

DiCarlo, J. J., Zoccolan, D., & Rust, N. C. (2012). How does the brain solve visual object recognition? *Neuron, 73*(3), 415–434.

Dolan, P., Leat, D., Mazzoli Smith, L., Mitra, S., Todd, L., & Wall, K. (2013). Self-organised learning environments (SOLEs) in an English school: An example of transformative pedagogy? *Online Education Research Journal, 3*(11), 1-21. ISSN 2044-0294

Dolcos, F., Iordan, A. D., & Dolcos, S. (2011). Neural correlates of emotion–cognition interactions: A review of evidence from brain imaging investigations. *Journal of Cognitive Psychology, 23*(6), 669–694.

Domahs, F., Moeller, K., Huber, S., Willmes, K., & Nuerk, H. C. (2010). Embodied numerosity: Implicit hand-based representations influence symbolic number processing across cultures. *Cognition, 116*(2), 251–266.

Drake, S. M., Savage, M. J., Reid, J. L., Bernard, M.L., & Beres, J. (2015). *An exploration of the policy and practice of transdisciplinarity in the IB PYP Programme*. The Hague: International Baccalaureate Organisation.

Dunn, M., Greenhill, S. J., Levinson, S. C., & Gray, R. D. (2011). Evolved structure of language shows lineage-specific trends in word-order universals. *Nature, 473*(7345), 79–82.

Dweck, C. S. (2006). *Mindset: The new psychology of success*. New York: Random House.

Edelenbosch, R., Kupper, F., Krabbendam, L., & Broerse, J. E. (2015). Brain-based learning and educational neuroscience: Boundary work. *Mind, Brain, and Education, 9*(1), 40–49.

Eggen, P. D. & Kauchak, P. P. (1998). *Strategies for teacher: Teaching content and thinking skills* (6th ed.). Boston, MA: Pearson.

Eggen, P. D. & Kauchak, D. (2001). *Educational psychology: windows on classrooms* (5th ed). Upper Saddle River, NJ: Merrill-Prentice Hall.

Eisenberger, N. I. & Lieberman, M. D. (2004). Why rejection hurts: a common neural alarm system for physical and social pain. *Trends in Cognitive Sciences, 8*(7), 294–300.

Eisenberger, N. I., Taylor, S. E., Gable, S. L., Hilmert, C. J., & Lieberman, M. D. (2007). Neural pathways link social support to attenuated neuroendocrine stress responses. *Neuroimage, 35*(4), 1601–1612.

Eisner, E. (1979). *The educational imagination* (Vol. 103). New York: Macmillan.

Ekman, P. & Friesen, W. V. (2003). *Unmasking the face: A guide to recognizing emotions from facial clues.* Los Altos, CA: Malor Books.

Elkind, D. (2007). Preschool academics: Learning what comes naturally. *Exchange: The Early Childhood Leaders' Magazine since 1978, 178*, 6–8.

Elliott, M. A., Kelly, J., Friedel, J., Brodsky, J., & Mulcahy, P. (2015). The golden section as optical limitation. *PloS One, 10*(7), e0131045.

Emberson, L. L., Richards, J. E., & Aslin, R. N. (2015). Top-down modulation in the infant brain: Learning-induced expectations rapidly affect the sensory cortex at 6 months. *Proceedings of the National Academy of Sciences, 112*(31), 9585–9590.

Emery, A., Sanders, M., Anderman, L. H., & Yu, S. L. (2017). When mastery goals meet mastery learning: Administrator, teacher, and student perceptions. *Journal of Experimental Education, 86*(3), 419–441.

Emmorey, K. & Reilly, J. S. (2013). *Language, gesture, and space.* East Sussex, UK: Psychology Press.

Enrici, I., Adenzato, M., Cappa, S., Bara, B. G., & Tettamanti, M. (2011). Intention processing in communication: A common brain network for language and gestures. *Journal of Cognitive Neuroscience, 23*(9), 2415–2431.

Erickson, K. I., Hillman, C. H., & Kramer, A. F. (2015). Physical activity, brain, and cognition. *Current Opinion in Behavioral Sciences, 4*, 27–32.

Ericsson, K. A., Prietula, M. J., & Cokely, E. T. (2007). The making of an expert. *Harvard Business Review, 85*(7/8), 114.

Esquith, R. (2007). *Teach like your hair's on fire: The methods and madness inside room 56.* New York: Penguin.

Fairhurst, M. T., Janata, P., & Keller, P. E. (2013). Being and feeling in sync with an adaptive virtual partner: Brain mechanisms underlying dynamic cooperativity. *Cerebral Cortex, 23*(11), 2592–2600.

Fan, C., Chen, S., Zhang, L., Qi, Z., Jin, Y., Wang, Q., . . . & Luo, W. (2015). N170 changes reflect competition between faces and identifiable characters during early visual processing. *NeuroImage, 110*, 32–38.

Fedorenko, E., & Thompson-Schill, S. L. (2014). Reworking the language network. *Trends in Cognitive Sciences, 18*(3), 120–126.

Fehr, T., Code, C., & Herrmann, M. (2007). Common brain regions underlying different arithmetic operations as revealed by conjunct fMRI–BOLD activation. *Brain Research, 1172*, 93–102.

Fengler, A., Meyer, L., & Friederici, A. D. (2016). How the brain attunes to sentence processing: Relating behavior, structure, and function. *NeuroImage, 129*, 268–278.

Fera, F., Passamonti, L., Herzallah, M. M., Myers, C. E., Veltri, P., Morganti, G., . . . & Gluck, M. A. (2014). Hippocampal BOLD response during category learning predicts subsequent performance on transfer generalization. *Human Brain Mapping, 35*(7), 3122-3131.

Ferguson, S. (2015). Developing place value understanding. *Prime Number, 30*(1), 10.

Ferman, S. & Karni, A. (2010). No childhood advantage in the acquisition of skill in using an artificial language rule. *PloS One, 5*(10), e13648.

Feuerstein, R., & Jensen, M. R. (1980). Instrumental enrichment: Theoretical basis, goals, and instruments. *The Educational Forum, 44*(4), 401–423.

Field, S. (1992). The effect of temperature on crime. *The British Journal of Criminology, 32*(3), 340–351.

Fingelkurts, A. A., Fingelkurts, A. A., & Neves, C. F. (2010). Natural world physical, brain operational, and mind phenomenal space–time. *Physics of Life Reviews, 7*(2), 195–249.

Fink, L. D. (2013). *Creating significant learning experiences: An integrated approach to designing college courses.* Hoboken, NJ: John Wiley & Sons.

Fischer, K. W. (1980). A theory of cognitive development: The control and construction of hierarchies of skills. *Psychological Review, 87*(6), 477–531.

Fischer, K. W. (2008). Dynamic cycles of cognitive and brain development: Measuring growth in mind, brain, and education. *The Educated Brain*, 127–150.

Fischer, K. W. & Yan, Z. (2002). The development of Dynamic Skill Theory. In D. J. Lewkowicz & R. Lickliter (Eds.), *Conceptions of development: Lessons from the laboratory* (pp.279–312). London, UK: Psychology Press.

Fischer, K. W. & Rose, L. T. (2001). Webs of skills: How students learn. *Educational Leadership, 59*(3), 6–12.

Fischer, K. W., Rose, L. T., & Rose, S. P. (2007). Growth cycles of mind and brain: Analyzing developmental pathways of learning disorders. In K. W. Fischer, J. H. Bernstein, & M. H. Immordino-Yang (Eds.), *Mind, brain, and education in reading disorders*, (pp.101–123). New York: Cambridge University Press.

Fischer, K. W., Yan, Z., & Stewart, J. (2003). Adult cognitive development: Dynamics in the developmental web. In *Handbook of Developmental Psychology*, (pp.491–516). Thousand Oaks, CA: Sage.

Fisher, D., Frey, N., Quaglia, R. J., Smith, D., & Lande, L. L. (2017). *Engagement by design: Creating learning environments where students thrive.* Thousand Oaks, CA: Corwin Press.

Flegal, K. E., Marín-Gutiérrez, A., Ragland, J. D., & Ranganath, C. (2014). Brain mechanisms of successful recognition through retrieval of semantic context. *Journal of Cognitive Neuroscience, 26*(8), 1694–1704.

Fransson, P., Åden, U., Blennow, M., & Lagercrantz, H. (2011). The functional architecture of the infant brain as revealed by resting-state fMRI. *Cerebral Cortex, 21*(1), 145–154.

Frick, A., Hansen, M. A., & Newcombe, N. S. (2013). Development of mental rotation in 3- to 5-year-old children. *Cognitive Development, 28*(4), 386–399.

Friederici, A. D. (2012). Language development and the ontogeny of the dorsal pathway. *Frontiers in Evolutionary Neuroscience, 4*(3), 1–7 .

Friederici, A. D. & Gierhan, S. M. (2013). The language network. *Current Opinion in Neurobiology, 23*(2), 250–254.

Friedrich, R. M. & Friederici, A. D. (2013). Mathematical logic in the human brain: Semantics. *PloS One, 8*(1), e53699.

Fritz, T. H., Renders, W., Müller, K., Schmude, P., Leman, M., Turner, R., & Villringer, A. (2013). Anatomical differences in the human inferior colliculus relate to the perceived valence of musical consonance and dissonance. *European Journal of Neuroscience, 38*(7), 3099–3105.

Gagné, R. M. (1962). The acquisition of knowledge. *Psychological Review, 69*, 355–365.

Gagné, R. M. (1965). *The conditions of learning.* New York: Holt, Rinehart and Winston.

Gagné, R. M. (1968). Presidential address of division 15 learning hierarchies. *Educational Psychologist, 6*(1), 1–9.

Gagné, R. M. (1973). Learning and instructional sequence. *Review of Research in Education*, 3–33.

Geist, K., Geist, E. A., & Kuznik, K. (2012). The patterns of music. *Young Children, 2*, 75.

Georgieva, S., Peeters, R., Kolster, H., Todd, J. T., & Orban, G. A. (2009). The processing of three-dimensional shape from disparity in the human brain. *Journal of Neuroscience, 29*(3), 727–742.

Gerlach, C. & Marques, J. F. (2014). Visual complexity exerts opposing effects on object categorization and identification. *Visual Cognition, 22*(6), 751–769.

Gerou, T., & Lusk, L. (1996). *Essential dictionary of music notation*. Van Nuys, (Los Angeles), CA: Alfred Publishing Co.,

Gibbs, P. (Ed.). (2015). *Transdisciplinary professional learning and practice*. New York: Springer.

Gilmore, C., Attridge, N., De Smedt, B., & Inglis, M. (2014). Measuring the approximate number system in children: Exploring the relationships among different tasks. *Learning and Individual Differences, 29*, 50–58.

Goffin, C. & Ansari, D. (2016). Beyond magnitude: Judging ordinality of symbolic number is unrelated to magnitude comparison and independently relates to individual differences in arithmetic. *Cognition, 150*, 68–76.

Golestani, N. (2014). Brain structural correlates of individual differences at low- to high-levels of the language processing hierarchy: A review of new approaches to imaging research. *International Journal of Bilingualism, 18*(1), 6–34.

Goodfellow, I., Bengio, Y., Courville, A., & Bengio, Y. (2016). *Deep learning* (Vol. 1). Cambridge, MA: MIT press.

Gopnik, A. & Wellman, H. M. (2012). Reconstructing constructivism: Causal models, Bayesian learning mechanisms, and the theory. *Psychological Bulletin, 138*(6), 1085.

Grabner, R. H., Ansari, D., Koschutnig, K., Reishofer, G., Ebner, F., & Neuper, C. (2009). To retrieve or to calculate? Left angular gyrus mediates the retrieval of arithmetic facts during problem solving. *Neuropsychologia, 47*(2), 604–608.

Grafton, S. T., Hazeltine, E., & Ivry, R. (1995). Functional mapping of sequence learning in normal humans. *Journal of Cognitive Neuroscience, 7*(4), 497–510.

Gray, R. L. (2013). *Using brain-based strategies to increase motivation, cognition and long-term memory of biology concepts*. (Master's dissertation). Bozeman, MT: Montana State University.

Gray, S. A., & Reeve, R. A. (2016). Number-specific and general cognitive markers of preschoolers' math ability profiles. *Journal of Experimental Child Psychology, 147*, 1-21.

Greenberg, J. H. (1966). *Language universals: With special reference to feature hierarchies*. Berlin, Germany: Mouton.

Griffiths, J. D., Marslen-Wilson, W. D., Stamatakis, E. A., & Tyler, L. K. (2012). Functional organization of the neural language system: Dorsal and ventral pathways are critical for syntax. *Cerebral Cortex*, bhr386.

Grusec, J. E. & Hastings, P. D. (Eds.). (2014). *Handbook of socialization: Theory and research*. New York: Guilford Publications.

Guare, J. (1990). *Six degrees of separation: A play*. New York: Vintage.

Güçlü, U., Thielen, J., Hanke, M., van Gerven, M., & van Gerven, M. A. (2016). Brains on beats. In D. Schweizer (Ed.), *Advances in neural information processing systems* (pp. 2101–2109). Cambridge, MA: MIT Press.

Guerriero, S. (Ed.) (2017). *Pedagogical knowledge and the changing nature of the teaching profession*. Paris, France: OECD Publishing. DOI; http://dx.doi.org/10.1787/9789264270695-en

Gullick, M. M. & Wolford, G. (2014). Brain systems involved in arithmetic with positive versus negative numbers. *Human Brain Mapping, 35*(2), 539–551.

Gullick, M. M., Sprute, L. A., & Temple, E. (2011). Individual differences in working memory, nonverbal IQ, and mathematics achievement and brain mechanisms associated with symbolic and nonsymbolic number processing. *Learning and Individual Differences, 21*(6), 644–654.

Guskey, T. R. (2007). Closing achievement gaps: Revisiting Benjamin S. Bloom's "Learning for mastery." *Journal of Advanced Academics, 19*(1), 8–31.

Guskey, T. R. (2010). Lessons of mastery learning. *Educational Leadership, 68*(2), 52.

Guskey, T. R., & Pigott, T. D. (1988). Research on group-based mastery learning programs: A meta-analysis. *The Journal of Educational Research, 81*(4), 197–216.

Hadjikhani, N., Zürcher, N. R., Rogier, O., Ruest, T., Hippolyte, L., Ben-Ari, Y., & Lemonnier, E. (2015). Improving emotional face perception in autism with diuretic bumetanide: A proof-of-concept behavioral and functional brain imaging pilot study. *Autism, 19*(2), 149–157.

Haken, H. (2013). *Principles of brain functioning: A synergetic approach to brain activity, behavior and cognition* (Vol. 67). Berlin, Germany: Springer Science & Business Media.

Halinen, I. (2015). *What is going on in Finland?–Curriculum Reform 2016.* [Blog] *25.* Finnish National Agency For Education. Retrieved March 28, 2018 from http://oph.fi/english/current_issues/101/0/what_is_going_on_in_finland_curriculum_reform_2016.

Handjaras, G., Bernardi, G., Benuzzi, F., Nichelli, P. F., Pietrini, P., & Ricciardi, E. (2015). A topographical organization for action representation in the human brain. *Human Brain Mapping, 36*(10), 3832–3844.

Hannula, M. M., & Lehtinen, E. (2005). Spontaneous focusing on numerosity and mathematical skills of young children. *Learning and Instruction, 15*(3), 237-256.

Harris, I. M. & Miniussi, C. (2003). Parietal lobe contribution to mental rotation demonstrated with rTMS. *Journal of Cognitive Neuroscience, 15*(3), 315–323.

Harrison, A. G. & Croll, R.K. (2007). *Using analogies in middle and secondary school science classrooms: The FAR Guide-An interesting way to teach with analogies.* Thousand Oaks, CA: Corwin.

Hart, B. & Risley, T. R. (2003). The early catastrophe: The 30 million word gap by age 3. *American Educator, 27*(1), 4–9.

Hartline, D.K. (2008). What is myelin? *Neuron Glia Biology, 4,* 153–163 doi:10.1017/S1740925X09990263.

Hasson, U., Chen, J., & Honey, C. J. (2015). Hierarchical process memory: Memory as an integral component of information processing. *Trends in Cognitive Sciences, 19*(6), 304–313.

Hattie, J. A. (2009). *Visible learning: A synthesis of 800+ meta-analyses on achievement.* Abingdon, UK: Routledge.

Hattie, J. (2012). *Visible learning for teachers: Maximizing impact on learning.* London, UK: Routledge.

Hattie, J., & Anderman, E. M. (Eds.). (2013). *International guide to student achievement.* London, UK: Routledge.

Hauser, M. D., Chomsky, N., & Fitch, W. T. (2002). The faculty of language: What is it, who has it, and how did it evolve?. *Science, 298*(5598), 1569–1579.

Herrington, J., Reeves, T. C., & Oliver, R. (2014). Authentic learning environments. In M. J. Spector, M. D. Merrill, J. Elen, & M. J. Bishop (Eds.), *Handbook of research on educational communications and technology* (pp. 401–412). New York: Springer.

Hickman, H. (1980). *Miscellanea musicologica (Vies et travaux).* Organization des antiquites de l'Egypte, Service des musees. ISBN 977-02-0334-3. ISBN 978-977-02-0334-7.

Ho, M. W. (2014). Golden music of the brain. *Science in Society, 62,* 1-8.

Hoff, E. (2013a). Interpreting the early language trajectories of children from low-SES and language minority homes: Implications for closing achievement gaps. *Developmental Psychology, 49*(1), 4.

Hoffman, E. M. (2014). Faculty and student relationships: Context matters. *College Teaching, 62*(1), 13–19.

Holland, D., Chang, L., Ernst, T. M., Curran, M., Buchthal, S. D., Alicata, D., . . . & Dale, A. M. (2014). Structural growth trajectories and rates of change in the first 3 months of infant brain development. *JAMA Neurology, 71*(10), 1266–1274.

Holland, J. L. (1973). *Diagnostic scheme for specifying vocational assistance.* Baltimore, MD: Center for the Study of Social Organization of Schools, Johns Hopkins University.

Holland, J. L. (2014). *Train the brain to hear: Understanding and treating auditory processing disorder, dyslexia, dysgraphia, dyspraxia, short term memory, executive function, comprehension, and ADD/ADHD.* Irvine, CA: Universal-Publishers.

Holloway, I. D., Battista, C., Vogel, S. E., & Ansari, D. (2013). Semantic and perceptual processing of number symbols: evidence from a cross-linguistic fMRI adaptation study. *Journal of Cognitive Neuroscience, 25*(3), 388–400.

Holm, L. & Madison, G. (2013). Whenever next: Hierarchical timing of perception and action. *Behavioral and Brain Sciences, 36*(3), 217–218.

Horikawa, T. & Kamitani, Y. (2017). Generic decoding of seen and imagined objects using hierarchical visual features. *Nature Communications, 8,* 15037.

Horvath, J. C., & Donoghue, G. M. (2016). A bridge too far–revisited: Reframing Bruer's neuroeducation argument for modern science of learning practitioners. *Frontiers in Psychology, 7,* 377.

Hsieh, L. T. & Ranganath, C. (2015). Cortical and subcortical contributions to sequence retrieval: Schematic coding of temporal context in the neocortical recollection network. *NeuroImage, 121,* 78–90.

Hubers, F., Snijders, T. M., & De Hoop, H. (2016). How the brain processes violations of the grammatical norm: An fMRI study. *Brain and Language, 163,* 22–31.

Hudak, G. (Ed.). (2014). *Labeling: Pedagogy and politics.* London, UK: Routledge.

Hulshof, H. & Verloop, N. (2002). The use of analogies in language teaching: Representing the content of teachers' practical knowledge. *Journal of Curriculum Studies, 34*(1), 77–90.

Hunt, J. H. (2011). *The effects of a ratio-based teaching sequence on performance in fraction equivalency for students with mathematics disabilities.* (Doctoral dissertation). Orlando, FL: University of Central Florida.

Huth, A. G., Nishimoto, S., Vu, A. T., & Gallant, J. L. (2012). A continuous semantic space describes the representation of thousands of object and action categories across the human brain. *Neuron, 76*(6), 1210–1224.

Immordino-Yang, M. H. (2015). *Emotions, learning, and the brain: Exploring the educational implications of affective neuroscience* (The Norton Series on the Social Neuroscience of Education). New York: W. W. Norton & Company.

Immordino-Yang, M. H. (2016). Embodied brains, social minds: Toward a cultural neuroscience of social emotion. In *The Oxford handbook of cultural neuroscience, Part II: Cultural neuroscience of emotion,* (pp. 129–142). London, UK: Oxford University Press.

Inagaki, T. K. (2014). *Neurobiological bases of social connection.* (Doctoral dissertation). Los Angeles, CA: University of California at Los Angeles.

Ischebeck, A., Schocke, M., & Delazer, M. (2009). The processing and representation of fractions within the brain: An fMRI investigation. *NeuroImage, 47*(1), 403–413.

Ishai, A. (2011). Art compositions elicit distributed activation in the human brain. In A.P. Shimamura & S.E. Palmer (Eds.), *Aesthetic science: Connecting minds, brains, and experience* (pp. 337–355). New York: Oxford University Press.

Israel, S. (2016). Toward a mechanistic understanding of how variation in the oxytocin receptor gene shapes individual differences in brain and social behavior. *Biological Psychiatry, 80*(2), e7–e9.

Istók, E., Brattico, E., Jacobsen, T., Ritter, A., & Tervaniemi, M. (2013). 'I love Rock 'n'Roll'—Music genre preference modulates brain responses to music. *Biological Psychology, 92*(2), 142–151.

Izard, V., Streri, A., & Spelke, E. S. (2014). Toward exact number: Young children use one-to-one correspondence to measure set identity but not numerical equality. *Cognitive Psychology, 72*, 27-53.

Jaber, M. Y. (Ed.). (2016). *Learning curves: Theory, models, and applications.* Boca Raton, FL: CRC Press.

Jacob, S. N., Vallentin, D., & Nieder, A. (2012). Relating magnitudes: The brain's code for proportions. *Trends in Cognitive Sciences, 16*(3), 157–166.

Jain, A. K. & Li, S. Z. (2011). *Handbook of face recognition.* New York: Springer.

Jeong, J. H., Linderholm, H. W., Woo, S. H., Folland, C., Kim, B. M., Kim, S. J., & Chen, D. (2013). Impacts of snow initialization on subseasonal forecasts of surface air temperature for the cold season. *Journal of Climate, 26*(6), 1956–1972.

Jones, H. L., & Russell, J. M. (1979). Hierarchical learning paradigm. *Journal of Research in Science Teaching, 16*(6), 489–499.

Jukes, I. Dosaj, A., Macdonald, B. (2000). *NetSavvy: Building information literacy in the classroom* (2nd ed.). Thousand Oaks, CA: Corwin.

Kalénine, S., Shapiro, A. D., Flumini, A., Borghi, A. M., & Buxbaum, L. J. (2014). Visual context modulates potentiation of grasp types during semantic object categorization. *Psychonomic Bulletin & Review, 21*(3), 645–651.

Karinthy, K. (1929). *Chains (Láncszemek).* Budapest, Hungary: Author.

Karmiloff-Smith, A. (2006). The tortuous route from genes to behavior: A neuroconstructivist approach. *Cognitive, Affective, & Behavioral Neuroscience, 6*(1), 9–17.

Karmiloff–Smith, A. (2009). Preaching to the converted? From constructivism to neuroconstructivism. *Child Development Perspectives, 3*(2), 99–102.

Karmiloff-Smith, A. (2012a). Brain: The neuroconstructivist approach. *Neurodevelopmental disorders across the lifespan: A neuroconstructivist approach,* (pp. 37–58). Oxford, UK: Oxford University Press.

Karmiloff-Smith, A. (2012b). From constructivism to neuroconstructivism: Activity-dependent structuring of the human brain. *After Piaget, 1*(1), 1-14.

Karmiloff-Smith, A. & Farran, E. K. (2011). Future theoretical and empirical directions within a neuroconstructivist framework. In E. K, Farran & A. Karmiloff-Smith (Eds.), *Neurodevelopmental disorders across the lifespan: A neuroconstructivist approach,* (pp. 363–372). Oxford, UK: Oxford University Press.

Kaufmann, L., Vogel, S. E., Starke, M., Kremser, C., & Schocke, M. (2009). Numerical and non-numerical ordinality processing in children with and without developmental dyscalculia: Evidence from fMRI. *Cognitive Development, 24*(4), 486–494.

Kelly, S., Healey, M., Özyürek, A., & Holler, J. (2015). The processing of speech, gesture, and action during language comprehension. *Psychonomic Bulletin & Review, 22*(2), 517–523.

Kemmerer, D. (2017). Categories of object concepts across languages and brains: The relevance of nominal classification systems to cognitive neuroscience. *Language, Cognition and Neuroscience, 32*(4), 401–424.

Kennerley, H. & Kischka, U. (2013). The brain, neuropsychology and dissociation. In *Cognitive behavioural approaches to the understanding and treatment of dissociation,* (pp.67-80). London, UK: Routledge.

Kepinska, O., de Rover, M., Caspers, J., & Schiller, N. O. (2017). Whole-brain functional connectivity during acquisition of novel grammar: Distinct functional networks depend on language learning abilities. *Behavioural Brain Research, 320*, 333–346.

Khaligh-Razavi, S. M., Henriksson, L., Kay, K., & Kriegeskorte, N. (2014). Explaining the hierarchy of visual representational geometries by remixing of features from many computational vision models. *BioRxiv*, 009936.

Kherif, F., Josse, G., & Price, C. J. (2010). Automatic top-down processing explains common left occipito-temporal responses to visual words and objects. *Cerebral Cortex, 21*(1), 103–114.

Kibbe, M. M. & Feigenson, L. (2015). Young children 'solve for x' using the Approximate Number System. *Developmental Science, 18*(1), 38–49.

Kidd, C., Piantadosi, S. T., & Aslin, R. N. (2012). The Goldilocks effect: Human infants allocate attention to visual sequences that are neither too simple nor too complex. *PloS One, 7*(5), e36399

Kirk, D. (2014). *Physical education and curriculum study: A critical introduction.* Oxon, UK: Routledge.

Klein, A., Starkey, P. (2004). Fostering preschool children's mathematical knowledge: Findings from the Berkeley math readiness project. In D. H. Clements, J. Sarama, & A. M. DiBiase (Eds.) *Engaging young children in mathematics: Standards for early childhood mathematics education* (pp.343–360). New York: Routledge.

Klein, E., Suchan, J., Moeller, K., Karnath, H. O., Knops, A., Wood, G., . . . & Willmes, K. (2014). Considering structural connectivity in the triple code model of numerical cognition: differential connectivity for magnitude processing and arithmetic facts. *Brain Structure and Function*, 1–17.

Kononowicz, T. W., Van Rijn, H., & Meck, W. H. (2016). Timing and time perception: A critical review of neural timing signatures before, during, and after the to-be-timed interval. *Sensation, Perception and Attention, 2*, 1–35.

Kornilaki, E., & Nunes, T. (2005). Generalising principles in spite of procedural differences: Children's understanding of division. *Cognitive Development, 20*(3), 388–406.

Kourtzi, Z., & Connor, C. E. (2011). Neural representations for object perception: Structure, category, and adaptive coding. *Annual Review of Neuroscience, 34*, 45–67.

Kovic, V., Plunkett, K., & Westermann, G. (2010). The shape of words in the brain. *Cognition, 114*(1), 19–28.

Kozhevnikov, M., Blazhenkova, O., & Becker, M. (2010). Trade-off in object versus spatial visualization abilities: Restriction in the development of visual-processing resources. *Psychologic Bulletin & Review, 17*(1), 29–35.

Koziol, L. F., Budding, D. E., & Chidekel, D. (2012). From movement to thought: Executive function, embodied cognition, and the cerebellum. *Cerebellum, 11*(2), 505–525

Krause, F., Lindemann, O., Toni, I., & Bekkering, H. (2014). Different brains process numbers differently: Structural bases of individual differences in spatial and nonspatial number representations. *Journal of Cognitive Neuroscience, 26*(4), 768–776.

Krishnan, S., Watkins, K. E., & Bishop, D. V. (2016). Neurobiological basis of language learning difficulties. *Trends in Cognitive Sciences, 20*(9), 701–714.

Kucian, K. (2017). The importance of central-visual perception disorders for dyslexia and dyscalculia. *Neuropediatrics, 48*(S 01), KSS20–04.

Kuhl, P. K. (2004). Early language acquisition: Cracking the speech code. *Nature Reviews Neuroscience, 5*(11), 831–843.

Kuhl, P. K. (2011). Early language learning and literacy: neuroscience implications for education. *Mind, Brain, and Education, 5*(3), 128–142.

Kuperberg, G. R., Wlotko, E. W., Riley, S. J., Zeitlin, M., & Cuhna-Lina, M. L. (2017). The brain dissociates between different levels of prediction during language comprehension. In *Cognitive Neuroscience Society meeting in San Francisco, CA (March 25-28, 2017).*

Kuuluvainen, S., Nevalainen, P., Sorokin, A., Mittag, M., Partanen, E., Putkinen, V., . . . & Kujala, T. (2014). The neural basis of sublexical speech and corresponding nonspeech processing: A combined EEG–MEG study. *Brain and Language, 130,* 19–32.

Lamm, C., Batson, C. D., & Decety, J. (2007). The neural substrate of human empathy: Effects of perspective-taking and cognitive appraisal. *Cognitive Neuroscience 19*(1), 42–58.

LeCun, Y., Bengio, Y., & Hinton, G. (2015). Deep learning. *Nature, 521*(7553), 436–444.

LeFevre, J. A. & Morris, J. (1999). More on the relation between division and multiplication in simple arithmetic: Evidence for mediation of division solutions via multiplication. *Memory & Cognition, 27*(5), 803–812.

Leibovich, T. & Henik, A. (2013). Magnitude processing in non-symbolic stimuli. *Frontiers in Psychology, 4* 375.

Leibovich, T., Katzin, N., Harel, M., & Henik, A. (2017). From "sense of number" to "sense of magnitude": The role of continuous magnitudes in numerical cognition. *Behavioral and Brain Sciences, 40* .

Lemov, D. (2010). *Teach like a champion: 49 techniques that put students on the path to college (K-12).* Hoboken, NJ: John Wiley & Sons.

Lenay, C. & Steiner, P. (2010). Beyond the internalism/externalism debate: the constitution of the space of perception. *Consciousness and Cognition, 19*(4), 938–952.

Lewis, G. & Poeppel, D. (2014). The role of visual representations during the lexical access of spoken words. *Brain and Language, 134,* 1–10.

Libertus, M. E. (2015). The role of intuitive approximation skills for school math abilities. *Mind, Brain, and Education, 9*(2), 112–120.

Lieberman, J. S., Kyle, C. T., Schedlbauer, A., Stokes, J., & Ekstrom, A. D. (2017). A tale of two temporal coding strategies: common and dissociable brain regions involved in recency versus associative temporal order retrieval strategies. *Journal of Cognitive Neuroscience, 29*(4),739–754.

Lin, Y. P., Wang, C. H., Jung, T. P., Wu, T. L., Jeng, S. K., Duann, J. R., & Chen, J. H. (2010). EEG-based emotion recognition in music listening. *IEEE Transactions on Biomedical Engineering, 57*(7), 1798–1806.

Linsen, S., Verschaffel, L., Reynvoet, B., & De Smedt, B. (2015). The association between numerical magnitude processing and mental versus algorithmic multi-digit subtraction in children. *Learning and Instruction, 35,* 42–50.

Lipko-Speed, A., Dunlosky, J., & Rawson, K. A. (2014). Does testing with feedback help grade-school children learn key concepts in science? *Journal of Applied Research in Memory and Cognition, 3*(3), 171–176.

Livio, M. (2008). *The golden ratio: The story of phi, the world's most astonishing number.* New York: Broadway Books.

Long, C., Li, J., Chen, A., Qiu, J., Chen, J., & Li, H. (2015). Event-related potential responses to letter-string comparison analogies. *Experimental Brain Research, 233*(5), 1563–1573.

Lourenco, S. F. & Longo, M. R. (2011). Origins and development of generalized magnitude representation. In S. Dehaene & E. Brannon (Eds.), *Space, time, and number in the brain: Searching for the foundations of mathematical thought* (pp. 225–244). New York: Academic Press.

Lowenberg Ball, D., Thames, M. H., & Phelps, G. (2008). Content knowledge for teaching what makes it special? *Journal of Teacher Education, 59*(5), 389–407.

Lowenberg Ball, D. (2014). *The work of teaching.* President of AERA defending need for specialized math teachers to Congress. Retrieved March 28, 2018 from https://www.youtube.com/watch?v=nrwDM4ejNqs

Lucio, R., Hunt, E., & Bornovalova, M. (2012). Identifying the necessary and sufficient number of risk factors for predicting academic failure. *Developmental Psychology, 48*(2), 422.

Luria, A. R. & Vygotsky, L. S. (1930). *Studies on the history of behavior.* Hillsdale, NJ: LEA.

Lyons, S. (2007). *Horace's Odes and the mystery of do-re-mi with full verse translation of the Odes.* Oxford: Aris & Phillips, 2007. ISBN 978-0-85668-790-7.

Lyons, I. M. & Ansari, D. (2015). Foundations of children's numerical and mathematical skills: The roles of symbolic and nonsymbolic representations of numerical magnitude. *Advances in Child Development and Behavior, 48*, 93–116.

Lyons, I. M. & Beilock, S. L. (2013). Ordinality and the nature of symbolic numbers. *Journal of Neuroscience, 33*(43), 17052–17061.

Lyons, I. M., Ansari, D., & Beilock, S. L. (2015). Qualitatively different coding of symbolic and non-symbolic numbers in the human brain. *Human Brain Mapping, 36*(2), 475–488.

MacInnis, D. J., Park, C. W., & Priester, J. W. (2014). *Handbook of brand relationships.* New York: Routledge.

Madec, S., Le Goff, K., Anton, J. L., Longcamp, M., Velay, J. L., Nazarian, B., . . . & Rey, A. (2016). Brain correlates of phonological recoding of visual symbols. *NeuroImage, 132*, 359–372.

Mahon, B. Z. & Caramazza, A. (2011). What drives the organization of object knowledge in the brain? *Trends in Cognitive Sciences, 15*(3), 97–103.

Marceau, K., Ram, N., Houts, R. M., Grimm, K. J., & Susman, E. J. (2011). Individual differences in boys' and girls' timing and tempo of puberty: Modeling development with nonlinear growth models. *Developmental Psychology, 47*(5), 1389.

Mareschal, D. (2007). *Neuroconstructivism: How the brain constructs cognition* (Vol. 1). Oxford, UK: Oxford University Press.

Mareschal, D. (2011). From NEOconstructivism to NEUROconstructivism. *Child Development Perspectives, 5*(3), 169–170.

Mareschal, D., Johnson, M. H., Sirois, S., Spratling, M., Thomas, M. S., & Westermann, G. (2007). *Neuroconstructivism-I: How the brain constructs cognition.* Oxford, UK: Oxford University Press.

Mareschal, D., Sirois, S., Westermann, G., & Johnson, M. H. (2007). *Neuroconstructivism Vol. 2: Perspectives and Prospects.* Oxford University Press.

Martin, A., Wiggs, C. L., Ungerleider, L. G., & Haxby, J. V. (1996). Neural correlates of category-specific knowledge. *Nature, 379*(6566), 649.

Marzilli, C. (2016). Concept analysis of value. *International Journal of Recent Advances in Multidisciplinary Research 3*(11), 1919–1921.

Matejko, A. A., & Ansari, D. (2015). Drawing connections between white matter and numerical and mathematical cognition: a literature review. *Neuroscience & Biobehavioral Reviews, 48*, 35–52.

Mathieu, R., Epinat-Duclos, J., Sigovan, M., Breton, A., Cheylus, A., Fayol, M., . . . & Prado, J. (2017). What's behind a "+" sign? Perceiving an arithmetic operator recruits brain circuits for spatial orienting. *Cerebral Cortex, 28*(5),1673–1684.

Matthews, W. J. (2015). Time perception: the surprising effects of surprising stimuli. *Journal of Experimental Psychology: General, 144*(1), 172.

Mazza, V. & Caramazza, A. (2011). Temporal brain dynamics of multiple object processing: the flexibility of individuation. *PloS One, 6*(2), e17453.

McClelland, M. M., Acock, A. C., & Morrison, F. J. (2006). The impact of kindergarten learning-related skills on academic trajectories at the end of elementary school. *Early Childhood Research Quarterly, 21*(4), 471-490.

McGaghie, W. C., Barsuk, J. H., & Wayne, D. B. (2017). The promise and challenge of mastery learning. *Advances in Medical Education and Practice, 8*, 393.

McGaghie, W. C., Issenberg, S. B., Barsuk, J. H., & Wayne, D. B. (2014). A critical review of simulation–based mastery learning with translational outcomes. *Medical Education, 48*(4), 375–385.

McManus, J. N., Li, W., & Gilbert, C. D. (2011). Adaptive shape processing in primary visual cortex. *Proceedings of the National Academy of Sciences, 108*(24), 9739–9746.

Mell, J. C., Howard, S. M., & Miller, B. L. (2003). Art and the brain The influence of frontotemporal dementia on an accomplished artist. *Neurology, 60*(10), 1707-1710.

Mills, D., C. Prat, R. Zangl, C. Stager, H. Neville, & Werker, J. (2004). Language experience and the organization of brain activity to phonetically similar words: ERP evidence from 14- and 20-month-olds. *Journal of Cognitive Neuroscience 16*(8),1452–1464.

Milner, D. & Goodale, M. (2006). *The visual brain in action*. Oxford, UK: Oxford University Press.

Misyak, J. B., Christiansen, M. H., & Bruce Tomblin, J. (2010). Sequential expectations: The role of prediction–based learning in language. *Topics in Cognitive Science, 2*(1), 138–153.

Mitra, S. (2003). Minimally invasive education: a progress report on the "hole–in–the–wall" experiments. *British Journal of Educational Technology, 34*(3), 367–371.

Mitra, S. & Crawley, E. (2014). Effectiveness of self-organised learning by children: Gateshead experiments. *Journal of Education and Human Development, 3*(3), 79–88.

Mix, K. S. (1999). Similarity and numerical equivalence: Appearances count. *Cognitive Development, 14*(2), 269–297.

Moon, C., Lagercrantz, H., & Kuhl, P. K. (2013). Language experienced in utero affects vowel perception after birth: A two–country study. *Acta Paediatrica,102*(2), 156–160.

Muckli, L., Petro, L. S., & Smith, F. W. (2013). Backwards is the way forward: Feedback in the cortical hierarchy predicts the expected future. *Behavioral and Brain Sciences, 36*(3), 221–221.

Mudrik, L., Lamy, D., & Deouell, L. Y. (2010). ERP evidence for context congruity effects during simultaneous object–scene processing. *Neuropsychologia, 48*(2), 507–517.

Mullally, S. L. & Maguire, E. A. (2014). Memory, imagination, and predicting the future: A common brain mechanism?. *The Neuroscientist, 20*(3), 220–234.

Mulligan, J. (1992). Children's solutions to multiplication and division word problems: A longitudinal study. *Mathematics Education Research Journal, 4*(1), 24–41.

Mulligan, J. T. & Mitchelmore, M. C. (1997). Young children's intuitive models of multiplication and division. *Journal for Research in Mathematics Education, 28*(3), 309–330.

Murre, J. M. (2014). *Learning and categorization in modular neural networks*. East Sussex, UK: Psychology Press.

Mussolin, C., Nys, J., Leybaert, J., & Content, A. (2012). Relationships between approximate number system acuity and early symbolic number abilities. *Trends in Neuroscience and Education, 1*(1), 21-31.

NAEYC & NCTM (National Association for the Education of Young Children/National Council of Teachers of Mathematics, USA). (2002). *Early childhood mathematics: Promoting good beginnings* (position statement). Retrieved Mar 28, 2018 from http://oldweb.naeyc.org/about/positions/psmath.asp

Nakatani, H. & Yamaguchi, Y. (2014). Quick concurrent responses to global and local cognitive information underlie intuitive understanding in board-game experts. *Scientific Reports, 4*, 5894.

Nehring, I., Kostka, T., von Kries, R., & Rehfuess, E. A. (2015). Impacts of in utero and early infant taste experiences on later taste acceptance: A systematic review–3. *Journal of Nutrition, 145*(6), 1271-1279.

Newman, A. J., Supalla, T., Fernandez, N., Newport, E. L., & Bavelier, D. (2015). Neural systems supporting linguistic structure, linguistic experience, and symbolic communication in sign language and gesture. *Proceedings of the National Academy of Sciences*, 201510527.

Noguchi, Y. & Murota, M. (2013). Temporal dynamics of neural activity in an integration of visual and contextual information in an esthetic preference task. *Neuropsychologia, 51*(6), 1077–1084.

Notebaert, K., Nelis, S., & Reynvoet, B. (2011). The magnitude representation of small and large symbolic numbers in the left and right hemisphere: An event-related fMRI study. *Journal of Cognitive Neuroscience, 23*(3), 622–630.

Nucci, L., Krettenauer, T., & Narváez, D. (Eds.). (2014). *Handbook of moral and character education.* London, UK: Routledge.

Nuthall, G. (2004). Relating classroom teaching to student learning: A critical analysis of why research has failed to bridge the theory-practice gap. *Harvard Educational Review, 74*(3), 273–306.

Nyberg, L., Kim, A. S., Habib, R., Levine, B., & Tulving, E. (2010). Consciousness of subjective time in the brain. *Proceedings of the National Academy of Sciences, 107*(51), 22356–22359.

Oliva, A., & Torralba, A. (2007). The role of context in object recognition. *Trends in Cognitive Sciences, 11*(12), 520–527.

Orban, G. A. (2011). The extraction of 3D shape in the visual system of human and nonhuman primates. *Annual Review of Neuroscience, 34*, 361–388.

Orban, P., Peigneux, P., Lungu, O., Debas, K., Barakat, M., Bellec, P., . . . & Doyon, J. (2011). Functional neuroanatomy associated with the expression of distinct movement kinematics in motor sequence learning. *Neuroscience, 179*, 94–103.

Oriental Institute of the University of Chicago, The. (2018). *The Nippur expedition* [website]. Retrieved 2 July 2018 from https://oi.uchicago.edu/research/projects/nippur-expedition.

Osterhout, L., Kim, A., & Kuperberg, G. R. (2012). The neurobiology of sentence comprehension. In M. Spivey, M. Joanisse, & K. McRae (Eds.), *The Cambridge handbook of psycholinguistics*, (pp. 365–389). Cambridge, UK: Cambridge University Press.

Oyserman, D. (2013). Not just any path: Implications of identity-based motivation for disparities in school outcomes. *Economics of Education Review, 33*, 179–190.

Ozernov–Palchik, O., & Gaab, N. (2016). Tackling the 'dyslexia paradox': reading brain and behavior for early markers of developmental dyslexia. *Wiley Interdisciplinary Reviews: Cognitive Science, 7*(2), 156-176.

Pallett, P. M., Link, S., & Lee, K. (2010). New "golden" ratios for facial beauty. *Vision Research, 50*(2), 149–154.

Pariyadath, V., Plitt, M. H., Churchill, S. J., & Eagleman, D. M. (2012). Why overlearned sequences are special: Distinct neural networks for ordinal sequences. *Frontiers in Human Neuroscience, 6* .

Park, J., Berg, B., Chiang, C., Woldorff, M. G., & Brannon, E. M. (2017). Developmental trajectory of neural specialization for letter and number visual processing. *Developmental Science, 21*(3), e12578. DOI: 10.1111/desc.12578

Park, J., Li, R., & Brannon, E. M. (2014). Neural connectivity patterns underlying symbolic number processing indicate mathematical achievement in children. *Developmental Science, 17*(2), 187-202.

Passolunghi, M. C., Lanfranchi, S., Altoè, G., & Sollazzo, N. (2015). Early numerical abilities and cognitive skills in kindergarten children. *Journal of Experimental Child Psychology, 135*, 25-42.

Pattamadilok, C., Dehaene, S., & Pallier, C. (2016). A role for left inferior frontal and posterior superior temporal cortex in extracting a syntactic tree from a sentence. *Cortex, 75*, 44–55.

Patterning. (2017). Merriam-Webster Online Dictionary. Downloaded August 9, 2017 from https://www.merriam-webster.com/dictionary/patterning

Pavlidis, T. (2013). *Structural pattern recognition* (Vol. 1). New York: Springer.

Peña, M., Maki, A., Kovačić, D., Dehaene-Lambertz, G., Koizumi, H., Bouquet, F., & Mehler, J. (2003). Sounds and silence: An optical topography study of language recognition at birth. *Proceedings of the National Academy of Science, 100*(20), 11702–11705.

Pereira, L. (2018). Japanese alphabet: Kanji, Hiragana, Katakana. *Japanese with Anime* [blog]. Retrieved March 28, 2018 from https://www.japanesewithanime.com/2016/08/japanese-alphabet-hiragana-katakana-kanji.html

Perin, R., Berger, T. K., & Markram, H. (2011). A synaptic organizing principle for cortical neuronal groups. *Proceedings of the National Academy of Sciences, 108*(13), 5419–5424.

Perkins, D. (2010). *Making learning whole. How seven principles of teaching can transform education.* San Francisco: Jossey-Bass.

Perrodin, C., Kayser, C., Abel, T. J., Logothetis, N. K., & Petkov, C. I. (2015). Who is that? Brain networks and mechanisms for identifying individuals. *Trends in Cognitive Sciences, 19*(12), 783–796.

Pessoa, L. (2014). Understanding brain networks and brain organization. *Physics of Life Reviews, 11*(3), 400-435.

Petersen, S. E. & Posner, M. I. (2012). The attention system of the human brain: 20 years after. *Annual Review of Neuroscience, 35*, 73–89.

Phillips, D. C. & Kelly, M. E. (1975). Hierarchical theories of development in education and psychology. *Harvard Educational Review, 45*(3), 351–375.

Piaget, J. (1952). *The origins of intelligence in children* (Vol. 8, No. 5). New York: International Universities Press.

Piaget, J. (1954). *The construction of reality in the child.* London, UK: Routledge.

Piazza, M., Izard, V., Pinel, P., Le Bihan, D., & Dehaene, S. (2004). Tuning curves for approximate numerosity in the human intraparietal sulcus. *Neuron, 44*, 547–555.

Piazza, M., Mechelli, A., Price, C. J., & Butterworth, B. (2006). Exact and approximate judgements of visual and auditory numerosity: An fMRI study. *Brain Research, 1106*(1), 177–188.

Pinel, P. & Dehaene, S. (2010). Beyond hemispheric dominance: Brain regions underlying the joint lateralization of language and arithmetic to the left hemisphere. *Journal of Cognitive Neuroscience, 22*(1), 48–66.

Pinker, S. (2003). *The language instinct: How the mind creates language.* London, UK: Penguin.

Planton, S., Longcamp, M., Péran, P., Démonet, J.-F., & Jucla, M. (2017). How specialized are writing-specific brain regions? An fMRI study of writing, drawing and oral spelling. *Cortex, 88*, 66–80. https://doi.org/10.1016/j.cortex.2016.11.018

Platt, P. (1977). Grapho-linguistics: Children's drawings in relation to reading and writing skills. *The Reading Teacher, 31*(3), 262–268.

Poulin-Dubois, D., Bialystok, E., Blaye, A., Polonia, A., & Yott, J. (2013). Lexical access and vocabulary development in very young bilinguals. *International Journal of Bilingualism, 17*(1), 57–70.

Price, C. J. & Devlin, J. T. (2011). The interactive account of ventral occipitotemporal contributions to reading. *Trends in Cognitive Sciences, 15*(6), 246–253.

Price, G. R. & Ansari, D. (2013). Dyscalculia: Characteristics, causes, and treatments. *Numeracy, 6*(1), 2.

Price, G. R., Mazzocco, M. M., & Ansari, D. (2013). Why mental arithmetic counts: Brain activation during single digit arithmetic predicts high school math scores. *Journal of Neuroscience, 33*(1), 156–163.

Pulvermüller, F. (2010). Brain embodiment of syntax and grammar: Discrete combinatorial mechanisms spelt out in neuronal circuits. *Brain and Language, 112*(3), 167–179.

Pulvermüller, F. (2013). How neurons make meaning: Brain mechanisms for embodied and abstract-symbolic semantics. *Trends in Cognitive Sciences, 17*(9), 458–470.

Purcell, J., Turkeltaub, P., Eden, G., & Rapp, B. (2011). Examining the central and peripheral processes of written word production through meta-analysis. *Frontiers in Psychology, 2*, 1–16. https://doi.org/10.3389/fpsyg.2011.00239

Putnam, R. T., & Borko, H. (2000). What do new views of knowledge and thinking have to say about research on teacher learning?. *Educational Researcher, 29*(1), 4-15.

Ragni, M. & Strube, G. (2014). Cognitive complexity and analogies in transfer learning. *KI-Künstliche Intelligenz, 28*(1), 39–43.

Ramanathan, K., Luping, S., Jianming, L., & Chong, C. T. (2012). Hierarchical network models for memory and learning. In N. M. Seel (Ed.), *Encyclopedia of the sciences of learning* (pp. 1424–1426). New York: Springer US.

Reber, A. S. & Lewis, S. (1977). Implicit learning: An analysis of the form and structure of a body of tacit knowledge. *Cognition, 5*(4), 333–361.

Reber, A. S., Kassin, S. M., Lewis, S., & Cantor, G. (1980). On the relationship between implicit and explicit modes in the learning of a complex rule structure. *Journal of Experimental Psychology: Human Learning and Memory, 6*(5), 492.

Reigeluth, C. M., Merrill, M. D., Wilson, B. G., & Spiller, R. T. (1980). The elaboration theory of instruction: A model for sequencing and synthesizing instruction. *Instructional Science, 9*(3), 195–219.

Revill, K. P., Namy, L. L., DeFife, L. C., & Nygaard, L. C. (2014). Cross-linguistic sound symbolism and crossmodal correspondence: Evidence from fMRI and DTI. *Brain and Language, 128*(1), 18–24.

Rilling, J. K., Glasser, M. F., Jbabdi, S., Andersson, J., & Preuss, T. M. (2011). Continuity, divergence, and the evolution of brain language pathways. *Frontiers in Evolutionary Neuroscience, 3* .

Ripley, B. D. (2007). *Pattern recognition and neural networks.* Cambridge, UK: Cambridge University Press.

Ritchhart, R., Church, M., & Morrison, K. (2011). *Making thinking visible: How to promote engagement, understanding, and independence for all learners.* Hoboken, NJ: John Wiley & Sons.

Rivera, G. M. Bilbao La Vieja (2013). *Prácticas docentes para la enseñanza de la lectura a partir de los hallazgos científicos del estudio de Mente, Cerebro y Educación* [tesis de Maestría]. Quito, Ecuador: Universidad San Francisco de Quito.

Rivera, F. D. (2014a). Counting and cardinality in kindergarten. In F. D. Rivera (Ed.), *Teaching to the math Common Core State Standards* (pp. 31–39). Boston, MA: SensePublishers.

Rivera, F. D. (2014b). Numbers and operations–fractions. In F. D. Rivera (Ed.), *Teaching to the math Common Core State Standards* (pp. 89–109). Boston, MA: SensePublishers.

Robbins, S. E. (2010). Special relativity and perception: The singular time of psychology and physics. *Journal of Consciousness Exploration & Research, 1*(5) .

Rock, I. (1957). The role of repetition in associative learning. *The American Journal of Psychology, 70*(2),186–193.

Roenneberg, T. (2013). Chronobiology: the human sleep project. *Nature, 498*(7455), 427–428.

Rose, L. T. & Fischer, K. W. (2009). Dynamic systems theory. In *The child: An encyclopedic companion.* Chicago: University of Chicago Press.

Rosenberg-Lee, M., Barth, M., & Menon, V. (2011). What difference does a year of schooling make? Maturation of brain response and connectivity between 2nd and 3rd grades during arithmetic problem solving. *Neuroimage, 57*(3), 796–808.

Rosenberg-Lee, M., Chang, T. T., Young, C. B., Wu, S., & Menon, V. (2011). Functional dissociations between four basic arithmetic operations in the human posterior parietal cortex: A cytoarchitectonic mapping study. *Neuropsychologia, 49*(9), 2592–2608.

Rousselet, G. A., & Pernet, C. R. (2011). Quantifying the time course of visual object processing using ERPs: It's time to up the game. *Frontiers in Psychology, 2*, 107. DOI: https://doi.org/10.3389/fpsyg.201 107

Rubinsten, O. & Sury, D. (2011). Processing ordinality and quantity: the case of developmental dyscalculia. *PLoS One, 6*(9), e24079.

Rueda, M. R., Checa, P., & Cómbita, L. M. (2012). Enhanced efficiency of the executive attention network after training in preschool children: Immediate changes and effects after two months. *Developmental Cognitive Neuroscience, 2*, S192–S204.

Rugg, M. D. & Vilberg, K. L. (2013). Brain networks underlying episodic memory retrieval. *Current Opinion in Neurobiology, 23*(2), 255–260.

Salimpoor, V. N., Zald, D. H., Zatorre, R. J., Dagher, A., & McIntosh, A. R. (2015). Predictions and the brain: How musical sounds become rewarding. *Trends in Cognitive Sciences, 19*(2), 86–91.

Samarasinghe, S. (2016). *Neural networks for applied sciences and engineering: From fundamentals to complex pattern recognition*. Boca Raton, FL: CRC Press.

Sampaio-Baptista, C., Khrapitchev, A. A., Foxley, S., Schlagheck, T., Scholz, J., Jbabdi, S., . . . & Kleim, J. (2013). Motor skill learning induces changes in white matter microstructure and myelination. *Journal of Neuroscience, 33*(50), 19499–19503.

Sarama, J., & Clements, D. H. (2009). *Early childhood mathematics education research: Learning trajectories for young children*. Abingdon-on-Thames, UK: Routledge.

Schleppegrell, M. J. (2014 Apr). Plenary speech: Content-based language teaching with functional grammar in the elementary school. *Language Teaching*. Available on CJO 2014 doi: 10.1017, S0261444814000093.

Schmithorst, V. J. & Brown, R. D. (2004). Empirical validation of the triple-code model of numerical processing for complex math operations using functional MRI and group Independent Component Analysis of the mental addition and subtraction of fractions. *Neuroimage, 22*(3), 1414–1420.

Schroeder, C. M., Scott, T. P., Tolson, H., Huang, T. Y., & Lee, Y. H. (2007). A meta-analysis of national research: Effects of teaching strategies on student achievement in science in the United States. *Journal of Research in Science Teaching, 44*(10), 1436–1460.

Schwartz, M. S., Sadler, P. M., Sonnert, G., & Tai, R. H. (2009). Depth versus breadth: How content coverage in high school science courses relates to later success in college science coursework. *Science Education, 93*(5), 798-826.

Segev, I., Martinez, L. M., & Zatorre, R. J. (2014). Brain and art. *Frontiers in Human Neuroscience, 8*, 1.

Sehatpour, P., Dias, E. C., Butler, P. D., Revheim, N., Guilfoyle, D. N., Foxe, J. J., & Javitt, D. C. (2010). Impaired visual object processing across an occipital-frontal-hippocampal brain network in schizophrenia: An integrated neuroimaging study. *Archives of General Psychiatry, 67*(8), 772–782.

Shaywitz, S. E., Shaywitz, B. A., Pugh, K. R., Fulbright, R. K., Constable, R. T., Mencl, W. E., . . . & Gore, J. C. (1998). Functional disruption in the organization of the brain for reading in dyslexia. *Proceedings of the National Academy of Sciences, 95*(5), 2636–2641.

Sheldon, S., Farb, N., Palombo, D. J., & Levine, B. (2016). Intrinsic medial temporal lobe connectivity relates to individual differences in episodic autobiographical remembering. *Cortex, 74*, 206–216.

Shulman, L. S. (1986). Those who understand: Knowledge growth in teaching. *Educational Researcher, 15*(2), 4–14.

Siegler, R. S., & Booth, J. L. (2005). Development of numerical estimation. In J.A. Campbell's *Handbook of mathematical cognition*, (pp.197-212). London, UK: Psychology Press.

Siegler, R. S., Fazio, L. K., Bailey, D. H., & Zhou, X. (2013). Fractions: the new frontier for theories of numerical development. *Trends in Cognitive Sciences, 17*(1), 13–19.

Silson, E. H., McKeefry, D. J., Rodgers, J., Gouws, A. D., Hymers, M., & Morland, A. B. (2013). Specialized and independent processing of orientation and shape in visual field maps LO1 and LO2. *Nature Neuroscience, 16*(3), 267–269.

Simons, G. F. & Fennig, C.D. (Eds.). (2018). *Ethnologue: Languages of the world* (21st ed.). Dallas, Texas: SIL International. Online version: http://www.ethnologue.com

Sirois, S., Spratling, M., Thomas, M. S., Westermann, G., Mareschal, D., & Johnson, M. H. (2008). Precis of neuroconstructivism: How the brain constructs cognition. *Behavioral and Brain Sciences, 31*(03), 321–331.

Sloan Science. (2017). *Quantity - Quantity in physical science*. Downloaded August 22, 2017 from http://sloan.org

Smolensky, P., Goldrick, M., & Mathis, D. (2014). Optimization and quantization in gradient symbol systems: A framework for integrating the continuous and the discrete in cognition. *Cognitive Science, 38*(6), 1102–1138.

Smolleck, L. A. & Nordgren, S. B. (2014). Transforming standards-based teaching: Embracing the teaching and learning of science as inquiry in elementary classrooms. *Journal of Education and Human Development, 3*(2), 1–19.

Snaidero, N. & Simons, M. (2014). Myelination at a glance. *Journal of Cell Science, 127*, 2999–3004. doi:10.1242/jcs.151043

Søby, M. (2015). Finnish education system. *Nordic Journal of Digital Literacy, 10*(2), 64–68. Retrieved 10 June 2018 from http://www.idunn.no/file/pdf/66781940/finnish_education_system.pdf

Society for Neuroscience. (2018), *The brain facts book*. Washington, D.C.: Author.

Sokolowski, H. M., Fias, W., Mousa, A., & Ansari, D. (2017). Common and distinct brain regions in both parietal and frontal cortex support symbolic and nonsymbolic number processing in humans: A functional neuroimaging meta-analysis. *NeuroImage, 146*, 376–394.

Sommers, F. & Englebretsen, G. (2017). *An invitation to formal reasoning: The logic of terms*. Abingdon-on-Thames, UK: Routledge.

Sophian, C. (2000) Perceptions of proportionality in young children: Matching spatial ratios. *Cognition 75*, 145–170.

Sprengelmeyer, R., Rausch, M., Eysel, U. T., & Przuntek, H. (1998). Neural structures associated with recognition of facial expressions of basic emotions. *Proceedings of the Royal Society of London. Series B: Biological Sciences, 265*(1409), 1927–1931.

Squire, L. R. (1987). Memory and brain. In S. L. Friedman, A. K., A. Klivington, & R.W. Peterson (Eds.). *The brain, cognition and education*, (pp. 171–202). New York: Academic Press.

Squire, S. & Bryant, P. (2002). From sharing to dividing: Young children's understanding of division. *Developmental Science, 5*(4), 452–466.

Srinivasan, M. & Carey, S. (2010). The long and the short of it: On the nature and origin of functional overlap between representations of space and time. *Cognition, 116*(2), 217–241.

Staiano, A. E. & Calvert, S. L. (2011). Exergames for physical education courses: Physical, social, and cognitive benefits. *Child Development Perspectives, 5*(2), 93–98.

Stansbury, D. E., Naselaris, T., & Gallant, J. L. (2013). Natural scene statistics account for the representation of scene categories in human visual cortex. *Neuron, 79*(5), 1025–1034.

Starkey, G. S., & McCandliss, B. D. (2014). The emergence of "groupitizing" in children's numerical cognition. *Journal of Experimental Child Psychology, 126*, 120-137.

Steele, J. (2003). Children's gender stereotypes about math: The role of stereotype stratification. *Journal of Applied Social Psychology, 33*(12), 2587–2606.

Steele, J. R. & Ambady, N. (2006). "Math is hard!" The effect of gender priming on women's attitudes. *Journal of Experimental Social Psychology, 42*(4), 428–436.

Steele, J., James, J. B., & Barnett, R. C. (2002). Learning in a man's world: Examining the perceptions of undergraduate women in male-dominated academic areas. *Psychology of Women Quarterly, 26*(1), 46–50.

Stein, J. (2014). Dyslexia: The role of vision and visual attention. *Current Developmental Disorders Reports, 1*(4), 267–280.

Stigler, J. W. & Hiebert, J. (2009). *The teaching gap: Best ideas from the world's teachers for improving education in the classroom.* New York: Simon & Schuster.

Stilla, R. & Sathian, K. (2008). Selective visuo-haptic processing of shape and texture. *Human Brain Mapping, 29*(10), 1123–1138.

Stratford, E., Compton, L & Wagg, F., (2017). *Do we learn in utero? Does it matter?, Learning over the life-course: A series of conversations with Leon Compton,* [ABC Radio 936, Hobart], Tasmania, 24 October 2017, p. 2. [Media Interview].

Strauß, A., Kotz, S. A., Scharinger, M., & Obleser, J. (2014). Alpha and theta brain oscillations index dissociable processes in spoken word recognition. *NeuroImage, 97,* 387–395.

Strickland, D. S. & Morrow, L. M. (1989). *Emerging literacy: Young children learn to read and write.* Newark, DE: International Reading Association.

Striemer, C. L., Chouinard, P. A., Goodale, M. A., & de Ribaupierre, S. (2015). Overlapping neural circuits for visual attention and eye movements in the human cerebellum. *Neuropsychologia, 69,* 9-21.

Szegedy, C., Toshev, A., & Erhan, D. (2003). Deep neural networks for object detection. In M. I. Jordan, Y. LeCun and S.A. Solla's *Advances in neural information processing systems* (pp. 2553–2561). Cambridge, MA: MIT Press.

Tan, L. H., Spinks, J. A., Gao, J. H., Liu, H. L., Perfetti, C. A., Xiong, J., . . . & Fox, P. T. (2000). Brain activation in the processing of Chinese characters and words: A functional MRI study. *Human Brain Mapping, 10*(1), 16–27.

Taylor, J. S. H., Rastle, K., & Davis, M. H. (2013). Can cognitive models explain brain activation during word and pseudo word reading? A meta-analysis of 36 neuroimaging studies. *Psychological Bulletin, 139*(4), 766.

Terasawa, Y., Kurosaki, Y., Ibata, Y., Moriguchi, Y., & Umeda, S. (2015). Attenuated sensitivity to the emotions of others by insular lesion. *Frontiers in Psychology, 6,* 13-14.

Thierry, G. (2016). Neurolinguistic relativity: How language flexes human perception and cognition. *Language Learning, 66*(3), 690–713.

Thompson, J. M., Nuerk, H. C., Moeller, K., & Kadosh, R. C. (2013). The link between mental rotation ability and basic numerical representations. *Acta Psychologica, 144*(2), 324–331.

Thomson, A. (2011). Memory and remembering in oral history. *The Oxford Handbook of Oral History,* 77–95.

Tokuhama-Espinosa, T. (2008a). *The scientifically substantiated art of teaching: A study in the development of standards in the new academic field of neuroeducation (Mind, Brain, and Education Science).* Dissertation (Ph.D.), St. Paul, MN: Capella University. AAT 3310716.

Tokuhama-Espinosa, T. (2008b). *Living languages: Multilingualism across the lifespan.* Westport, CT: Greenwood. ISBN-10: 9780275999124

Tokuhama-Espinosa, T. (2010). *The new science of teaching and learning: Using the best of mind, brain, and education science in the classroom.* New York, NY: Teachers College Press.

Tokuhama-Espinosa, T. (2014). *Making classrooms better: 50 practical applications of mind, brain, and education science.* New York: W. W. Norton & Company.

Tokuhama-Espinosa, T. (2015a). *Paper 1: Theoretical foundations for the theory of the five pillars.* Quito, Ecuador: Unpublished.

Tokuhama-Espinosa, T. (2015b). Celebrating the complexity and multidimensionality of "quality" in education: Toward a new process of choosing indicators that measure in ways that better reflect context. In *World Education Research Association (WERA) Yearbook* (pp.114-159). New York, NY: Routledge.

Tokuhama-Espinosa, T. & Rivera, G. M. Bilbao La Vieja (2013b). *Procesamiento inicial matemático y el fracaso escolar.* Contractado y publicado por el Gobierno Costa Rica, y el System for Integration for Central American CECC/SICA.

Tokuhama-Espinosa, T. & Rivera G. M. Bilbao La Vieja (2013a). *Estudio del arte sobre conciencia fonológica en lenguaje preescolar: El cerebro y fracaso escolar.* Contractado y publicado por el Gobierno Costa Rica, y el System for Integration for Central American CECC/SICA.

Tomlinson, C. A. (2014). *The differentiated classroom: Responding to the needs of all learners.* Alexandria, VA: ASCD.

Tomlinson, C. A. & McTighe, J. (2006). *Integrating differentiated instruction & understanding by design: Connecting content and kids.* Alexandria, VA: ASCD.

Tschentscher, N. & Hauk, O. (2014). How are things adding up? Neural differences between arithmetic operations are due to general problem solving strategies. *Neuroimage, 92,* 369–380.

Twomey, S. (2013). *Introduction to the mathematics of inversion in remote sensing and indirect measurements (Vol. 3).* Amsterdam, The Netherlands: Elsevier.

Tylén, K., Christensen, P., Roepstorff, A., Lund, T., Østergaard, S., & Donald, M. (2015). Brains striving for coherence: Long-term cumulative plot formation in the default mode network. *NeuroImage, 121,* 106–114.

Ulfarsson, M. O., Walters, G. B., Gustafsson, O., Steinberg, S., Silva, A., Doyle, O. M., . . . & Gisladottir, R. S. (2017). 15q11. 2 CNV affects cognitive, structural and functional correlates of dyslexia and dyscalculia. *Translational Psychiatry, 7*(4), e1109.

Ultanir, E. (2012). An epistemological glance at the constructivist approach: Constructivist learning in Dewey, Piaget, and Montessori. *Online Submission, 5*(2), 195–212.

van Atteveldt, N. & Ansari, D. (2014). How symbols transform brain function: A review in memory of Leo Blomert. *Trends in Neuroscience and Education, 3*(2), 44–49.

Van Rijn, H., Gu, B. M., & Meck, W. H. (2014). Dedicated clock/timing-circuit theories of time perception and timed performance. In H. Merchant & V. de Lafuente (Eds.), *Neurobiology of interval timing* (pp. 75–99). New York: Springer US.

Varona, P., & Rabinovich, M. I. (2016). Hierarchical dynamics of informational patterns and decision-making. The Royal Society. *Proceedings in Research in Social Biology, 283*(1832), 20160475.

Venneri, A. & Semenza, C. (2011). On the dependency of division on multiplication: Selective loss for conceptual knowledge of multiplication. *Neuropsychologia, 49*(13), 3629–3635.

Vessel, E. A., Starr, G. G., & Rubin, N. (2012). The brain on art: Intense aesthetic experience activates the default mode network. *Frontiers in Human Neuroscience, 6,* 66.

Villagrasa, F., Baladron, J., & Hamker, F. H. (2016). Fast and slow learning in a neuro-computational model of category acquisition. In A. E. P. Villa, P. Masulli, & A. J. Pons Rivero (Eds.), *Artificial neural networks and machine learning-ICANN 2016* (pp. 248–255). New York: Springer International Publishing.

Voelker, P., Piscopo, D., Weible, A. P., Lynch, G., Rothbart, M. K., Posner, M. I., & Niell, C. M.

(2017). How changes in white matter might underlie improved reaction time due to practice. *Cognitive Neuroscience, 8*(2), 112-118.

Vogel, S. E., Goffin, C., & Ansari, D. (2015). Developmental specialization of the left parietal cortex for the semantic representation of Arabic numerals: An fMR-adaptation study. *Developmental Cognitive Neuroscience, 12*, 61–73.

Von Glasersfeld, E. (1995). *Radical constructivism: A way of knowing and learning. Studies in mathematics education series: 6.* Bristol, PA: Falmer Press, Taylor & Francis Inc.

Vuust, P., Gebauer, L. K., & Witek, M. A. (2014). Neural underpinnings of music: the polyrhythmic brain. In *Neurobiology of interval timing* (pp. 339–356). New York: Springer.

Vygotsky, L. (1934/1986). *Thought and language.* Trans. A. Kozulin. Cambridge, MA: Harvard University Press.

Vygotsky, L. (1998). *The collected works of L. S. Vygotsky*, Volume V. New York: Springer.

Vygotsky, L. S. (1933). *Play and its role in the mental development of the child.* (Trans. N. Schmotlze.) Leningrad, Russia: Hezen Pedagogical Institute. Retrieved May 22, 2018 from https://files.eric.ed.gov/fulltext/EJ1138861.pdf

Wagenmakers, E. J., van der Maas, H. L., & Farrell, S. (2012). Abstract concepts require concrete models: Why cognitive scientists have not yet embraced nonlinearly coupled, dynamical, self-organized critical, synergistic, scale-free, exquisitely context-sensitive, interaction-dominant, multifractal, interdependent brain-body-niche systems. *Topics in Cognitive Science, 4*(1), 87–93.

Wang, J., Cherkassky, V. L., & Just, M. A. (2017). Predicting the brain activation pattern associated with the propositional content of a sentence: Modeling neural representations of events and states. *Human Brain Mapping, 38*(10), 4865-4881.

Wang, L. C., Tasi, H. J., & Yang, H. M. (2012). Cognitive inhibition in students with and without dyslexia and dyscalculia. *Research in Developmental Disabilities, 33*(5), 1453–1461.

Watson, D. M., Young, A. W., & Andrews, T. J. (2016). Spatial properties of objects predict patterns of neural response in the ventral visual pathway. *NeuroImage, 126*, 173–183.

Webb, A. R., Heller, H. T., Benson, C. B., & Lahav, A. (2015). Mother's voice and heartbeat sounds elicit auditory plasticity in the human brain before full gestation. *Proceedings of the National Academy of Sciences, 112*(10), 3152-3157.

Wehbe, L., Murphy, B., Talukdar, P., Fyshe, A., Ramdas, A., & Mitchell, T. (2014). Simultaneously uncovering the patterns of brain regions involved in different story reading subprocesses. *PloS One, 9*(11), e112575

Wei, W., Liu, J., Dai, R., Feng, L., Li, L., & Tian, J. (2014, March). Different brain activations between own- and other-race face categorization: An fMRI study using group independent component analysis. In *SPIE Medical Imaging* (Vol. 9038, p.903807). Bellingham WA: International Society for Optics and Photonics.

Welchman, A. E., Deubelius, A., Conrad, V., Heinrich, H. B., & Kourtzi, Z. (2005). 3D shape perception from combined depth cue in human visual cortex. *Nature Neuroscience, 8*(6), 820.

Westermann, G. (2016). Experience–dependent brain development as a key to understanding the language system. *Topics in Cognitive Science, 8*(2), 446–458.

Westermann, G., Mareschal, D., Johnson, M. H., Sirois, S., Spratling, M. W., & Thomas, M. S. (2007). Neuroconstructivism. *Developmental Science, 10*(1), 75–83.

Westermann, G., Thomas, M. S., & Karmiloff-Smith, A. (2010). Neuroconstructivism (p. 723). In J.E. Opfer, S.A. Gelman, & U. Goswami (Eds.), *The Wiley-Blackwell handbook of childhood cognitive development.* Hoboken, NJ: Wiley and Sons.

White, R. T. (1973). Research into learning hierarchies. *Review of Educational Research 43*(3), 361–375.

White, R. T. & Gagné, R. M. (1974). Past and future research on learning hierarchies 1. *Educational Psychologist, 11*(1), 19–28.

Whitebread, D. & Coltman, P. (Eds.). (2015). *Teaching and learning in the early years.* Abingdon-on-Thames, UK: Routledge.

Widmann, A., Schröger, E., Tervaniemi, M., Pakarinen, S., & Kujala, T. (2012). Mapping symbols to sounds: Electrophysiological correlates of the impaired reading process in dyslexia. *Frontiers in Psychology, 3,* 60 . https://doi.org/10.3389/fpsyg.2012.00060

Wiggins, G. P. & McTighe, J. (2005). *Understanding by design.* Alexandria, VA: ASCD.

Willingham, D. T. (2009). *Why don't students like school?: A cognitive scientist answers questions about how the mind works and what it means for the classroom.* Hoboken, NJ: John Wiley & Sons.

Wilson, A. J., Andrews, S. G., Struthers, H., Rowe, V. M., Bogdanovic, R., & Esldie, K. E. (2015). Dyscalculia and dyslexia in adults: Cognitive bases of comorbidity. *Learning and Individual Differences, 37,* 118–132.

Woese, C., Kandler, O., & Wheelis, M. (1990). Towards a natural system of organisms: Proposal for the domains Archaea, Bacteria, and Eucarya. *Proceedings of the National Academy of Science, USA 87*(12), 4576–4579.

Woollams, A. M., Silani, G., Okada, K., Patterson, K., & Price, C. J. (2011). Word or word-like? Dissociating orthographic typicality from lexicality in the left occipito-temporal cortex. *Journal of Cognitive Neuroscience, 23*(4), 992–1002.

World Heritage Encyclopedia. (2017). Outline of academic disciplines. *World Heritage Encyclopedia.* New York: World Public Library Association.

Xenidou-Dervou, I., van der Schoot, M., & van Lieshout, E. C. (2015). Working memory and number line representations in single-digit addition: Approximate versus exact, nonsymbolic versus symbolic. *The Quarterly Journal of Experimental Psychology, 68*(6), 1148-1167.

Xenidou-Dervou, I., van Lieshout, E. C., & van der Schoot, M. (2014). Working memory in non-symbolic approximate arithmetic processing: A dual-task study with preschoolers. *Cognitive Science, 38*(1), 101-127.

Xu, F. (2003). Numerosity discrimination in infants: Evidence for two systems of representations. *Cognition 89,* B15–B25 10.1016/S0010-0277(03)00050-7

Xu, K., Ba, J., Kiros, R., Cho, K., Courville, A., Salakhudinov, R., . . . & Bengio, Y. (2015, June). Show, attend and tell: Neuronal image caption generation with visual attention. In *International conference on machine learning, Lille. France, July 6-11,* (pp. 2048–2057). New York: Springer. Downloaded 1 July 2018 from https://icml.cc/2015/booklet-icml2015.online.pdf

Yonelinas, A. P., Otten, L. J., Shaw, K. N., & Rugg, M. D. (2005). Separating the brain regions involved in recollection and familiarity in recognition memory. *Journal of Neuroscience, 25*(11), 3002–3008.

Yoo, S., Chung, J. Y., Jeon, H. A., Lee, K. M., Kim, Y. B., & Cho, Z. H. (2012). Dual routes for verbal repetition: Articulation-based and acoustic–phonetic codes for pseudoword and word repetition, respectively. *Brain and Language, 122*(1), 1–10.

Your Dictionary. (2017). What are the fourteen punctuation marks in English grammar? *LoveToKnow.* Downloaded August 22, 2017 from http://grammar.yourdictionary.com/punctuation/what/fourteen-punctuation-marks.html

Yuan, Y. & Brown, S. (2015). Drawing and writing: An ALE meta-analysis of sensorimotor activations. *Brain and Cognition, 98,* 15–26. https://doi.org/10.1016/j.bandc.2015.05.004

Yuan, P. & Raz, N. (2014). Prefrontal cortex and executive functions in healthy adults: A meta-analysis of structural neuroimaging studies. *Neuroscience & Biobehavioral Reviews, 42,* 180–192.

Zatorre, R. J., Fields, R. D., & Johansen-Berg, H. (2012). Plasticity in gray and white: Neuroimaging changes in brain structure during learning. *Nature Neuroscience, 15*(4), 528–536.

Zebian, S., & Ansari, D. (2012). Differences between literates and illiterates on symbolic but not nonsymbolic numerical magnitude processing. *Psychonomic Bulletin & Review, 19*(1), 93-100. Zeki, S. & Nash, J. (1999). *Inner vision: An exploration of art and the brain* (Vol. 415). Oxford, UK: Oxford University Press.

Zemelman, S., Daniels, H., & Hyde, A. (2005). *Best practice: Today's standards for teaching in America's schools.* Portsmouth, NH: Heinemann.

Zvyagintsev, M., Clemens, B., Chechko, N., Mathiak, K. A., Sack, A. T., & Mathiak, K. (2013). Brain networks underlying mental imagery of auditory and visual information. *European Journal of Neuroscience, 37*(9), 1421–1434.

Appendix A: Curricular Example: Applying the Pillars to Early Math Learning

What follows is a narrative of what the Five Pillars of the Mind means in a child's life from birth to about age three related to math to get a sense of what they look like in real life.

When a child is born, she has an **innate number sense** (Dehaene, 1997). Even before she can speak, she also uses her senses to explore and experience order, size, quantity, sequence, and type to confirm this number sense of the world. One of the first concepts a child understands, thanks to this general number sense, is "more" vs. "less," which is the first order of **magnitude**. "More" and "less" can be expressed in symbols or through patterns, order, categories, and relationships, and is a pre-verbal understanding of the world. That is, within the first year of life, there is evidence that she understands magnitude.

If a child successfully understands "more" and "less," she can then grasp "different" and "similar," which are in turn prerequisites for "equal," which means she has the foundations of **relationships**. Once "different" and "similar" are understood, the child can learn "high" and "low" (but only relative to herself and mainly as a **relation**). Following "high" and "low," the child begins the first sense of measure and learns "short" and "long." If the child understands both "high-low" and "short-long," she will have the first notion of **proximity** ("near" and "far"), which in turn lays the foundation for "posterior" (behind) and "anterior" (before). "Before" and "after" can be understood in both space and time, which makes the conceptual notion so important. Parents can motivate understanding of this key notion by putting one toy animal ahead of another, calling out how "Nick is going before Ann, then it is our turn," or

Table 21. Early Math: 0–12 Months

RELATIONS	Level	CATEGORIES	Level	ORDER	Level	PATTERNS	Level	SYMBOLS	Level
Short-Long	0	Short-Long	0	Symbols, Patterns, Categories, Relationships	0	Symbols, Order, Categories, Relationships	0	Patterns, Order, Relationships, Categories	0 (10–12 mons.)
High-Low	0	High-Low	0	Symbols, Patterns, Categories, Relationships	0	Symbols, Order, Categories, Relationships	0	High-Low	0 (10 mons)
Different-Similar	0	Different-Similar	0	Symbols, Patterns, Categories, Relationships	0	Different-Similar	0		0 (6 mons)
More-Less	0	More-Less	0	Symbols, Patterns, Categories, Relationships	0	More-Less	0	More-Less	0 (newborn)
Sensorial experience of order, size, quantity, sequence, and type	0	Sensorial experience of order, size, quantity, sequence, and type	0	Sensorial experience of order, size, quantity, sequence, and type	0	Sensorial experience of order, size, quantity, sequence, and type	0	Sensorial experience of order, size, quantity, sequence, and type	0 (newborn)

SOURCE: TOKUHAMA-ESPINOSA, 2015

Table 22. Early Math: 12–20 Months

RELATIONS	Level	CATEGORIES	Level	ORDER	Level	PATTERNS	Level	SYMBOLS	Level
Symbols, Patterns, Order, Categories	0	Line	0	Symbols, Patterns, Categories, Relationships	0	Symbols, Order, Categories, Relationships	0	Line	0 (12–20 mons)
Symbols, Patterns, Order, Categories	0	Point	0	Symbols, Patterns, Categories, Relationships	0	Symbols, Order, Categories, Relationships	0	Point	0 (12–20 mons)
Estimation	0	Symbols, Patterns, Order, Relationships	0	Symbols, Patterns, Categories, Relationships	0	Symbols, Order, Categories, Relationships	0	Patterns, Order, Relationships, Categories	0 (12–20 mons)
Symbols, Patterns, Order, Categories	0	Symbols, Patterns, Order, Relationships	0	Positive-Negative	0	Symbols, Order, Categories, Relationships	0	Patterns, Order, Relationships, Categories	0 (12–20 mons)
Posterior-Anterior	0	Symbols, Patterns, Order, Relationships	0	Posterior-Anterior	0	Symbols, Order, Categories, Relationships	0	Patterns, Order, Relationships, Categories	0 (12–20 mons)
Close-Far/Proximity	0	Close-Far/Proximity	0	Symbols, Patterns, Categories, Relationships	0	Symbols, Order, Categories, Relationships	0	Patterns, Order, Relationships, Categories	0 (12–20 mons)

SOURCE: TOKUHAMA-ESPINOSA, 2015

establishing the **order** of daily activities (*let's put your socks on* before *your shoes*; *let's eat* after *going to the park*; *we'll read the book* during *lunch*).

Nearly simultaneously to proximity, when "before" (anterior) and "after" (posterior) are learned, the child can conceptually understand "positive" and "negative." Whereas previous concepts were purely about magnitude, "positive-negative" is often first learned related to behavior (*You slept through the night, that was good!* or *Fighting with Jason was bad [negative]*) though it will later serve other purposes, including understanding not only emotional reasoning but also laying the foundation of notions that will help the child learn math, language, and other academic subjects as well. To extend "positive" and "negative" (and further reinforce the understanding of "equal"), parents can count aloud, forward and backward, as they do daily activities or chores (i.e., hold a baby tight while sitting on a swing and say *backward. . .forward. . .* [**order** and **pattern**]; comment on quantity or relativity; highlight order, processes, or steps; and so on. *I have just two glasses of water and there are three of us. I am missing one glass, aren't I? I am one glass short.*)

Once a core foundation for "positive-negative" is understood, the child can begin to understand **estimation** in relation to other things. The ability to estimate begins relative to the individual. For example, a child learning to walk must estimate, relative to her position, the distance between a caregiver's arms, or from the edge of the table to the couch. After estimation, the first mathematical symbol can be explicitly learned: the point ("."). Whereas earlier mathematical expressions were of magnitude (i.e., a lot of toys vs. fewer toys), this is the first **symbol** that is explicitly learned, because without a point there can be no other shapes. As a child begins to grasp crayons and scribble, all will begin with that first point. Whereas parents naturally motivate kids to go beyond points and draw lines, it's all important to celebrate that first dot on the page, as nothing can be made without it.

After dots or points, kids can scribble lines. The very first **symbols** known to man and documented as written language were tally marks, used to count. Young children evolve through dots to lines to tally marks in parallel with understanding magnitude through other senses, such as rhythmic beats. Children who are sung to, listen to music, and learn to use their own bodies to keep the beat (as in clapping) are laying the foundation of counting. Kids have a sense of counting (the **order** of objects in **sequence**) before they can actually count out loud, which happens around the age of two, give or take six or seven

Table 23. Early Math: 20–24 Months

RELATIONS	Level	CATEGORIES	Level	ORDER	Level	PATTERNS	Level	SYMBOLS	Level
Shapes/Forms and Characteristics	0	Shapes/Forms and Characteristics	0	Shapes/Forms and Characteristics	0	Shapes/Forms and Characteristics	0	Shapes/Forms and Characteristics	0 (20–24 mons)
1, 2, 3, 4, 5, 6, 7, 8, 9, 10. . .	0	Symbols, Patterns, Order, Relation-ships	0	1, 2, 3, 4, 5, 6, 7, 8, 9, 10. . .	0	1, 2, 3, 4, 5, 6, 7, 8, 9, 10. . .	0	1, 2, 3, 4, 5, 6, 7, 8, 9, 10. . .	0 (20–24 mons)
Number Line (Physical)	0	Symbols, Patterns, Order, Relation-ships	0	Number Line (Physical)	0	Number Line (Physical)	0	Number Line (Physical)	0 (20–24 mons)
Whole/Natural numbers/Integers	0	Whole/Natural numbers/Integers	0	Whole/Natural numbers/Integers	0	Symbols, Order, Categories, Rela-tionships	0	Whole/Natural numbers/Integers	0 (20–24 mons)
Penny (one cent) (associating sym-bols with quantity)	0	Penny (one cent) (associating sym-bols with quantity)	0	Symbols, Patterns, Categories, Rela-tionships	0	Symbols, Order, Categories, Rela-tionships	0	Penny (one cent) (associating sym-bols with quantity)	0 (20–24 mons)
Properties (Triple Code)	0	Symbols, Patterns, Order, Relation-ships	0	Symbols, Patterns, Categories, Rela-tionships	0	Properties (Triple Code)	0	Properties (Triple Code)	0 (20–24 mons)
Symbols, Patterns, Order, Categories	0	Symbols, Patterns, Order, Relation-ships	0	Counting verbally (out loud)	0	Counting verbally (out loud)	0	Patterns, Order, Relationshipships, Categories	0 (20–24 mons)
Symbols, Patterns, Order, Categories	0	Symbols, Patterns, Order, Relation-ships	0	Counting objects	0	Counting objects	0	Patterns, Order, Relationshipships, Categories	0 (20–24 mons)
Symbols, Patterns, Order, Categories	0	Symbols, Patterns, Order, Relation-ships	0	Count by beats	0	Count by beats	0	Patterns, Order, Relationshipships, Categories	0 (20–24 mons)
Symbols, Patterns, Order, Categories	0	Symbols, Patterns, Order, Relation-ships	0	Symbols, Patterns, Categories, Rela-tionships	0	Symbols, Order, Categories, Rela-tionships	0	Tally mark	0 (20–24 mons)

SOURCE: TOKUHAMA-ESPINOSA, 2015

Table 24. Early Math: 24–48 Months

RELATIONS	Level	CATEGORIES	Level	ORDER	Level	PATTERNS	Level	SYMBOLS	Level
Addition	**1**	**Addition**	**1**	**Addition**	**1**	**Addition**	**1**	**Addition Plus sign (+)**	**1**
1st, 2nd, 3rd, 4th, 5th, 6th, 7th, 8th, 9th, 10th. . .	0	Symbols, Patterns, Order, Relation-ships	0	1st, 2nd, 3rd, 4th, 5th, 6th, 7th, 8th, 9th, 10th. . .	0	1st, 2nd, 3rd, 4th, 5th, 6th, 7th, 8th, 9th, 10th. . .	0	1st, 2nd, 3rd, 4th, 5th, 6th, 7th, 8th, 9th, 10th. . .	0 (36–48 mons)
Decomposition	0	Symbols, Patterns, Order, Relation-ships	0	Decomposition	0	Decomposition	0	Decomposition	0 (36–48 mons)
Base-10 blocks	0	Symbols, Patterns, Order, Relation-ships	0	Base-10 blocks	0	Base-10 blocks	0	Base-10 blocks	0 (30–48 mons)
Magnitude	0	Symbols, Patterns, Order, Relation-ships	0	Symbols, Patterns, Categories, Rela-tionships	0	Symbols, Order, Categories, Rela-tionships	0	Patterns, Order, Relationshipships, Categories	0 (24–30 mons)
Increase-Decrease	0	Symbols, Patterns, Order, Relation-ships	0	Symbols, Patterns, Categories, Rela-tionships	0	Symbols, Order, Categories, Rela-tionships	0	Patterns, Order, Relationshipships, Categories	0 (24–30 mons)
First-Last	0	First-Last	0	First-Last	0	Symbols, Order, Categories, Rela-tionships	0	Patterns, Order, Relationshipships, Categories	0 (24–30 mons)
Approximate Number System	0	Symbols, Patterns, Order, Relation-ships	0		0	Symbols, Order, Categories, Rela-tionships	0	Patterns, Order, Relationshipships, Categories	0 (24–30 mons)

	0	Symbols, Patterns, Order, Relationships	0	Limit	0	Limit	0	Limit	0 (24–30 mons)
Counting	0	Counting	0	Counting	0	Counting	0	Counting	0 (24–30 mons)
Number Line (Mental)	0	Symbols, Patterns, Order, Relationships	0	Number Line (Mental)	0	Symbols, Order, Categories, Relationships	0	Number Line (Mental)	0 (22–30 mons)
Unit	0	Symbols, Patterns, Order, Relationships	0	Symbols, Patterns, Categories, Relationships	0	Symbols, Order, Categories, Relationships	0	Unit	0 (20–24 mons)
Numeral	0	Numeral	0	Symbols, Patterns, Categories, Relationships	0	Symbols, Order, Categories, Relationships	0	Numeral	0 (20–24 mons)

SOURCE: TOKUHAMA-ESPINOSA, 2015

months. Some kids will "learn to count" or appear to do so, but they have only rehearsed the sources. Just as they can respond to "What's your name?" children can be trained to parrot back what looks like counting "one-two-three") without understanding of what exactly "one" or "two" or "three" means. If the child actually does understand the quantity behind the words "one" "two" "three," then he can comprehend the properties of the symbols and eventually the "triple code ("3"; three, ****) (**symbol** and **relation**). After points, lines, and tally marks, this is the first symbolic representation he understands.

Without this major milestone as prerequisite knowledge, other symbolic representations, such as coin value (a penny or nickel) will elude the child. It is vital for future learning that the child sees the **equivalencies** among multiple representations. For example, the three candles on the birthday cake are the same or equivalent to the number "3," which is also the same as the word "three" and his three fingers. Only after the triple code has been solidified can a child comprehend number sense and number lines. Once a child recognizes the multiple representation of **quantity**, he can identify individual numerals out of context, then be introduced to units, and eventually form a mental number line of relative qualities in a specific **order**. This enables the child to count objects, not only parrot numbers. If he can do this, he can then recognize small groups of objects at a glance and relate them to a number. All this occurs before the child is 4 and often even earlier (2.5 to 3 years old), depending on the environment.

This design is based on a combination of learning trajectories from education and neuroscience. This curriculum example of the development of math notions in the early years is meant to illustrate what Level 0 of math might look like in the pillars.

Appendix B: Neuroconstructivist Design Levels for Mathematics

The following is a learning trajectory of math notions gleaned from the combination of state standards in the United States, research into the area of trajectories, hierarchies and core notions in math (e.g., Clement & Sarama, 2014; McClelland et al., 2006), and information from neuroscience (e.g., work by Dehaene; Ansari; De Smedt, among others).

For the pillars to function in Options B and C (Chapter 8), a mapping such as the one below would have to be made for all subjects normally taught in school. The subjects would then be overlaid upon one another to reveal a pillars curriculum (as suggested in Figure 43 in Chapter 8).

Appendix A suggests a general trajectory for infant learning of math concepts from birth to three. If a child began by implicitly and explicitly learning about math as suggested in Appendix A, she would begin to build the foundations for higher order concepts in math. Appendix B suggests that if we use Backward Design (identify objective; decide evaluation criteria; execute activities [explained in Chapters 7 and 8]), we should begin creating a pillars curriculum design by identifying our objective. Let's presume, for the sake of this exercise, that at the end of formal schooling, we hope students can "creatively use mathematical thinking to resolve problems in the real world," which coincides with several government statements for standards and objectives.

If we look at the figure below, we can see that at Level 14 and beyond, the goal is, indeed, the ability to create "New Representations" with what they know. However, to create something "new" the learner must have a strong command of the prerequisite knowledge, or lower order concepts, (related to constructivist and neuroconstructivist design, as explained Chapter 7). The key to the pillars hierarchy is neuroconstructivist design.

Table 25. Neuroconstructivist Design Levels 14, 13, 12 (approx. ages 16–19)

RELATIONS	CATEGORIES	ORDER	PATTERNS	SYMBOLS	Level
(New) Representations Linear algebra Parabola	(New) Representations Linear algebra Parabola	(New) Representations Linear algebra Parabola	(New) Representations Linear algebra Parabola	(New) Representations Linear algebra Parabola Contour integral ("∮") Integral ("∫") Logical consequence ("∴") Because ("∵") Inference/Is derived from ("⊢")	14+
Calculus (integral, multivariate, differential) Fourier analysis Fluid dynamics Bayesian inference Pre-calculus	Calculus (integral, multivariate, differential) Fourier analysis Fluid dynamics Bayesian inference Pre-calculus Hyperbolic geometry Reconfiguration	Calculus (integral, multivariate, differential) Fourier analysis Fluid dynamics Bayesian inference Pre-calculus Hyperbolic geometry Reconfiguration	Calculus (integral, multivariate, differential) Fourier analysis Fluid dynamics Bayesian inference Pre-calculus Hyperbolic geometry Reconfiguration	Calculus (integral, multivariate, differential) Fourier analysis Fluid dynamics Bayesian inference Pre-calculus Hyperbolic geometry	14
		sec cot tan cos sin Omega Epsilon Delta Gamma Beta Alpha Pi	sec cot tan cos sin	sec cot tan cos sin Omega ω Epsilon ε Delta Δ Gamma Γ Beta β Alpha α Pi π	13
unctions roportionality actorial xponents articles actors Iodularity Iodels hree-dimensional planes	**Functions** Imaginary numbers Factors Modularity Models Three-dimensional planes	**Functions** Imaginary numbers Factorial Factors Modularity Models Trigonometry	**Functions** Proportionality Factors Modularity Models Three-dimensional planes	**Functions** [f(x)] Imaginary numbers Proportionality ("∝") Logical negation ("¬") Factorial ("!") Exponents Particles Factors Trigonometry Three-dimensional planes	12

JRCE: TOKUHAMA-ESPINOSA, 2015

Table 26. Neuroconstructivist Design Levels 11, 10, 9, 8, 7, 6 (approx. ages 15–10

RELATIONS	CATEGORIES	ORDER	PATTERNS	SYMBOLS	Leve
Mapping	Mapping		Mapping	Mapping	11
Configuration	Configuration		Configuration	Configuration	
				Dichotomy Graph (bar)	
Two-dimensional planes	Two-dimensional planes	Two-dimensional planes	Two-dimensional planes		
Statistics	Statistics	Statistics		Statistics	
Probability distribution		Probability distribution	Probability distribution	Probability distribution ("~")	
Probability		Probability	Probability		
				Cover/Order theory ("<•")	
Maps to ("↦")	Maps to ("↦")			Maps to ("↦")	
Superset ("⊇")	Superset ("⊇")			Superset ("⊇")	
Subset ("⊆")	Subset ("⊆")			Subset ("⊆")	
Subgroup ("◁")				Subgroup ("◁")	
If . . . then . . . ("⇒" or "→")			If . . . then . . . ("⇒" or "→")	If . . . then . . . ("⇒" or "→")	
Material implication /			Material implication /	Material implication /	10
		End of proof		End of proof ("n")	
		Logically equivalent (":⇔")		Logically equivalent (":⇔")	
		Material equivalent ("⇔")		Material equivalent ("⇔")	
		Definition (":=")		Definition (":=")	
Venn diagram	Venn diagram			Venn diagram	
Primary numbers	Primary numbers	Primary numbers	Primary numbers	Primary numbers	
	Variables	Variables		Variables	
Circumference		Circumference	Circumference	Circumference	
Dimension		Dimension	Dimension	Dimension	
Parameters		Parameters	Parameters	Parameters	
Data		Data			9
Range	Range	Range	Range	Range	
	Romulo	Romulo	Romulo	Romulo	
	Prism	Prism	Prism	Prism	
	Cylinder	Cylinder	Cylinder	Cylinder	
	Cone	Cone	Cone	Cone	
	Pyramid	Pyramid	Pyramid	Pyramid	
	Cube	Cube	Cube	Cube	
Area	Area	Area	Area	Area	
	Arch	Arch	Arch	Arch	
	Planes	Planes	Planes	Planes	
Geometry	Geometry	Geometry	Geometry	Geometry	
			Variants	Variants	
Contralateral		Contralateral	Contralateral	Contralateral	
	Lateral		Lateral	Lateral	
Linear	Linear	Linear		Linear	
		Congruence ("≡" or "≅")		Congruence ("≡" or "≅")	
	Component	Component	Component	Component	

isect ertices btuse angle cute angle ight angle ngles arallel isjointed union “Λ”) **ivision** uotient	Columns Ellipse Decagon Pentagon Octagon Hexagon Trapezoid Parallelogram Pyramid Bisect Vertices Obtuse angle Acute angle Right angle Angles **Division**	Bisect Contralateral lines **Division**	Columns Ellipse Decagon Pentagon Octagon Hexagon Trapezoid Parallelogram Pyramid Bisect Vertices Obtuse angle Acute angle Right angle Angles Contralateral lines Parallel **Division**	Columns Ellipse Decagon Pentagon Octagon Hexagon Trapezoid Parallelogram Bisect Vertices Obtuse angle Acute angle Right angle Angles Contralateral lines Parallel Disjointed union (“Λ”) Square root sign (“√”) **Division** Quotient	8
uared (“n^2”) **rcentage** to deci- nals and fractions **ultiplication** iagram art aph tio cimals to actions nominator- umerator actions to wholes finity (“∞”) ich less than “≪”) ich greater than “≫”) equal/Not Much reater than (“≫”) ual to (“≠”)	**Percentage** **Multiplication** Ratio Decimals Denominator-Numerator Fractions	Brackets (“|x|” or “[]”) Parentheses (“()”) **Percentage** **Multiplication** Diagram Chart Graph Ratio Decimals Fractions Infinity (“∞”) Much less than (“≪”) Much greater than (“≫”) Unequal/Not equal to (“≠”)	Squared (“n^2”) **Percentage** **Multiplication** Graph Ratio Decimals Fractions	Divisor (“÷” or “/”) Brackets (“|x|” or “[]”) Parentheses (“()”) Squared (“n^2”) **Percentage sign** (“%”) **Multiplication** Diagram Chart Graph Ratio (“:”) Decimals Denominator-Numerator Fractions Infinity (“∞”) Much less than (“≪”) Much greater than (“≫”) Unequal/Not equal to (“≠”)	7
an dian/Middle		Mean Average Median/Middle	Mean/Middle	Mean (“$\bar{x}$”) Average Median/Middle Mode Less than or equal to (“≤” or “≦”) Greater than or equal to (“≥” or “≧”) Less Than (“<”)	6

CE: TOKUHAMA-ESPINOSA, 2015

Table 27. Neuroconstructivist Design Levels 6, 5, 4, 3, 2, 1, 0 (approx. ages 10–1)

RELATIONS	CATEGORIES	ORDER	PATTERNS	SYMBOLS	Level
				Greater Than (“>”)	6
				Sum of (“Σ”)	
Series	Series	Series	Series		
	Lines		Lines	Lines	
	Rows	Rows	Rows	Rows	
		Operations	Operations		
	Absolute values		Absolute values	Absolute values	
Rectangle	Rectangle		Rectangle	Rectangle	
Line of symmetry		Line of symmetry	Line of symmetry	Line of symmetry	
Rational numbers	Rational numbers	Rational numbers	Rational numbers	Rational numbers	
Triangle to square	Triangle			Triangle	5
	Square			Square	
Arc	Arc			Arc	
to Circle	Circle			Circle	
to Curve	Curve			Curve	
Component					
Ounce (oz.) / gram (gr.)				Ounce (oz.) / gram (gr.)	
Pound sign / Kilo (kl)				Pound sign / Kilo (kl)	
Degree		Degree		Degree sign (°)	
Inch (‘) / centimeter (cm)	Inch (‘) / centimeter (cm)	Inch (‘) / centimeter (cm)		Inch (‘) / centimeter (cm)	
Foot (“) / millimeter (mm)	Foot (“) / millimeter (mm)	Foot (“) / millimeter (mm)		Foot (“) / millimeter (mm)	
Time	**Time**	**Time**	**Time**	**Time**	
AM-PM		AM-PM		AM-PM	
Analog clock face representation of time		Analog clock face representation of time		Analog clock face representation of time	
Number-line		Number-line	Number-line	Number-line	
Zero	Zero	Zero		Zero	
Position		Position	Position		
Diagonal				Diagonal	
	Calendar representation of time	Calendar representation of ti e	Calendar representation of time	Calendar representation of time	
Space	**Space**	**Space**	**Space**	**Space**	
Horizontal-Vertical	Horizontal-Vertical	Horizontal-Vertical		Horizontal-Vertical	
		Central			
Analogy		Analogy			4
Perimeter					
One dollar to quarter, dimes, nickels, pennies					
Value		Value			
Half		Half	Half	Half	
Quarter (25 cents) to dimes, nickels, pennies	Quarter (25 cents)			Quarter (25 cents)	
Subtraction	**Subtraction**	**Subtraction**	**Subtraction**	**Subtraction/ Minus sign (“-”)**	
Comparison		Comparison	Comparison		
Evaluation		Evaluation			
Equivalency	Equivalency		Equivalency		
				Approximately equal to (“≈”)	
				Plus or minus (“±”)	

ts and dollars tation ("¢" and) kel (five cents) dime and nies e (ten cents) to nies "{3, 4, 5, 6}") -modal pairing ing numbers numbers	Cents and dollars notation ("¢" and "$") Nickel (five cents) Dime (ten cents) Set ("{3, 4, 5, 6}") Sorting Odd numbers Even numbers	Set ("{3, 4, 5, 6}") Uni-modal pairing Odd numbers Even numbers	Set ("{3, 4, 5, 6}") Uni-modal pairing Sorting Odd numbers Even numbers	Cents and dollars notation ("¢" and "$") Nickel (five cents) Dime (ten cents) Odd numbers Even numbers Equal sign ("=")	3
ition 2nd, 3rd, 4th, , 6th, 7th, 8th, , 10th . . . -10 blocks e/Forms t **ns and** **racteristics** 3, 4, 5, 6, 7, 8,) . . . y (one cent) ociating bols with ntity)	**Addition** Shape/Forms Digit **Forms and Characteristics** Penny (one cent) (associating symbols with quantity)	**Addition** 1st, 2nd, 3rd, 4th, 5th, 6th, 7th, 8th, 9th, 10th . . . Base-10 blocks Shape/Forms **Forms and Characteristics** 1, 2, 3, 4, 5, 6, 7, 8, 9, 10 . . .	**Addition** 1st, 2nd, 3rd, 4th, 5th, 6th, 7th, 8th, 9th, 10th . . . Base-10 blocks Shape/Forms **Forms and Characteristics**	**Addition** Plus sign ("+") 1st, 2nd, 3rd, 4th, 5th, 6th, 7th, 8th, 9th, 10th . . . Base-10 blocks Shape/Forms Unit Digit **Forms and Characteristics** 1, 2, 3, 4, 5, 6, 7, 8, 9, 10 . . . Penny (one cent) (associating symbols with quantity)	2
erties rior-Anterior -Far -Long	Properties Close-Far Short-Long	Counting verbally (out loud) Counting manipulatives Positive-Negative Posterior-Anterior	Properties Counting verbally (out loud) Counting manipulatives	Properties Tally mark Line Point	1
-Low rent-Similar rial experi- of order, size, ntity, sequence	High-Low Different-Similar	Sensorial experience of order, size, quantity, sequence	Different-Similar	High-Low Sensorial experience of order, size, quantity, sequence	0

TOKUHAMA-ESPINOSA, 2015

Appendix C: Evidence for Mathematical Neuroconstructivism

It was once believed that young children were incapable of higher cognitive processes. Only in the 1950s did a boom of new publications begin to offer insight into the complexities of young children's minds and their advanced mental processes. It is only even more recently, since the turn of the 21st century, that neuroimaging studies have offered definitive proof of the changes occurring during learning in infants—including important changes indicative of cognitive development such as typical growth rate, myelination, top-down modulation, and increased use of cortical hubs (Dempsey et al., 2015; Deoni et al., 2011; Emberson et al., 2015; Fransson et al., 2011; Holland et al, 2014). This means that while many appreciate the role of early stimulation, few people understand how stimulating children's learning from the moment they are born occurs in the brain. For example, few teachers and parents know that infants have a preverbal early number sense, meaning children have already begun to estimate quantities, gauge relative size, and judge spatial orientation. More people should have access to this information.

While our understanding of the human brain is still young, better technology and more detailed studies provide insights not yet incorporated into general pedagogical knowledge. At a minimum, teachers should know that neuronal networks are composed of multiple pathways, which in turn are created by synapses. Synapses pass signals between neurons and form the communicative bonds of new learning. New learning is stimulated by experience and is the basis for synaptic proliferation.

In the case of math, in a meta-analysis of available literature, we found that there are at least 16 neuronal networks related to early math skills (Tokuhama-Espinosa & Rivera, 2013a). Each of the four global strands of studies branch into 16 important neural networks for early math. The four global strands are: (A) Physiological networks; (B) Cultural-Social-Emotional networks; (C) General cognitive networks; and (D) Specific cognitive networks (for math in this case.) The table below shows the four strands and the 16 networks. As you can see, the pillars fall under the specific cognitive domain strand (D).

Based on the literature reviewed, these networks branch out into 118 pathways in the case of math and 90 pathways in the case of language. The language networks and pathways are outlined below. Each of the 16 networks branch out into one or more pathways that has neuroscientific studies that explain their development and identify distinct hubs in the brain, confirming their uniqueness as compared with other pathways. While all people seem to share

Table 28. Neural Networks Related to Early Math Skills

GLOBAL STRAND	16 NEURONAL NETWORKS FOR LITERACY
Physiological (sensory perception) (n=3)	I. Hearing
	II. Vision
	III. Touch and Graphomotor
Cultural-Social-Emotional (n=4)	IV. Social contagion; cultural contexts
	V. Relations with caregivers
	VI. Self-esteem
	VII. Motivation and self-regulation
	VIII. Memory
Cognitive (general) (n=3)	IX. Attention
	X. Executive functions
Cognitive (domain specific) (n=6)	XI. Math/Language Sense
	XII. Symbols
	XIII. Patterns
	XIV. Order
	VX. Categories
	XVI. Relationships

SOURCE: TOKUHAMA-ESPINOSA, 2015

the same networks, the precise pathways vary, presumably based on individual experiences and synaptogenesis influenced by radical constructivism (the role of individual experiences on synaptic potentiation).

Table 29. Pathways, Including the Pillars, Related to Language

16 NEURONAL NETWORKS FOR LITERACY	PATHWAYS EVIDENT IN THE NEUROSCIENTIFIC LITERATURE
I. Hearing	1. Pitch 2. Tempo 3. Tone 4. Prosody and intonation 5. Loudness 6. Background-to-foreground sounds 7. Left vs. right sounds 8. Speech vs. non-speech sounds
II. Vision	9. Color 10. Luminance 11. Motion 12. Size, Monocular-Binocular 13. Proximity 14. Perception vs. Action 15. Spatial-temporal contrast 16. Faces vs. other objects 17. Search and Saliency 18. Visual crowding 19. Spatial frequency
III. Touch and Graphomotor	20. Visual-Motor integration 21. Scribbling and Tracing 22. Tactile recognition of shapes 23. Writing 24. Drawing 25. Variant Expressions
IV. Social cognition, cultural context	26. Cultural awareness 27. Theory of Mind (class position)
V. Relations with caregivers	28. Cognitive-Affective dimension 29. Modeling for resiliency
VI. Self-esteem	30. Self-belief: efficacy, worth
VII. Motivation and self-regulation	31. Self-regulation 32. Intrinsic motivation

VIII. Memory	33. Short-term 34. Working 35. Long-term (fact retrieval; semantic) 36. Long-term autobiographical 37. Long-term episodic 38. Long-term procedural
IX. Attention	39. Sustained 40. Alerting 41. Orienting 42. Executive (decision making)
X. Executive Functions	43. Cognitive flexibility 44. Working memory 45. Inhibitory control
XI. "Language Sense" Start of Receptive and Productive Language	46. Initial Language Sense (nonverbal grouping [categorization, patterning]) 47. Secondary Language Sense (comparative references)
XII. Symbols	48. Coding (abstract to tangible to symbolic) 49. Analogic quality system 50. Coding (Phoenician alphabet, symbol to sound) 51. Triple code, print/cursive, small/capital, hand written/typed 52. Symbolic vs. Non-symbolic letters (identification/labeling) 53. Symbolic vs. Non-symbolic letters (production) 54. Symbolic vs. Non-symbolic letters (sentence formation) 55. Coding (alphabet symbols) 56. Forms/Shapes (begin to produce written and keyboard language) 57. Forms/Shapes (matching) 58. Spatial orientation 59. Forms/Shapes (part-whole comprehension) 60. Forms/Shapes (shape identification and mapping) 61. Forms/Shapes (shape matching) 62. Forms/Shapes (preliminary alignment) 63. Forms/Shapes (space and rotation) 64. Forms/Shapes (letter description) 65. Forms/Shapes (shape reproduction)
XIII. Order	66. Ordinality (rank [including before-after; first-last]) 67. Ordinality (fixed order) 68. Ordinality (unique) 69. Ordinality (inverse) 70. Ordinality (oral rehearsal of alphabet) 71. Sequence order 72. Sequence value, phoneme combinations

XIV. Patterns	73. Repetition and Regularity 74. Understands context for humor 75. Identification (in multiple formats) 76. Process grammar (word order)
XV. Categories	77. Classification (characteristics) 78. Classification (relations) 79. Matching (forms) 80. Matching (names and forms) 81. Matching (advanced names and forms)
XVI. Relationships	82. Parts of speech (e.g., relationship of adjectives to nouns) 83. Nonsense words vs. real words 84. Synonyms 85. Antonyms 86. Decomposition (present tense) 87. Decomposition (past tense) 88. Decomposition (equivalencies) 89. Equivalencies (CAPITAL vs. lower case letters) 90. Proportions (page layout)

SOURCE: TOKUHAMA-ESPINOSA, 2015

These pathways, including the pillars, branch out into observable behavior (Tokuhama-Espinosa & Rivera, 2013a). After identifying the pathways that came from the literature, we matched the neuroscience studies with educational research to see if it was possible to make micro-level studies observable to teachers. A sample of this from the early math brain analysis used to order the studies can be seen in the table below.

Table 30. Examples of Neuroscientific and Educational Evidence for the Pillars

Current School Level	Preschool
Approximate Age	36–48 months
Network	Cognitive (domain specific)
Current School Label	QUANTITY
Pathway	Secondary Number Sense (comparative value or magnitude)
Evidence in Neuroscience	Baroody, 2004; Booth & Siegler, 2005; Bueti & Walsh, 2009; Dehaene, Bossini, Giraux 1993; De Smedt, Noël, Gilmore & Ansari, 2013; Fias, Lammertyn, Hyde, Porter, Flom & Stone, 2013; Reynvoet, Dupont & Orban, 2003; Lourenco & Longo, 2011; Maclellan, 2012; Santens, Roggeman, Fias & Verguts, 2010; Walsh, 2003; Whyte & Bull, 2008

continues

Quotes from Neuroscience and Brain Hubs mentioned in texts	"... Numerous studies have identified the intraparietal sulcus (IPS) as an area critically involved in numerical processing. ...An area in posterior superior parietal cortex was identified as a substrate for the intermediate number-sensitive steps required for processing nonsymbolic quantities. .. a larger central–parietal P3 amplitude effect was present for active versus passive numerosity processing. This result was not influenced by numerosity itself and could not be explained by response processing. It therefore appears to reflect general cognitive processes. Together, our results show that we do not (automatically) extract numerosity from a visual scene during passive or active processing of numerosity. Instead, these results are consistent with the notion that we rely on the continuous sensory properties of numerosity stimuli to make numerosity judgments ... (Santens, Roggeman, Fias & Verguts, 2010, doi: 10.1093/cercor/bhp080); " ... In studies with both children and adults, the left and the right intraparietal sulci (IPS) have been found to be important neural correlates of numerical magnitude processing ..." (De Smedt, Noël, Gilmore, & Ansari, 2013, p.8).
Quotes from Educations and Standards mentioned in the texts	Child can identify objects as "the same" or "different," and then "more" or "less," on the basis of attributes that they can measure. They identify measurable attributes such as length and weight and solve problems by making direct comparisons of objects on the basis of those attributes (NCTM, 2006, p.11); "Children learn the foundations of data analysis by using objects' attributes that they have identified in relation to geometry and measurement (e.g., size, quantity, orientation, number of sides or vertices, color) for various purposes, such as describing, sorting, or comparing. For example, children sort geometric figures by shape, compare objects by weight ("heavier," "lighter"), or describe sets of objects by the number of objects in each set" (NCTM, 2006, p.11); Children observed "distinguishing between "some" and "all") (Epstein, 2003, p.6); Displays understanding of perceptual grasp of quantity and sensory coordination (begins to use fingers and five-frame conceptual understanding of numeracy (McGuire, Kinzie & Berch, 2012, p. 213).

SOURCE: TOKUHAMA-ESPINOSA, 2015

Even if we can't do brain scans on all students, we can better understand what is going on in their minds by improving our interpretion of their behavior in our classrooms. All levels of the pillars 0-6 for math had evidence in both neuroscience and education, which created a one-on-one comparison of educational standards and neuroscientific findings. This permitted the creation of a hierarchy, or "trajectory of learning," as educators call it, which included both educational standards and neuroscientific evidence for hierarchical placement or key notions. Finally, the pathways were mapped hierarchically, and education studies were listed alongside the neuroscientific information to compare current curricular recommendations with neuroscientific evidence. This comparative international literature review provided the synthesis needed to establish a baseline of the distinct skills that subserve math and language development. The studies that do exist point to promising information in support of the five pillars.

As mentioned in Chapter 2–6, there are multiple studies in each pillar area. Some concrete examples divided by subject area—math, in this case—rather than by pillar include how the brain learns to code mathematical symbols and to distinguish between "3," "three," and "***" in a "triple code" that shows the different **symbolic** representations of number quantities (e.g., Dehaene et al., 1999; Klein et al, 2014; Schmithorst & Brown, 2004). There are other studies about how the brain distinguishes and organizes **patterns** (e.g., Bergeson & Trehub, 2006; Geist et al., 2012) that include numerals, as well as shapes, form, and context. There is also evidence for the way the brain rotates **shapes,** which goes beyond concrete contexts and extends into manipulating forms; applying past knowledge of them to imaginatively transform their location in space (e.g., Bruce & Hawes, 2015; Frick et al., 2013; Harris & Miniussi, 2003; Thompson et al., 2013).

There are studies that show the brain's understanding of the importance of **order** in regard to symbolic number magnitude, formulas, patterns, sequencing, cycles, and series (e.g., Cassia et al., 2012; Kaufmann et al., 2009; Lyons & Beilock, 2013; Rubinsten & Sury, 2011). Other research clarifies the neuronal networks related to the role of fixed **sequence,** which is highly related to patterns, but follows distinct neuronal pathways (e.g., Grafton et al., 1995; Kidd et al., 2012; Orban et al., 2011; Pariyadath et al., 2012). Additionally, there are studies that show how the brain understands and manages **place-value** and distinguishes from ones ("1s") and tens ("10s") related to ordering and symbolic magnitude, as well as placement (e.g., Butterworth et al., 2011; Ferguson, 2015).

There are studies on how the brain estimates **magnitude:** varying amounts, sizes, weights, quantities, speeds, and so on (e.g., Linsen et al., 2015; Lourenco & Longo, 2011; Lyons & Ansari, 2015; Notebaert et al., 2011). Studies on magnitude in the brain range from a general understanding of "less" and "more" to actual calculations, which have been conducted on both symbolic and nonsymbolic representations (e.g., De Smedt, et al., 2013). The global skill set of how the brain determines a general sense of "numerosity" (**magnitude**) is related to symbolic and nonsymbolic estimation, but can be even broader, depending on different neuronal pathways (e.g., Anobile et al., 2013; Domahs et al., 2010; Piazza et al., 2004; Piazza et al., 2006; Xu, 2003). The way the brain creates **approximations** and **estimations** has also been studied and uses a combination of neuronal networks dependent on memory and magnitude (e.g., Gilmore et al., 2014; Kibbe & Feigenson, 2015). Related, but different in terms of networks for estimation, is the understanding of **equivalencies** (e.g., Chesney et al., 2014; Hunt, 2011; Mix, 1999; Price et al., 2013).

If you compare mathematical curriculum hierarchies with evidence from neuroconstructivism, you can identify an orderly way of teaching mathematics from infancy through high school (see Appendix B).

The key is the order of introduction to concepts with a goal of mastery. That is, the broader hierarchy suggests a child will understand "before" and "after" before he understands "first," "second," and "third"; he will name shapes before he can decompose them; he will identify repetition and regularity in a pattern before he can design a pattern himself; he will learn to match sets before he can produce sets; and so on. This will come as no surprise to teachers, as most of the findings from neuroscience confirm traditional curriculum order with just a handful of exceptions (i.e., the age children can learn division). This suggests that a pillars curriculum would add a new dimension for explicit teaching, and only change a handful of content areas. The main change, of course, would be in the mastery structure, rather than by age groups.

Evidence for Linguistic Neuroconstructivism

There is a similar wealth of information in documenting early language in the brain. Language can be mapped in a similar fashion to math, except that the domain-specific networks are for language and not math. The literature is rich with studies exploring the neural correlation of human language development.

For example, there is research in neuroscience documenting how infants comprehend speech **patterns** (e.g., Kuhl, 2004; Moon et al., 2013; Peña et al., 2003) and the neuronal foundations of receptive language. This complex structure involves not only auditory pathways, but also affective and semantic memory networks. There are also longitudinal studies on the general structural changes in cognitive development as language develops over time (e.g., Binder et al., 1997; Brauer et al., 2011; Fedorenko & Thompson-Schill, 2014; Friederici & Gierhan, 2013; Rilling et al., 2011), including how memory and attention pathways are strengthened with rehearsal. There are other studies that establish how **symbolic** gestures change language understanding (e.g., Andric & Small, 2012; Emmorey & Reilly, 2013; Enrici et al., 2011; Kelly et al., 2015; Newman et al., 2015), which explains how memory is enhanced by movement of other body parts, especially the hands. Other research establishes how the neuronal pathways related to lexical access **relationships** (e.g., Almeida & Poeppel, 2013; Lewis & Poeppel, 2014) give access to the personal dictionaries of each individual in a strikingly similar way through phonemic understanding (**symbols**) and semantic recall (**categories**) (e.g., Mills et al., 2004). There are other studies that consider the microanalysis of specific sounds (phonemes) and just how the brain considers them individually, and then collectively, to come up with words and their meanings.

The neuronal pathways for correct order and use of different words are managed in a complex network that determines how the brain comprehends correct grammar (**order**) (e.g., Ardila, 2012). Some of these networks explain how the brain processes past tense (**patterns**), (e.g., Budd et al., 2013) as compared with present tense and thus locates the speaker or reader in the context of time. Additionally, studies try to break down how more sophisticated elements of language emerge on the stepping stones of more rudimentary studies and create sophisticated **language** and the ability to process analogies (**relationships**) (e.g., Christie & Gentner, 2014). Other aspects of languages rely heavily on attention systems, as in how the brain distinguishes between "what" and "where" (**relationships**) information (e.g., Griffiths et al., 2012). A large part of communication and language processing depends on prediction (**patterns**) (e.g., Misyak et al., 2010), and the way the brain anticipates specific patterns in an effort to conserve energy to be efficient. There are other studies that consider the greater role of language development in general cognition (e.g., Kuhl, 2011), and expansion of general cognitive abilities based on new language learning (e.g., Bialystok & Poarch, 2014; Cao et al., 2014). Finally, there are only a handful of studies on the brain's most complex language act, writing. Suggestions that writing involves more areas of the brain simultaneously than any other skill set (e.g., Barnhardt et al., 2005; Planton et al., 2017; Purcell et al., 2011; Yuan & Brown, 2015) have surfaced only recently in educational neuroscience. Every element studied to date maps onto the pillars design.

To conclude, it is important to note that there is important longitudinal evidence from both early math and early language education that indicates how skills developed in children as young as one year of age lay the foundation for future learning in these areas (Clements & Sarama, 2014; Hoff, 2013), meaning that a more thorough understanding of all the neuronal networks implicated in early math and early language acquisition should be better understood.

There are very few neuroscientific studies on children, however. As Matejko and Ansari showed in 2015, most neuroimaging studies are done on children 10 to 11 years old, and there are none with an average age of 6 or younger. If the learning trajectory for all levels of all subjects can be disaggregated in the same way as early math and early language skills shown above, the burden will pass from evidence in neuroscience to evidence of improved learning in classrooms.

Index

In this index, *f* denotes figure and *t* denotes table.

About the Author

Tracey Tokuhama-Espinosa, Ph.D., is a Professor at Harvard University's Extension School (The Neuroscience of Learning) and is currently an educational researcher affiliated with the Latin American Social Science Research Faculty (FLACSO) in Quito, Ecuador. She is a former member of the Organisation For Economic Co-Operation and Development (OECD) expert panel to redefine Teachers' New Pedagogical Knowledge due to contributions from Technology and Neuroscience and is the founder of *Connections: The Learning Sciences Platform*, which provides evidence-based resources to teachers. Conexiones and MESH, a UK-based charity, have constructed a new, free, online, evidence-based platform to help fill in gaps of pedagogical knowledge for the 21st century, which was presented to the UNESCO 10th Policy Dialogue on the Teaching Profession.

Tracey has taught kindergarten through university and works with schools, universities, governments, and NGOs in more than 40 countries around the world. She is the former Director of the Institute for Teaching and Learning (IDEA) and Director of Online Learning at the Universidad San Francisco de Quito, and founding Dean of Education at the American University in Quito. She currently heads "Connections," which seeks to improve the quality of education through research, teacher training, and student support. Tracey's vision is to better the social, democratic, and economic structures of countries through a better educated population.

Tracey's main areas of research are improved indicators to measure educational quality; the expansion of the Mind, Brain, and Education field; learning in the digital age and paradigm shifts using appropriate technologies; bilingualism and multilingualism; and the general improvement of teacher education practices.